The Women We Become

The Women ~We Become

MYTHS, FOLKTALES, AND STORIES

ABOUT GROWING OLDER

Ann G. Thomas, Ed.D.

Prima Publishing

PRIMA PUBLISHING and colophon are registered trademarks of
Prima Communications, Inc.

Library of Congress Cataloging-in-Publication Data

Thomas, Ann G.
    The women we become: myths, folktales, and stories about
growing older / by Ann G. Thomas.
      p. cm.
   ISBN 0-7615-0654-3
   1. Women—Folklore. 2. Women—Mythology. 3. Old age—
folklore. 4. Psychoanalysis and folklore. I. Title.
GR470.T56   1996
398′.354′082—dc20   96-31215
                                            CIP

96 97 98 99 00 01 AA 10 9 8 7 6 5 4 3 2 1
Printed in the United States of America

How to Order
Single copies may be ordered from Prima Publishing, P.O. Box
1260BK, Rocklin, CA 95677; telephone (916) 632-4400. Quantity
discounts are also available. On your letterhead, include information
concerning the intended use of the books and the number of books you
wish to purchase.

Visit us online at http://www.primapublishing.com

Contents

Acknowledgments   vii
Introduction   viii

1. Snow Maidens and Silver Linden Trees   *1*
   THE REALITY OF DEATH

      No One Lives Forever
      How Do I Look?
      The Snow Maiden
      I Have Sent Them My Death
      Baucis and Philemon

2. Vinegar and Beans   *45*
   ACCEPTING LIFE'S LIMITS

      The Aged Mother
      We'll See
      The Old Woman Who Lived in a Vinegar Bottle
      The String Bean That Went
         Through the Roof of the World
      The Hedley Kow

3. Snakes, Worms, and Rice Cakes   *93*
   AN INTERNAL SHADOW

      What the Snake Had in Mind
      How a Worm Destroyed a Tribe
      The Old Woman and the Rice Cakes

4. Which Witch?   *139*
   RELATING TO THE DARK FEMININE

      The Owl
      Frau Trude
      The Witch's Shoes
      Nyanbol

5. *Spindles and Spiders* 181
   THE GOOD MOTHER
      Mother Holle
      Grandmother Spider Steals the Sun
      Rizpah

6. *Islands and Falcons* 225
   THE MASCULINE WITHIN
      Ariadne
      Inanna
      The Feather of Finist the Bright Falcon

7. *A Golden Bird* 261
   THE SEARCH FOR MEANING
      The Golden Bird

Epilogue 277

Index 281

Acknowledgments

I would like to thank Dr. Eileen Maday for her continual reading and enthusiasm during this process, and Dr. Nancy Robinson for hours of discussion and feedback on symbolism. Paul Corkery provided invaluable editing help and encouragement; Jim Wyre brought me into the computer age, and I am grateful to each. I thank my agent, Sheree Bykofski, for all her effort to find the right publisher.

I am also grateful to all the women I have worked with over the years. Although clients described in these pages are fictional, my long years in the therapy room have taught me more than I can ever repay, and I am enormously enriched by the contact I have had with so many.

Finally, I thank all my family and friends for their continued support, patience, and love during this process.

Introduction

As a psychotherapist I have worked over the years with countless women facing issues associated with aging. During that time I have found that myths and folktales were often helpful. These stories convey wisdom in ways that seem to touch women emotionally, enabling them to understand and remember in a deeper way the meaning of their aging. Countless times a woman has called or written to say, "Such and such was happening to me, and I remembered that story you told me about . . ."

Within this book I have combined retellings of some powerful folktales with some of the cognitive information psychologists have learned about aging. It used to be that psychologists thought all the growth and change that humans need for healthy, purposeful living occurs during the first five to twenty years of life. Now we know what the tellers of these folktales have known for thousands of years: To have a healthy, hopeful old age, one must continue one's emotional growth. If our lives are to be successful, we must do more than just keep our bodies and intellects functioning. We must also address our psychological and spiritual needs. Without this work our spirits will shrivel and die.

What psychologists, religious leaders, and ancient storytellers from the days of the oral traditions all have understood is that while cultures, societies, and times may change, the inner nature of humans, along with the nature of the universe itself, remains constant. Those who are to reach wisdom and peace, the mega-goal of age, must venture on an internal heroine's or hero's journey.

This book speaks of the tasks or pathways of that journey, retelling ancient tales and discussing how, within each tale's metaphors, we find insights as fresh and relevant as those from a modern psychologist's theory.

Let me begin with the story of how I came to write this book.

There's a warm breeze wafting in my bedroom window, bringing with it the smell of jasmine. I have no office hours scheduled: what a perfect beginning for this day.

I feel as I had in days past when school vacation would begin—light and free in an expectant, magical way. The day ahead holds all the promises that come with the prospect of free time.

In the bathroom, I splash water on my face and happen to look up into the mirror. Looking back at me with an intensity that I can feel reflected in my own face, is the face of an old woman.

We stare for a moment in silence.

Then—

"You are old," I find myself saying.

She stares back, waiting patiently while I examine her wrinkles and creases, poring over them as if for the first time.

"You really are old aren't you?" I find myself saying. "You're an old woman. It's a beautiful summer morning; I was feeling about twenty, and, then, here you are—"

She raises an eyebrow, and presents me with a slightly crooked smile, as if to say, "Talking to yourself, are you? Isn't that something your grandmother used to do?"

I nod my head in disbelief. I had awakened to a magical day of play, but now the magic is of a different sort.

The magic has conjured up an old woman from somewhere, and she has materialized in my rather ordinary suburban bathroom. I need to think about this some more.

"This confrontation in the mirror," I find myself thinking, "isn't about getting older. This is about being old."

"But you're not old yet. Probably you just slept wrong on your face. Besides, what's so horrible about old?"

I had no problem answering that. One by one, I went down the list of horribles: wrinkles, stretch marks, age spots, and cellulite.

Then there is also diminishing energy, and phone books become difficult to read, needles hard to thread. Coordination may decrease—old age can restrict physical movement. As if this weren't enough, there are the years, the simple numerical counting of years. A large enough number and one is designated as obsolete by many.

To be seen as an old woman is to risk being viewed as a crone or hag. While these once were titles of respect for women who had been able to develop their wisdom and spirituality, today these labels are pasted on old women who present themselves to the world in negative, angry ways. These once prestigious titles now serve as warnings to women not to create trouble or become unpleasant as they age.

No wonder one wants to resist acknowledging that one is growing old. Our culture devalues the prospect. Family and friends reflect that cultural bias. The natural losses and changes that accompany aging are frightening, indeed. As I contemplate this, I feel both fear and anger.

Yet there are many old people who maintain that old age can be peaceful and internally rich. There is some nonapparent truth these people seem to know. In talking with them, they appear calm, enthusiastic, and full of hope.

How does this transformation occur? My encounter with the old woman in the mirror made me feel that suddenly I was at the unexpected, surprising end of my own personal road. I felt a terror that accompanies any unexpected brush with death. Simultaneous with that terror was a realization that time is a trickster. I was, in the mirror, a woman who the young would see as an "old lady." Time seemed to be going faster. Beneath my day was a feeling of spinning, of spinning out of control, spinning out of control toward death. Was my time over?

Until that encounter, through all of youth and midlife, there was always a sense of having enough time. Until that encounter in the mirror, there was always plenty of time. Everyone I knew was oriented to the present or the future. We raised our children with an eye to the adults we envisaged. We worked to accumulate the things we wanted to own; pondered ways to develop the power bases we felt we needed; and we contributed our energy to cleaning up our chosen cultural mess, whether that was poverty, ignorance, or disease. Our lives were devoted to goal-oriented behaviors, with plenty of time . . . and then one morning there was an old woman in the mirror bringing what seemed like no gift at all—the gift of terror.

I began to seek out those old people who had a sense of hope and to collect from many cultures stories about aging. What I found from both people and stories was an understanding that there is a purpose to aging. It is this purpose that western psychology is rediscovering.

The old woman who appeared that summer morning wasn't a chimera. She was a connection—a tricky and trickster connection—to a world whose language I needed to learn. She was showing me that growing into an older woman with a meaningful life depends on more than just cognitive understanding of psychological terms or participating in senior center activities. We must also focus on our inner worlds, for it is here that we find the key to our futures.

～

Six tasks or pathways toward meaning and fulfillment in old age are explored within this book. The first, strangely enough, seems to emerge for women around the age of forty, long before the advent of old age. The task is this: we must each accept, intellectually and *emotionally* the reality of our own personal death. A woman who attempts to avoid this early developmental task will be unable to find the meaning and joy of her life since she will, from that point on, be held captive by fear.

Accepting that life is finite allows us to begin questioning our place within the cosmic plan or, indeed, whether or not there is a cosmic plan. Acceptance means searching for new questions and answers not previously considered and, in the process, finding the necessary tools for a solo journey into the unknown.

A second task involves exploring how we have lived our lives. For most of us, along with the joys and successes, there are dreams unfulfilled, goals unreached, and mistakes that have been made. Most of us have put these disappointments behind us. After all, we didn't know better, or it wasn't our fault, or it's all water over the dam anyway. To understand and claim our lives fully, however, we need to accept how these disappointments and failures have contributed to the total fabric of our lives.

What we find is that there are no longer enough days to make everything better. Alienation *has* occurred within families. People *have* died with words unsaid. Opportunities *have* passed. There is no longer any way we can fool ourselves into thinking that someday everything will be different.

To continue to hide from these issues of our past allows a sense of failure to run through the fabric of our lives. Many escape into alcohol, depression, and illness rather than struggle with meaning and acceptance. However, opening up this closet of disappointments provides the opportunity to reconcile with the reality that much of what we find painful and disappointing has meaning. To find meaning and acceptance is to find the route to forgiveness and healing. It is this road that leads to the sense of wisdom we experience with some elder friends.

Along with understanding what has occurred in our lives with others, aging provides each of us with the opportunity to discover more of our inner nature. Some of this inner self includes aspects of ourselves repressed over the years because at the time we judged them unacceptable or ugly. Jungians identify the part of each person's psyche where these traits are stored the *shadow*.

Although most of us believe we have successfully overcome those aspects of our personalities, we are usually fooling ourselves.

That early proclivity toward self-inflation, the intolerance of certain types of people, that speaking without thinking because of anger may still be alive, buried within the shadow, waiting to pop out when stress or age or something else weakens our defenses. When any of us act in this inadvertent manner, we risk hurting people we care about and embarrassing ourselves.

It is also true that at least some of our most hated invisible traits are quite visible to those around us. For example, others may clearly see us as controlling or angry while we tell ourselves we are only being helpful or necessarily forceful in order to get something done.

The opportunity of age, in exploring this task, is to bring our repressions out into the light of our consciousness to clearly see what is there. Only then are we able to decide where a particular quality belongs within our lives. If we push it down at that point, we still know it is there and can exercise some control when it pops up.

While each person's shadow is unique, there is a still-deeper level of the human psyche that Jungians call the *collective unconscious*. It is within this deepest level we find archetypes, those psychological representations of human instincts. Because archetypes are common to all, they link us one to another within this universe. While no one *is* an archetype, archetypes live within each of us, influencing our lives.

The Dark Feminine is one of these archetypes that affects the lives of all women, especially as we age. It is an important archetype to explore because many old women become caricatures of the Dark Feminine, taking on the sharp, angry tones of the wicked witch or of the hag. These women stand out in bold contrast to the wise women who have met and learned what to do with the Dark Feminine energy.

As we age, our ability to be tactful and long-suffering often decreases. If the witch has been lurking, she will be the one to appear. An important task is to discover how to view her and to determine what type of relationship we may be able to form with this part of our psyches.

Still another task appropriate for us as women growing older is the discovery of the archetype of the Good Mother. While most women understand how to nurture or to mother others, few of us have become skilled at mothering ourselves. A common mistake is to assume that adult women have passed the age of needing what the Good Mother has to offer. We fail to recognize that deep within our psyches is this great source of increased strength and well-being. One task awaiting us is locating this archetype within ourselves and learning from her what mothering ourselves can and ought to be.

There also exists within this deep collective unconscious aspect of each woman's psyche a masculine archetype. This psychological embodiment of human instinctual energy is what the Chinese call yang energy and what Jungians call the *animus.* The masculine archetype has nothing to do with gender or being manlike.

Many women, busy with children and homemaking, have been unaware of this internal potential during their young years. Other women, fighting their way within the patriarchal corporate structure, have developed a hard, seemingly masculine mask in order to survive. Neither type of woman, along with many of the rest of us who don't fall into these categories, have experienced an integration of the available animus energy. But the energy is there: it often sits dormant until age has removed some of the external restraints and has provided us with the time to explore this aspect of ourselves. This task leads to a sense of "being one with oneself."

Women who fail to find or integrate their animus energy often become overly aggressive and abrasive as they age. Instead of self-assurance, they grasp for aggression. Instead of acceptance, they find bitterness. Instead of becoming wise sages, they have become shrews. Or they go to the other extreme, falling into a childish dependency.

Finally there is the need to understand how each identified task connects with all the others. Continuing to grow is an ongoing process, not a short-term self-improvement course. Accepting life as a process allows each of us to confront the essence of our personal meaning. The consciousness of this quest continues throughout later life, allowing each of us to unfold, like the Western rose or the Eastern lotus.

To reach toward wholeness is the final psychological and spiritual task. Once a woman is on this journey, she discovers an outpouring of creativity, a renewal of energy, and a sense of simultaneously letting go and connecting.

And now . . . *Once upon a time . . .*

Snow Maidens and Silver Linden Trees

THE REALITY OF DEATH

Once upon a time an Old Woman sat on a stool next to the hearth. The night was cold. Even the extra log the man had added to the fire couldn't keep out the evening chill. She pulled a black shawl more snugly around her shoulders.

Crowded around her were children and their parents, all related somehow to each other and to her—but in a complicated genealogy she no longer clearly remembered. The room was quiet except for the crackling of the fire and the breathing of the hound, who slept at her feet.

She watched these people whom she loved as they sat watching her. In the space between them swirled the energy of their contact at the moment.

The Old Woman examined that energy carefully, separating the various threads of distress, pain, joy, and expectation from the tangled host of emotions. She followed each separate strand back to its human origin.

Although the Old Woman had never learned to read writing, she knew how to read people . . . and their energy.

She searched for new information. Who was struggling? Who was in pain? Whose life was changing now? Who was grieving?

Each time a corner of life is turned there is a need. People's inner spirits send forth whatever they find difficult to put into words, as though the words might be: "How do I get through this place? Why am I here? Has anyone ever been here before? I am frightened in this strange, new land and need to find a path, a guide."

What the Old Woman read in the faces and spirits of the people would determine which stories she told. Each night she could tell only a few from the hundreds in her mind. Her stories were never told merely for fun, although the children and the simpler among the adults may have thought so.

Her stories were told to be sent into the inner, knowing places of those who listened. If the story connected, if it were meaningful, there was a creation, a birth of a new entity in the life of that person. Something within that person would be sparked, nourished by the recognition of companionship. For it is a truth, even if not known, that no one travels alone: When a story connects, something within the person begins to sense meaning.

But when a story is without meaning for its listener, the story is stillborn. The Old Woman had seen that often enough to recognize that was also a truth.

That night across the continent by the side of a campfire, another old woman sat telling stories to her group. These listeners, traveling as they did in caravans from one spot to another, were related, if not by blood, then by history. Yet they, too, needed healing stories, and they, too, often gathered in the dark, waiting for this old woman to search their souls and relate from her stock of hundreds of stories, the one that would bring meaning that night to the people she traveled with, and loved.

But that was hundreds of year ago. What of our own hearth and our own old women?

Today our fireplaces are seldom lit, seldom crowded around. And campfires burn only for a few on summer vacations.

And the old women? At a time when more of us live past menopause into old age, where are the wise old women? Ironically, few are there to serve as our guides. Although more and more of us are beginning to understand that old age is also a strange new land for which we need guides, we live in a culture that places little value on becoming old.

Many old women have not become wise because they believe what the culture has taught. They see no value in their own old age. They accept the idea that their technologically illiterate generation has little of value to contribute, and they move away from us into retirement villages or nursing homes, unavailable. These elders take with them whatever wisdom they have gleaned.

It appears that all of us—those already old and those at midlife—have forgotten that meaning, belonging, coping with evil, fostering love, and being fully present in one's own life are timeless issues. It appears that we have also forgotten that paying attention as one lives a life and thoughtfully reflecting on that life produces insight and wisdom not available in some mechanical, external manner. These are the opportunities of living long. These are the insights needed by anyone considering a long life.

While many of us may not have access to wise old women who will serve as guides, we do have stories. In days past, wisdom was often conveyed in story form. Parables, folktales, and myths were as familiar as today's popular TV shows. While many of these stories have been forgotten, they were not lost. As we read and tell these stories once more, we find they are filled with symbols containing great wealth. The wealth is an abundance of insight into ways women of old created a meaningful old age. The stories also contain examples of mistakes which led women astray. Because the universal concerns of life do not change with time, these insights are as golden today as they were in those days of village storytellers.

One audience for these stories would have been, and still is, women in midlife who are interested in preparing for their latter years. The guidance we need involves how we can find a pathway for successful aging. If we want old age to be meaningful, we need direction. We want stories that point the way. We want stories that give road maps. We want stories that identify dangers and dead ends. And often, very often, we want to hear stories that will help us find courage for the journey.

Many of the stories selected for this book feature an old woman protagonist who serves as a mentor. Some point the way. Others warn brilliantly, through symbols, of dangers. All speak to the unique emotional and spiritual work involved. Many of these stories alert us to the reality that life is filled with paradox and we will be unable to find meaning or direction unless we struggle to understand the paradoxes within our own lives.

This quality of paradox becomes more obvious as we age. It is not as easy to understand life as a simple black-or-white proposition. It no longer feels accurate to see most events as all good or all bad. Even the logical sequence and order of life seems less simple.

We begin our inquiry into aging, therefore, with a paradox. Logic would suggest that we outline the steps from youth to age and follow them one at a time. We would begin with the loss of some opportunities or physical attributes and end with death. We might discuss the order of the steps *in between,* but there would be little argument that death is the end. This is where we meet our first paradox. There is no way to find the meaning we are searching to find unless we begin at the end and work *backward.* The information about how to live the last third of life in a meaningful way is found by exploring the reality that we will cease living.

The issue of death comes up automatically for most people sometime in their forties. We all experience it as what some have labeled *midlife crisis.* Midlife crisis has at its core the panic and denial surrounding the shortness of life, that is, panic about our own personal death and the need to move our focus from those things around us, the external, to those things within. Anyone who becomes stuck at this place will spend the remainder of her life running faster and faster in order to bolster the denial. Underneath, the panic remains.

This is the reason the issue of death must be resolved. When we avoid this issue, we will be forced to use our energy to bolster the denial in order to keep from feeling panic. As long as we maintain that defensive position, we will be unable to go in any other direction. We will not be open to growth. Instead, we will grow into old women pretending to be someone we are not. We become caricatures of ourselves.

Death is also a metaphor. Early in our lives we must keep our focus outward. It is necessary to work to understand the world. It is important that we find our place in this world. By midlife this task should be completed and we need to let go and make the transition to an internal focus.

There have been many stories told about death. From these stories two major ideas emerge. The first is that death is a transition. The second is that finding meaning for one's life is the only replacement for fear. The stories help us understand more about these ideas.

The power of stories lies in their functioning as metaphor. Ancient and modern storytellers convey their messages through symbols. Although it is a strange idea to our conscious, rational twentieth-century minds, the unconscious understands symbols that our conscious minds must work to translate. Symbols are indirect, complex, and multilayered. Logic and rationality are straightforward and very helpful when we need to understand how something works. When it comes to the meaning of aging and death, this rational approach is not very helpful. We are all quite clear *how* we arrive at old age and death: We simply keep on living.

When I was young I remember hearing my grandmother say of someone she knew, "She needs to just lay down and die." I have no idea if that was a southern expression or one unique to Grandmother. Either way, it horrified me as a child. It also puzzled me since Grandmother was one of the kindest people I knew and never sounded angry when she made this statement. In recent years her words have come back to me. I think her meaning is the same as that of the following story.

～ No One Lives Forever ～

THERE ONCE LIVED a woman who feared death. "If only I could find a way to live forever," she would say. "If only I did not have to die."

"Death comes," everyone said to her. "No one lives forever."

"I would like to find a way," she would answer.

One day she left her village and journeyed to a wise man she had heard of who lived some distance away. When she arrived, she asked, "Can you tell me how to live forever?"

"Oh no," he answered. "No one lives forever. I can tell you only how to live for two hundred years, which I think is quite enough. If you want to live longer, then you must go to the old woman who lives in the woods. She is older and perhaps she knows."

So the woman set out and after many days she arrived at the cottage of the old woman of the woods. "Can you tell me how to live forever?" she asked.

"Oh no," answered the old woman. "No one lives forever. I can tell you only how to live for five hundred years, which I think is quite enough. If you want to live longer, you must go to the man who lives on top of the mountain. He is older than I and perhaps he knows."

So the woman set out and after many days she arrived on top of the mountain where a very, very old-looking man sat quite still. At first the woman thought he was dead, but finally he turned and looked at her.

"Can you tell me how to live forever?" the woman asked.

"I don't know," the old man answered. "I don't think anyone will live forever, but I have lived a long, long time, and you may stay here if you want and learn what I know."

And so the woman stayed with him for hundreds of years. One day she decided she wanted to return to her village, just to look around. The old man advised her not to go, but she was so determined that he finally gave her a horse to ride.

"Do not get down from the horse," he warned her. "Ride into the village, look around, and then come directly back. You must be back before the sun sets."

The woman promised and left. When she got to her village, she did not recognize anything, for it had been so many years. She rode around a bit, then left to go back to the mountain.

On the way she was stopped on the road by a wagon that had spilled its contents. Scattered across the road were piles and piles of worn shoes. It was impossible to pass on either side. The oldest looking man she had ever seen was picking up the shoes, one shoe at a time. He was moving very slowly because it was clear that his back hurt when he bent down to pick up a shoe. He was also having difficulty raising his arms to toss the shoes into the wagon.

"Please hurry," the woman said. "I need to return to my mountain home."

"I can't hurry any faster," the old man said. "Perhaps you could help me."

The woman looked at the huge piles and thought, "It will be days before he has all this picked up." She looked at the old, old man, struggling with his task, and thought, "Poor old man."

So she began to dismount from her horse, saying as she did, "Where did you get all these worn-down shoes?"

"I have worn them out myself," the old man said. "I have been walking around the earth, year after year after year, searching for you. My name is Father Death."

And as her feet touched the earth, the woman crumbled into bones. Father Death tenderly gathered her remains. "No one lives forever," he gently whispered as he carried her off.

~

There has always been a reluctance to die. Death is the one change that cannot be reversed. People feel helpless with something so final.

You may postpone death, this story from Italy tells us, but no one lives forever. Today we might understand the postponement in terms of diet and exercise and genetics. Those are all logical responses to the question of how to evade death. But the statement "No one lives forever" is as true today as when this story was first told.

Why, then, do some people go easily toward that final time while others are anxious, frightened, even angry? What information do we need and what experiences are necessary in order for us to feel whole rather than fragmented; peaceful instead of tormented; cognizant of the meaning of our lives instead of bewildered and confused?

Every character in a story, like every person in a dream, can be understood as parts of the lead character or dreamer. We find very few characters in this story. In addition to the central figure, there are those identified as "everyone." Then there are three figures: a wise man, an old woman on a hill, and the final old man on the mountain. And finally, there is Death. There was no room in the central woman's inner or outer life to sing and dance and love. There was no room for village life or family interaction and no room for friends, relatives, or loved ones. There was no room to be open to all of the richness within her own psyche. Because she was afraid, she had to close out most of her external and internal life.

The figures that are present represent different versions of some internal wisdom figure. With the exception of the man on the mountain, they all say the same thing: "No one lives forever." Within this woman's psyche is the information that she refuses to hear. "This idea of yours is not going to be successful," she was being told by her intuition or instincts. "Do not continue. Find another way to go."

There are countless times when this way of knowing happens for all of us. We know something without having to be told. Some inner voice warns us not to ask certain questions, not to go in certain directions. The story woman is unable to profit from her inner voices and continues her quest.

This is the paradox. If we want to live the days we have, we must face our fear of death. We cannot run from death out of fear.

One of the ways we have learned to run and hide is to focus on our bodies as the part of us that is the most real. After all, the body has been our home during this life. We become so identified with our bodies that we begin to believe that they are who we are. "I am tall, short, fat, thin, pretty, plain . . . ," we say as we describe ourselves. Having identified with the body we inhabit, we are in danger of growing old as that body grows old.

Since physical changes are inevitable, this can be a dreary task that ages the spirit. Some of the women I know have seemed very old for many years. They have lost their sense of play. Fun, humor, and adventure have been replaced by habit, routine, and preoccupation with bodily functions. Their descriptions of themselves sound like, "I am sick . . . constipated . . . feeble . . . in pain . . . forgetful . . . tired . . . old . . . ."

Other women, of even more years, as the calendar measures time, seem filled with life. While they, too, may acknowledge that their bodies are wearing out, there are other aspects of life that attract their attention. They have chosen not to chain their spirits to their bodies.

The differences appear to be the result of how a woman answers the question: "Who am I?" Women who see themselves as body grow old. Women, whose identity resides in their spirit, age differently.

As we begin to consider questions of who we are, terror fades. I have been told by some with whom I faced those final hours that there was no longer fear. Death was viewed as one more transformation: a birth into the next phase. These women had a sense of inner peace and continuity. What do we need to do to arrive at that place?

We must begin by questioning: How do we find a process that will lead us to wholeness, peace, self-cohesiveness, and meaning? Where do we discover who we are? In what ways can we find our spirit? How can one die healed in this way? These are not easy questions with simple answers like, "Just do this!"

Our next story, an Inuit tale, tells of a woman who received insight about the consequences of focusing on her physical appearance.

⌒ How Do I Look? ⌒

THERE WERE TWO WOMEN living together in the far cold north. Everyone from their tribe had left and the two old women huddled together in their tent, talking of the cold winter which was fast approaching.

"We have some food," said the one. "We must just ration it and hope for the best. If we die, we die."

The other woman disliked that solution. Although she felt discontented, she could think of nothing else to do. Both women fell asleep.

As they were sleeping, the discontented woman woke to a noise. She got up and looked outside where she saw a handsome young man. He held out his hand to her, and when she grabbed hold of him, they both rose into the air. They kept ascending until they reached a hole in the sky.

Once on the other side, the woman found herself in a beautiful house. It was warm there and food was all around. She felt filled with energy and quite happy. She and the young man lived together for some months.

One morning the young man said to her, "Today I must leave for a while. There are dangers around for you, so please be careful." And with that strange warning, the young man left.

The woman walked around the house and yard but soon grew bored. "My young man is so handsome," she thought. "I wonder how I look to him?" With that thought, she began walking toward a distant pond in order to see her reflection.

As she reached the pond, she found a tiny house by the shore. A young woman there greeted her and they began to talk. The old woman said to her, "I have come to see my reflection in the pond for I am worried that I may not be attractive enough for my young man."

The young woman smiled knowingly. "I can help you," she said. Together they bent over the water while the younger woman pointed out a wrinkle here and a brown spot there. "And," she said, "there are some gray hairs coming back."

The old woman looked at the places the young woman pointed to on her body. As she looked, she began to see more and more signs of aging and she grew more and more tired and feeble. By the time she was finished looking, she felt so discouraged she could hardly make it back to the house. The young woman cut a stick for her to use to steady her walk.

Once back at the house, the old woman had to rest. It was while she was resting that the young man returned. He took one look at her and knew what had happened. He turned away, and as he did, the old woman felt a falling sensation. She closed her eyes for a moment, then opened them to discover that once more she was in her tent with her old friend.

∼

To understand this story's symbolism and its meaning for us today, we must remember to approach it as we would a dream. We let the literal fade to background.

It is not difficult to understand that we must approach stories and dreams in a similar manner when we understand that they have similar origins within the unconscious. While a dream comes from our personal unconscious, giving us information in a way we had not previously considered, a folktale comes from the unconscious of its tellers and listeners who through the ages have polished and refined it into its present form. A dream will have unique significance for the person who dreamed it. A folktale will have collective significance for the community who embraces it.

So let us interpret this story, which is about the collective experience of aging from the perspective of an old woman, for the insight the story has for us about female aging.

This is the story of one woman who was allowed to experience a truth. While one part of her slept, solidly resting on the ground of everyday reality, another facet of this woman moved into a different plane. She began to move in the world of the spirit. As she did, she experienced herself as young in the way that our spirits are always young.

One aspect of learning to live within the world of the spirit is fostering our ability to bring together the various dualities in our lives.

The "either/or" way we've come to understand life must be transformed into an ability to see that what we've always seen as opposites are united. For the woman in this story, body/spirit united into one "Self." As long as she understood this, she was happy.

This is an incredibly difficult truth for our Western minds to hold. We are convinced that what we see and know is what is true. and therefore, the opposite of a particular that we see and know must be untrue. The idea of duality, the belief that both are true seems as crazy as the world of *Alice in Wonderland*. How can it be that my hand, which feels so solid, is actually more empty space than it is solid matter or cells? How can it be that the individual cells in my body are constantly communicating with each other in order to regulate my body functions? How can it be that as we spin in the universe we experience stability; or that as we view ourselves as unique we are also the same? How can it be that as a woman I have within me both female and male, happy and sad, kind and unkind? It will not do to say that we are able to do these things sequentially: First I'm sad, then I'm happy. That is too simple. Just as fall comes and the marigold dies, the flower is producing the seeds of its continuing life. One contains the other. The moment a new life is conceived it is on a path toward its own demise. The moment night descends and the moon rises, the earth begins its turn toward day and sunshine.

My clients often come into therapy because they are stuck with the extremes of some either/or. "I could do this," they will say, "or I could do that. I can't decide."

The struggle is really with the feeling that keeps them in the middle. It is there, right in the heart of this duality or paradox, that their truth or meaning will reside.

"I hate my husband and I want to leave him," someone will say, "but I really don't know if getting a divorce is the right thing."

"I want to go back to college and get a degree. But somehow I never get over there to pick up a catalog or register."

"My husband and I keep arguing about where to move. We each have our own idea and they're very different. I don't want to go where he does, but I don't want him to be unhappy, either. I want to win, but I don't want him to lose."

Our story woman remains sleeping on the ground as she rises in the air. She is old yet she is young. She is sure of herself, unmindful of the physical, and she is insecure and critical of her appearance.

All goes well in this story/dream until she begins to focus once more on the split between body and spirit. When she reattaches meaning to her body, her senses and emotions follow, and she once again experiences herself as an old woman. She falls back to earth, losing contact with her spirit world. She wakes to find herself in her tent.

There is one more meaning to consider from this story. The story begins with the woman being told the way she must live the remainder of her life if she wants to feel alive. She is told in this way.

"There is not enough to eat," one part of her states. "There is too little of substance for this upcoming winter of my life. Because there is so little, I may die."

"There is not a thing you can do to change things," another part of her responds. "There may not be enough. If we die, we die."

"There is another way to look at old age and death," a third aspect of her psyche says. "You must learn to change your focus. Stop focusing on your body. Stop noticing its aging and remembering its youth. You and your body are not the same and when you believe they are, you become trapped in age and death."

The old woman in our story experiences this truth from the depth of her unconscious. It is given to her through a dream, which is one of several ways we know what is real.

In our next story an old Russian woman discovers she is lonely at the end of her life. While the story presents the loneliness as external, we know that the storyteller is showing us a metaphor for a type of internal emptiness that occurs when we first begin to contemplate the issue of death. This old woman makes the very human mistake of believing that the solution is external. She believes that by adding something to her life, she will be able to avoid the feelings of loneliness—never realizing that those very feelings are a key to help her face her own life and its meaning.

⌇ The Snow Maiden ⌇

ONCE, LONG AGO in a village in Russia, there lived an old woman and her husband. The old woman felt lonely and unhappy and thought if she only had a child, all would be well. So one day she and her husband made a beautiful girl from snow. The snow child was very pale and cold, but nonetheless, she came alive and went inside to live with the couple.

The old woman was happy and she cared for the girl night and day. The child grew more quickly then anyone had ever seen before and she soon began to help the old woman with the day's work. It seemed, to all who watched, that this was a happy family. Many people believed they heard the child singing although perhaps it was only the wind from the steppe.

Winter passed as winters always do, and spring returned to the village in Russia. The snows melted, flowers began to bloom, and the birds returned from the warm southern lands where they had spent the winter. As the days grew warmed and brighter, the Snow Maiden grew sadder and sadder. There were some in the village who believed they saw the child cry, although perhaps it was only the spring rain.

Once the old woman asked, "What is wrong little daughter?" but the Snow Maiden only sighed and did not answer, and the old woman did not ask again. Yet it seemed very clear that the maid was not happy.

Spring passed and warm summer came to the Russian countryside. By now the Snow Maiden was weeping each day, but the old woman pretended not to notice. Then one day the other children from the village came to the old woman's cottage. "We are going into the forest to play," they said. "We want the Snow Maiden to go with us."

The old woman sent the weeping girl, hoping that the time with the other children would cheer her. But the Snow Maiden did not play, for she was too sad.

As evening came the girls felt cold in the forest, so they gathered wood and lit a fire. They sat around singing, but the Snow Maiden's voice did not join with theirs. They told stories, but the Snow Maiden appeared not to hear. Finally they began to play a game of jumping—jumping, one at a time, over the coals of the fire. When all the girls had jumped, they pulled the Snow Maiden toward the fire. "Jump," they all said. "It's your turn now. It's fun. Jump."

And so the Snow Maiden jumped, but the heat from the coals, as she passed over the top, melted her away, and she disappeared in a hiss of steam, which sounded very much like a sigh.

～

My reaction to this story has always been one of at least a slight sadness. A tale of winter, it reminds me of one of those glass domes where a shake of the globe produces a sparkling winter's scene with fresh, new snowflakes. But the story has an ending, and it is not a happy one.

This is the story of a woman who has reached old age only to discover a great lack in her life. She identifies the lack as her childless circumstance.

Immediately we wonder what this symbolizes. There are many associations with the image of a child. A child is an image of newness, freshness, innocence. To produce a child is to create something deep within oneself that is new. This new creation begins as a speck so small it cannot be seen by a human eye and emerges, after time, as a separate entity, able to live on its own.

As we move toward old age and death, the story suggests, we begin to experience sadness for what has not occurred within our lives. In this example, the woman has not been creative. She has done nothing to renew herself or her spirit. She now wants to create. This yearning and the beginning creative energy it inspires came as a gift. Thus far we see a normal progression.

The problem begins when the old woman goes out into the snow and in short time creates a child who seems to her unique, pure, and most importantly of all, alive. The woman appears not to know that creation is a slow process that cannot be rushed without dire results.

Life, even in symbols, comes from life, and snow is not a life symbol. A child called forth from water, earth, a forest, a garden, or from spring seeds would have been a meaningful symbol of new life within the woman's internal world. But when the newness is created from snow, which holds no life, what then? What are we to understand from such a symbol?

Of course, snow is water, and perhaps in a story of Russian origin, snow suggests water. But when water is fluid and flowing, in a liquid state, only then is it alive. Water is the feminine symbol of ocean and stream, container of life from which we all came. When water becomes solid, however, we think of death. Ice and snow are without color, frozen and cold, not moving, like death itself.

The old woman recognizes the need that occurs in the life process to create something new from within. She is even able to identify that the creation needs to be something with life, something that will live on beyond her. The image of children often conveys that which transcends our own lives.

However, something within our story woman is cold and frozen. Some instinct, some inner part, has become hard and lifeless. It is from this lifeless part that the old woman tries to create something new. The result is the birth of something that cannot really last in life. She creates something not really alive.

This story woman is the woman within each of us who acts impulsively without stopping to analyze. It is the impatient part of us who, recognizing the need for something new, sets out to have it occur quickly. It is the part of us who searches outside, in a frozen and barren place, for something that will satisfy those deep questions of our lives. Somewhere in each of us, the story woman lives.

There are many times in life when we are in need of renewal. Certainly growing older and facing the finiteness of life is one of those times. This story cautions us. You must be patient and not accept the first distraction. Distractions are cold and frozen. They are without warmth. You must not do things as you have always done. This is the time of life when you must find a new way.

It is very difficult to do what we cannot imagine, and this is the old woman's difficulty as well. She is surrounded by snow. Snow is what she knows and so she creates from what she knows. There is a high probability, the story tells us, that instead of the creativity you need, this will produce something that is not really alive and viable.

There is a story from India that tells of an unending battle between the gods of good and the gods of evil. First one, then the other, would be victorious and the battle would continue. So it is in our lives. Those are the dualities, the either/ors of life. We choose one side and battle another. There is happy/sad, loving/hateful, healthy/sick, married/single, thin/overweight, energetic/tired. There is no end to the opposites within our lives. We find ourselves ever choosing until we begin considering the final duality: alive/dead. Suddenly we panic for it seems we cannot choose. We freeze inside and reach for some half solution.

In the story from India, the gods call for a solution that is not a part of either side. They call for the intervention of Kali, a goddess who is able to end the battle. It takes something new to resolve the duality. In this Indian tale, Kali represents the feminine force of emotional energy. The two polarized sides needed that feeling, that small germ of creativity, that was separate from their rational extremes, yet lived in between, in the middle. This is another example of how the wisdom of old, no matter which country or culture it comes from, has a truth we need today.

"Don't keep doing the same old thing," we are told. "Bring in the new," which in this case, is once again, the focus on the feeling between the two. It is here that the germ of transformation will reside unseen until we form enough of a relationship—an objective, accepting, nonjudgmental relationship—with the feeling to see what is to be seen.

Our story woman has snow blindness. She treats this frozen girl—or cold, lifeless symptom within—as we often treat those neurotic symptoms that occur in our lives. She acts as if what she wanted to believe might be occurring actually is happening.

Ruth, a fifty-year-old teacher, came to see me. She was very depressed. "Life is so short," she told me, "and I feel I haven't done anything. I feel empty." As often happens, while she and I were working on the issue together in therapy, she was also working in other ways during the rest of her week to find a solution.

That solution turned up in the form of a man much younger than Ruth. She fell in love. Any suggestion I made of caution was rejected. The younger man, like the Snow Maiden, grew more lovely by the hour. Ruth broke off therapy, promising to return if her depression ever came back. About a year later she called.

Ruth, like the story woman, experienced a need to do some repair work because of a feeling of emptiness and loneliness. Like the story woman, she arrived at the truth that she was in need and had emotional work to do through both feeling and an understanding of what the feeling was about. It was unfortunate that she also paralleled the story woman in one more way. She acted before she understood what the feeling meant.

This was, to put it simply, an impulsive response to feeling. And impulsive responses to feeling are usually unproductive. Ruth and the old woman chose to fill the emptiness with something that wasn't life sustaining. They each selected something that appeared to fill the void and give meaning. When the young man came along, Ruth submerged herself in the fantasy that she was twenty years younger; she chose to fill the void by denying she was growing older.

For both Ruth and the story woman, things went on for a while, with little apparent problem. The coldness within the Snow Maiden/story woman continues, but it seems she is content. We are told she even sings. So it often is with neurotic responses. In the beginning of the response, we may even think we are better off than we were before.

But things do begin to go wrong. Spring comes, followed by summer. A Snow Maiden, so charming in winter, in spring—in the midst of green grass, flowers, and the birds—is just inappropriate. We can no longer pretend this is a charming story of family life. Even more importantly, the Snow Maiden herself is sad and weeps.

Ruth described a similar pattern. "At first," she said, "we spent most of our time alone. He brought me flowers. We made love. It was wonderful. Then it began to get a little tense.

"He would take me to parties, but I was really uncomfortable with his friends. The married ones had children the ages of my grandchildren. The unmarried ones were so—I don't know, sort of immature, somehow. He and his friends wanted to stay up most of the night.

"I would get tired and want to go home. When we'd go out somewhere, to dinner or the theater, people began to refer to me as his mother. I was so embarrassed.

"Then we began to quarrel over silly things. I began to get headaches. Instead of being concerned, he became angry. He changed, I think. He began to act younger, somehow—less responsible. Or maybe I just didn't see what he was really like in the beginning. Anyway, he's gone, and here I am, back where I was before."

Life for our story woman grows worse as well. Unlike Ruth who began to see what was happening, the woman in our story becomes more disconnected. She is that modern woman who, experiencing distress or depression from some internal source, becomes trapped in a pattern of shopping or other frantic activity. The worse the feelings become, the more she shops or drinks or eats, burying the need and feelings beneath layers of things or alcohol or fat. She is understandably fearful of the unpleasant feeling because she has not yet understood that the feeling will lead her to places of self-knowledge.

While the old woman did recognize in the beginning that she had a need for something creative, she fails to understand, when things sour, that her response to the need was wrong. Thus she is unable to try again. If she, like Ruth, had been able to acknowledge her mistake, she might have found a happier ending.

You may think that a younger man or a Snow Maiden is an aspect of your creativity. However, you must be willing to look closely and listen carefully. If your choice is wrong, you may feel uncomfortable, even embarrassed. You will hear crying or a sigh. When you look and listen, you will know. Then you will be free to find another way.

The story contains several hopeful, encouraging messages. It tells us that creative energy is there for us no matter what our age, and that the need for creativity in some form will surface as we face our mortality.

The story suggests that whatever that initial feeling may be—loneliness, depression, or some other feeling—it is a messenger inviting us to begin a process of self-discovery. To be useful, however, we must apply our newly learned skill of watching in order to discover exactly what this message means.

Creativity, we learn from the story, is a process that takes time, gestation. When rushed, the unfortunate occurs, mistakes happen, neurotic symptoms appear. But the symptoms themselves are not catastrophic.

Ruth lost nothing more than a few months and some pride as a result of her impulsive attempt at a quick solution. While a bruised self-image, a wounded pride, is painful, few people actually die from hurt pride.

There are clear cautions within the story, too. Solutions implemented without thinking them through usually contain pitfalls. It is important to take whatever amount of time is needed before activating a plan.

Denial, the story woman's behavior when she fails to respond to the girl's tears, causes our creative potential to become frozen and then pushes it beyond our reach. Creative energy is not helpful when pushed away from our feelings. We must have some relationship with the need to create as well as something to create. We cannot hope for wholeness when we create something external to ourselves and then fail to relate to it in a way that considers its nature and purpose. That approach is ill-fated and divides us into even more pieces. We are then separated from ourselves.

This is a very common problem for women. And it's a state that many of us experience in one form or another long before we reach that stage of life when we need to face our own mortality. But what are its signs?

We are separated from ourselves when we cease to notice how we feel or what is happening to us. We are separated from ourselves when we are swept along by external events. We are separated from ourselves when we live in the future or the past, when we're unaware of how much food or air or movement or rest we need, or when we seldom do any of the things we used to love.

This separation often begins early in adult life when we have children. From a warm and loving part within us, we respond to the needs of our children, and yet in becoming so giving, many of us lose the good sense of belonging to ourselves.

Some women speak of reaching midlife only to discover they are numb. "It's as if I'm not here," is how one woman described her feeling to me.

Another said, "People ask me if I want this or that and I honestly don't know. For so long I've worried about what others wanted that I no longer know what would interest me.

"My husband knows what he wants. My children and grandchildren know what they want. I must have some feelings, some preferences, some opinions, but I don't know where they are or what they might be."

In the language of stories, this is saying: Part of me is at home and another part is in the forest. A part of me is crying, but I don't notice. The parts can't see or hear each other and don't have a clue as to what the other is feeling.

Our patriarchal culture also fosters the separation of women from themselves, especially when it comes to our angry or aggressive sides. Words like *shrew, nag,* or *bitch* are three of hundreds of negative word-ways in which angry women are labeled in an attempt to prohibit those feelings. Women who have wanted to fit in or gain the approval of others have accepted and internalized these rules. We have cooperated in our own internal separation from ourselves.

When each of us begins to recognize in midlife that our own death is a reality, we feel the need to go inside ourselves and to begin picking up the scattered pieces. We feel a need to find what is real and whole, to discover where we belong in the universe. Where are we attached? Avoidance or running away serves only to separate us further. But what are the parts we are looking for? The parts we need to find are those parts that are deep and abiding, that will transcend obligations and social rules.

"Everyone dies alone," Grandmother was fond of saying. My response, as an adult, is to say, "Yes, but . . . there is alone and then there is really alone." Some, like the old woman in our story, live and die separated from themselves. We've met some of these women. They are bitter, blaming others for whatever pain they're experiencing. They are numb, having cut off feelings for so many years. They are continually needing others to fill them emotionally because there is no internal source of nourishment. They cannot connect with anything of substance within themselves and therefore cannot connect with others in any substantial manner.

That is a state of true loneliness. But when we are connected to ourselves, we also have a knowledge of connection to something beyond. To be connected with oneself is to feel whole and content. Connected to oneself within the universe, one does not feel lonely, even in one's aloneness.

The night after I had written about "The Snow Maiden," I went to sleep thinking about the ways in which its meaning might apply to my own life. Certainly I understood about losing parts of myself, but I wondered what else the storyteller might have been trying to communicate.

I knew she was trying to say our feelings give us clues when something is not right—even if we don't understand exactly what might be wrong. In the story the girl weeps, and we know that's a sign of disease and distress. But is there a way of knowing when we're on the right track? How can we know that we're on the right course when trying to find ourselves?

At that point I must have fallen asleep because the next thing I remembered it was morning and I awoke remembering this dream:

I FEEL QUITE young, perhaps about ten or eleven, but I have no image of my physical self. There is a feeling of childlike wonder and naïveté. I am at a large fair or exposition of some type with three other women.

There are miles of exhibition buildings, and we are walking through a building looking at the displays.

Somehow I become separated from the first two women, one of whom was the person I relied on to take care of me, although it didn't seem she was my mother. I am frightened and begin looking around. The third woman is nearby and I tell her I am lost.

"I'm worried that I won't find her," I say, referring to the first of the three women since she is the one who seems the most significant. "She will be upset and will worry as to where I am."

"We'll find them," the third woman answers. I don't feel reassured, but I go with her outside to the street corner where we get on a bus. As the bus travels around the blocks of exhibition buildings I feel increasingly upset. None of the buildings seems familiar and I feel we are getting farther away from the woman I need to find. Then the bus turns a corner and I see a church building. I immediately feel a flood of relief and then a feeling of safety.

"I know where we are. Stop the bus," I say.

The building is one at the entrance to the exposition. I know that is where I will find the woman I need. Although I hadn't known that was the building I was looking for, or even that I had seen it before, when I am there, it is perfectly clear that this is where I need to be.

～

What I experienced in the dream is a sense of rightness, of aptness, which is so difficult to describe in an intellectual or abstract manner but very easy to know when it is experienced. This kind of knowing transpires intuitively and in the psyche. When we experience this sense of order we know things are right, we know where we are, we are able to find missing parts of ourselves. This kind of knowing is also experienced intellectually—when we find ourselves perhaps remarking, "Of course . . . . Why didn't I think of that before! It's so simple." This knowing, which takes place within one's whole being, is a coming home to oneself!

"The Snow Maiden" is a story that tells us we will know when a change is needed because there will be a shift in our energy. This internal growth must create something new that will lead to the heart of the life/death paradox.

The story warns that we should honor these needs by acting carefully, not impulsively. Easy solutions change nothing internally. They do not lead to wholeness. The impulsive response will not postpone our aging or death. Instead it leads to a feeling of loneliness.

In spite of its dark warning, "The Snow Maiden" remains a story full of charm, redolent of a Christmas card or a lovely Russian lacquered box. Not all stories are as pleasing. "I Have Sent Them My Death" is a darker tale, but one equally magnetizing.

～ I Have Sent Them My Death ～

ONCE UPON A TIME, in a far northern village where the land lies frozen and the winters are dark, there lived an old woman. This woman had lived many, many winters and now she was so feeble that she could scarcely rise from her sleeping platform.

The old woman was most certainly too feeble to go with others on the hunt. To eat, she was now forced to rely on handouts from her neighbors. Although people gave her food at first, they quickly began to withhold.

"Winter is coming," they said. "The water will soon freeze. The salmon will have gone. The caribou will be far away. The seal will not swim near. The tundra will be covered deep with snow. Our drying racks are not yet filled. Do not throw away our food on this old woman who is about to die."

The old woman by now had become only a skeleton. She understood her neighbors were not going to give her any more food, and so she did a strange thing. She folded her skeleton body from the waist and placed her skull against her vagina. Then, in a low and rhythmic voice, she began to sing a charm song. As she sang, the skull grew and grew and grew until it had reached such an enormous size that it broke off from its own weight.

Once the skull was free from the body, it began to roll around the village. Some people were so frightened that they died on the spot. Others, seeing the skull approaching, ran away. When the skull rolled past the old woman's grandson, he called out.

"Stop, Grandmother. What is wrong? Why are you trying to frighten everyone to death?"

Grandmother's skull stopped. "I have sent them my death so that they will understand the consequences of not feeding a fellow human being."

She then gathered together all of her bones and buried herself deep within the sea.

～

This story is filled with helpful symbolism that we can use to understand more about our own inner nature. At the same time, it is also a story designed to warn a community about unacceptable behavior.

Be careful, the story cautions listeners who are still young and strong. Do not treat old people in cruel ways. Do not become selfish and self-centered, for if you do, something horrible may happen to you—as it did to the mean-spirited villagers in the story.

The story points out something that we'd rather not admit: When times are tight and there is not enough for all, many will become selfish and unkind.

The story also reveals that the fear that one will be abandoned, hungry and in need as one ages, is a common one. We see the old and abandoned every day, but often choose to deny their plight, perhaps fearing that it will someday be our plight as well. The story reminds us that this fear exists within all of us, as does the capacity for this all too common reaction to the old.

The story leads us to think about what happens to those who are abandoned in our society. There are, as we know, old women living on the streets of most American cities as bag ladies. These women have been abandoned both by society and by someone who once knew them well. They are often cold, sick, hungry, and so feeble they can scarcely push their shopping carts.

There are also many old women, warm and fed, but left in nursing homes without visits from friends or relatives. Some of these women are also abandoned people, often so feeble they can barely rise from their sleeping platforms. This is not an ending any of us would welcome.

We must also go deeper into "I Have Sent Them My Death" to see how it helps us understand inner meaning. What does it mean symbolically when the community, or the collective, ignores one's needs? One's life force, the story says, drains away.

Within each of us is access to a large inner world. It is here we will find our instincts, our emotional energy, our intuitive collective sense. To be abandoned or cut off from this aspect of the Self is to be trapped in a serious depression.

This old woman, cut off as she was, was unable to feed herself. Her only source of energy was her intense feeling of victimization. "It is the responsibility of others to care for me," she believed. As she continued to neglect herself, her rage grew until she quite literally lost her head.

This woman had no ability to consider other possibilities, tap into other emotions, or connect with any other part of her self. She was trapped, growing weaker and weaker.

My client Elizabeth was locked into this type of small internal space. Twenty-five years before her visit to me she had married a self-absorbed man named Bill. Through the years she had pampered Bill until one day she realized life was passing quickly and she had many needs that had never been met.

She had discovered, in raising her children and in taking care of her husband, that she was able to be a competent problem solver, creator, and nurturer. Also within her, there was a "Christopher Columbus," a great adventurer who had the courage to take off for parts unknown. Although it had been Bill who made the frequent decisions to change jobs, it had been Elizabeth who located the homes, found friends in new cities, and made the transitions smooth for everyone.

However at this time of need, none of these inner resources came forth for her. Instead she was locked into the idea that Bill owed her.

It was up to him, she insisted, to know what she needed and to begin meeting those needs of hers. Her rich internal resources, through her abilities as nurturer, problem solver, creator, and explorer, could have nourished her. These parts were filled with caring, love, curiosity, competence, bravery, and courage—an emotional feast. They were not feeding her though, because she was unable to see beyond her rage and desire to achieve symmetry with Bill.

Another client, Maude, was cut off from her inner resources in a different way. Maude was in the grips of an internal dragon who daily filled her with fear. She had been living alone since her husband's death, had no living family, and no contact with friends from long ago.

As she reacted to her fear, she pulled her world in tightly around her. She cut herself off from people who might have been interesting, lacking the motivation to venture out. She cut herself off from reading books that might have given her sustenance; she was unable to find the energy to even open the covers.

As her depression grew, she controlled her daily pattern of home-work-home with breaks in the pattern only for what was truly necessary: weekly groceries, church on Sundays, and the dentist twice a year. She kept on her narrow trail of sameness even when she very keenly felt the starvation that was killing her.

Although Maude is an extreme, most of us can point to some time in our life when we were in a rut, doing the same things over and over again until we began to realize we were emotionally starving to death.

What we experience, cut off from others, is an absence of feelings; or conversely, the presence—the overwhelming presence—of a single feeling. Many people are numb. Others, like Elizabeth and the old woman in this story, are in the grips of rage. Maude's overpowering feeling was fear.

Yet Maude, like many of us, also spent a great deal of energy denying that one feeling! As we use this energy for denial, it saps our ability for rational thought. This is the lock which keeps us lying feeble on our sleeping platforms. We stay weak and half asleep, starving. There is no food, for it is within the land of feeling that the nourishing, sustaining food of meaning, purpose, and spirituality will grow.

In midlife it is especially important to pay attention to feelings. Introspection, contemplation, meditation, or psychotherapy become increasingly important as we once again, quite naturally, question who we are and who we have been. No longer, however, is this questioning rising out of the inexperience of adolescence. By midlife, each of us has already lived a portion of the life we have been given and it is essential we begin to look for and connect with the depth inside. To avoid doing so means succumbing to numbness and from that we face starvation. To connect with the depth inside brings feelings and from these we are nourished.

In the story, the old woman's self-neglect builds until she finally explodes in an act of vengeance. Typically when a person is blocked from her own feelings, the first feeling to surface is almost always anger. If the block has been strong and long in building, as it was in the case of the old woman, the anger is rage. The surfacing is in an explosion.

The old woman's next action is interesting. She bends over, places her skull against her vagina and sings a charm song. Her skull grows enormous, breaks off, and rolls around the village frightening people.

What can we make of this startling picture presented by the storyteller? First consider some of the symbols. Long before Christianity, when religions centered around the goddess, the female genital area was seen as sacred. This is the source from which life emerges. It is an obvious symbol for the feminine.

The skull, however, has always been a symbol of death. In addition rational or intellectual understanding—nonemotional understanding—has always been associated with the head. And the head has always been a symbol for masculine energy.

And as for the charm song, well, chanting and singing connect with the magical and the sacred. Both the witch and the nun hope their words and notes soar to another dimension, so that transformation will ensue.

The old woman's action was an attempt to create something new and magical, a transformation. She placed her skull, the seat of masculine rationality, alongside the feminine source of life, and began her incantation. She clearly needed new feminine aspects, newly born or resurrected emotions, within her own life.

Her mistake was trying to achieve something new and purely life-giving by approaching the feminine through a rationality that was being distorted by her rage. Now that's a mouthful, but it's a simple idea that my grandmother used to express in this way: "I'm so mad I can't think straight."

That is exactly where this old woman found herself. She needed to do something about her rage before either her feminine or her rational nature could begin to help her.

Elizabeth, Maude, the old woman in our story, and countless other women are, in essence, dead. As they look at who they are, they discover their life spirit has left them. It is only that one small space where they are imprisoned that has not died.

"Stop!" says the grandson in our story. "Look at what is happening! Become conscious of what you are doing and how your behavior has meaning . . . . Stop running around, stop rolling around. Stop and relate to the issue."

The little boy knows where to begin. The old woman—all these women need to reconnect with themselves. They need to focus on whatever emotion is present to begin this process of reconnection. The old woman must sit with the feeling, meditate upon this rage that is so present for her. She must question herself.

"Why so angry?" she might ask. "You are striking out at others. What do you think they have done? What does that have to do with what is happening inside of you? Are you doing the same thing to yourself? Are you permitting it to be done? Are you avoiding something by having this happen?"

The questions should continue until feeling comes to tell the old woman that a good path to another aspect of herself had been located.

With the realization of death, which is how we started this examination of how to have a rich and full, rather than an empty or dismaying, later life, comes intense emotion. The emotion may be a feeling of emptiness like that which engulfed the old woman in the tale of the Snow Maiden. And along with that feeling may come a feeling of rage or fear, or overwhelming fatigue or numbness.

Whatever accompanies that first glimpse we have into the darkness will arrive as an invitation, not as a conclusion. It is an invitation to begin a journey; a journey to locate and make conscious those aspects of ourselves which have been so long beyond our consciousness.

This is a different approach to unpleasant feelings than most people know. This approach suggests we welcome whatever emotion we happen to experience as an important and significant guide.

Depression? Anger? Fear?

"Hello. Since you come from my unconscious, I can learn from you. I know you are only a 'first' feeling, a doorman standing at the entrance, but you are the only real, tangible starting point. I can see you. So I will observe you without judgment, and sooner or later you will open the door to let another piece of my unconscious out or to let me in."

The stories we have talked about have given us these truths about the meaning of a personal death:

It is not possible to avoid death.

As we identify with our bodies, we age as the body ages. As we come to know and identify with our spirits, we grow young, for the spirit is eternal.

Discovering our spirit is a creative process that must occur over time.

There are internal voices, called feelings, instincts, or intuitions, that will guide us when we learn to listen.

We must begin with whatever emotion is present and become conscious of what meaning exists. This will allow us to expand our self-awareness.

The solutions to the meaning of our own lives are all internal. External solutions ultimately fail to provide satisfaction.

Our task as we prepare for own mortality is to discover who we are. To begin this task we must search beneath the layers we have built up of who we think we are and who others think we are. We must search beneath the layers of the body, below the acts of doing, until we find our spirits.

This means we must come to terms with the parts of ourselves we may not approve of or like. We have to work with our own rejected parts in order to safely move into the unknown.

We have seen how one old woman rushes into her creativity by building a snow child as soon as she feels a need, without discovering what the need is about. We met a woman who acts on her rage without understanding why she is so enraged. We can see their rejected and repressed parts coming out and controlling who they are able to be.

"But I'm not like that," we're tempted to say.

"I'm nice—except for the times when . . .

"I'm kind—except for the time when I . . .

"I'm always thoughtful—well, almost always . . .

"And when I'm not—well—it was circumstances or someone else's fault."

What becomes clear as we explore further is that we all have a repressed side. The nicer we are, the more our unknown side is filled with the "nasties." The nicer we are, the more these nasties seem alien to our conscious mind. And the less we know about them, the more we are vulnerable as we age.

In our final story we meet a woman who has successfully dealt with much of her emerging unconscious. Although this story does not share how she did that, it does focus on how she comes to terms with death. It also shows what the wise woman of old knew, which is that once she is able to confront and accept the reality of her death, the remainder of life is filled with joy and meaning.

From Roman mythology comes the story of Baucis and Philemon.

∼ Baucis and Philemon ∼

IN A COUNTRY far from here, there is a very remarkable tree. This tree and the temple behind it are all that exist on a small island. The roots of this tree go deep into the earth. Its trunk is strong and solid, yet it splits partway up, becoming on one side an oak and on the other, a silver linden tree.

Once, during the days when Jupiter was the supreme god on Mount Olympus, this land and the water around it were all part of a village. One evening Jupiter decided to visit the village to see if the people who lived there were kind and hospitable. He and his son Mercury dressed themselves in beggars' clothes. Then they went from door to door, begging food and rest. At each door, however, they were turned away until finally they arrived at the cottage home of Baucis, an old woman, and her husband, Philemon.

Baucis and Philemon answered the door and invited the two weary travelers in.

The fire was fanned into flame, a bench was pulled close to the fire, and from her meager store of food, Baucis gathered a cabbage, a slab of salt pork, some eggs, olives, plums, endive, radishes, and cheese.

Water was brought to wash the strangers' feet.

A table was drawn near; one leg, long broken, was propped up with a broken bit of pottery. A wine bowl was placed on the table.

Once the food was cooked and served and the wine was poured, the beggars began to eat.

Wine was poured again and once more, but as much as was poured, the wine bowl remained full. As Baucis and Philemon noticed this, they began to wonder, and then to fear!—for surely as anything is sure, they were in the presence of gods.

"We are sorry," the old woman and man said, "to have offered you such poor food. We have a goose. We will catch it now and cook it for you."

And out they rushed after the goose, but as fast as the old woman and man could run, the goose ran faster, honking all the while. Finally the goose ran into the house and stayed by the side of the gods. The old couple came in, gasping for breath.

"Stop," Jupiter commanded. "You have been good while your neighbors were selfish and wicked. They will be punished. Come with us."

And the gods led the old pair up a nearby hill. When they were almost at the top and it seemed the old ones could continue no farther, the gods stopped.

"Turn around," they commanded. Baucis and Philemon turned and saw that the village, including their cottage, was under water.

They began to weep for the loss of their home and neighbors. As they wept and watched, dry land appeared in the center of the water, and on the land, a beautiful, large temple to Jupiter materialized.

"What would you like?" Jupiter asked the two. "What do you most desire?"

The two talked together, then spoke to Jupiter. "We would like to live our final years as priests in your temple, and when it is time for us to die, we would like to die together."

And so the two were granted their wish. They lived many years within the temple of Jupiter, happily and faithfully serving the gods, and when their time came, they were transformed, both at the same time, into a tree that was both one and two. Baucis became the silver linden, and Philemon the oak.

～

Looking at this story as a social tale, we find it is very similar to the teaching tale in the New Testament in which Jesus admonishes his followers to show hospitality with the words: "For I was hungered, and ye gave me meat / I was thirsty, and ye gave me drink / I was a stranger, and ye took me in / Naked and ye clothed me / I was sick, and ye visited me / I was in prison, and ye came unto me. . . . Verily I say unto you, Inasmuch as ye have done it unto one of the least of my brethren ye have done it unto me."

This concept of showing kindness to those in need is found within every culture whose stories I have studied. Indeed, the value is more than a cultural rule: it represents a religious imperative that or-dains that those who fulfill this obligation will be rewarded just as surely as punishment will fall upon those who disregard it. From a social perspective, "Baucis and Philemon" offers an example of moral behavior for a community.

We also know a story is a metaphor for each of our individual psyches. We see what each story holds for us internally by regarding all in it—Gods and humans—as different aspects of the central character. From this perspective, the story becomes one in which we are shown an image of wholeness and connection, both to oneself and beyond that to something universal, which transcends death.

Remembering the guideline that everyone in a story can be understood as aspects of one person, we see that the central character Baucis/Philemon has a feminine side, Baucis, and a masculine side, Philemon. The development of a sound person depends on the recognition and healthy growth of both the feminine and masculine qualities.

Two gods pay a visit and we are immediately faced with a paradox. Everything within the story is to be viewed as an aspect of the internal psyche—yet humans are not to believe they are really gods.

When we elevate ourselves above human status, something will inevitably cut us down. There was a custom among carpet makers of old that shows they understood the importance of remaining within the human sphere. Once a beautiful carpet was completed, the artisan would add a flaw. "Perfection," they would say, "is reserved for the gods." Today we understand that we cannot find our life spirit if we are pretending to be perfect.

In this story, Jupiter and Mercury are what Jungians call *archetypes*. Archetypes are universal patterns of ideas and impulses that all humans hold in common. Jungian psychology suggests that these ideas and impulses reside deep within the collective unconscious.

No one is taught the archetypes; we are born with them. Just as all humans are born with two eyes and one nose, all are also born with archetypal concepts, such as the concept of mother. We know that each human face appears different in spite of the two eyes and one nose because of the influence of family genetics. Both the sameness and the individuality exist side by side. So it is with the archetypes. The details of the concept of mother also are individually shaped by personal experience.

In this story, Jupiter and Mercury, as archetypal images, are aspects of the god within. Jupiter's role in Roman mythology was head of Olympus. The Jupiter archetype, powerful beyond the control or bidding of our personal egos, sees and understands all. Mercury, also a powerful archetype, is another aspect of the ultimate power within the universe or of God. Mercury is the mercurial energy that causes us to lose our way in order to find another direction and who releases wisdom about our direction to us each night through our dreams.

There are many times in our lives when we are able to experience the power of archetypes. For women, the birth of a child is often one of those times. When I first held each of my children, I felt joined to all women of all times who had ever given birth. I felt the energy of Gaia, the earth mother, flowing through my body.

Weddings are another occasion at which archetypal energy may manifest. The tears that sometimes well up, even when the bride is not someone close, are an indication of how deeply one responds to the symbol of the archetypal energy of union. Most weddings are moments of the perfect union, no matter how the marriage may later turn out.

Within the story "Baucis and Philemon," the archetype of Jupiter and Mercury appears to test human ability to nurture under difficult circumstances. Two ragged strangers appear late in the day and ask to be fed and taken in. This is a difficult request. Yet the story says we, too, may be confronted in this way. There is a knock at our door. We may have a natural reluctance to even answer the knock and open the door. Most of us have lived reasonably good lives. We've done our work, perhaps raised children, have been good members of our community. We have friends and family members who like and respect us. Why, then, the knock at the door?

Many women in therapy tell me, "I just want to feel good. I don't want to go back into all that old stuff. That was a long time ago." That statement of resistance is, itself, a beginning feeling. It is a place to start. "Why is that feeling here?" we wonder. Maybe this is not a good time to explore. Perhaps there are other priorities.

Or perhaps the resistance leads elsewhere. There is no external rule that dictates a "right" time or a "right" way to live our psychological lives. The very best that any of us can do is to try to understand what meaning exists in the feelings we have. The only possible guide is an internal one. In order to know if we are to answer the door and what it means to find someone or something there is to pay attention to our feelings and go from that point on. Feel it. Write about it. Talk about it with people who can be helpful. Paint it. Join a group.

Other women in therapy will say, "I don't know where that feeling, or outburst, or strange behavior, came from. It's so unlike me."

"Invite it in," the storyteller suggests. "You may fear the worst, thinking this stranger comes from some dark land and you may be kidnapped, carried off in chains. But if you keep your eyes open and pay attention, *and* if you are kind to the feeling, you will receive the gift of understanding."

It is true that when there is a knock at the door, that knock is asking for extra work, work that was not a part of our daily lives. These visitations often come in the form of depression, anxiety, or some other emotion that gives us an added burden.

Once the door is open, Baucis/Philemon sees two ragged, dirty, smelly strangers. Jupiter and Mercury come disguised in this way. At our own emotional doors, the gods often arrive clothed in ugly feelings we want no part of, memories we've worked to forget, and dreams that wake us into terror or rage.

All our lives we've worked to become people worthy of respect. Now this strange feeling arrives at our doors. It seems very difficult to see these smelly strangers as arrivals who will enhance our lives. They aren't our type and they don't fit into the lives we've created. There is a strong urge to turn them away. We can understand the response of Baucis/Philemon's neighbors.

Baucis/Philemon does open the door, though, and invites the strangers in. She shows compassion by allowing them to rest, drink, and eat. She nurtures this aspect of life and of herself. Only slowly does she discover there is more here than she originally thought. A transformation occurs, but the reality of that transformation takes time to dawn on her.

So it is with real growth. The growth must take place naturally; it cannot be contrived. Baucis/Philemon did not welcome the strangers because she thought she would gain from their arrival—she welcomed them out of compassion for their need.

That the beggars were something more than beggars was a reality that did not manifest itself immediately but only over a period of time. The gods indeed waited until Baucis/Philemon knew the reality before they transformed themselves and revealed their god-like countenance.

In much the same way, the old woman in "I Have Sent You My Death" could have opened the door to her rage. But she didn't. After all, what was at the door looked like rage, and who wants that in the house? Jupiter and Mercury looked like dirty beggars, and who would want them in the house?

Within my own life as well as in the lives of many of my clients there have been times when I didn't like what was at my door. When I was very young, I ran around busily, fending off the feelings. "If I'm busy enough, if I'm tired enough, if I accomplish enough," I reasoned to myself, "the feelings will disappear."

And indeed they did. But I was left exhausted, no wiser, and eventually the feelings returned anyway.

Gradually I learned to invite them. "Let me get a good look at you," I learned to say. "This is a difficult time. Let me take good care of myself while I sit with these strange feelings. Let me feed myself regularly on nourishing food rather than on junk. Let me rest when I'm tired. I will show compassion to myself and my feelings."

Sometimes, but not always, the feelings led me to a new place. Sometimes there was something there that was magical and transforming, which emerged slowly from the experience.

The magical is there for Baucis. When the gods ask her what she would like, she responds by asking that she be allowed to continue to serve the spiritual aspect of life for as long as she lives. And then when she dies she will do so with her internal masculine and feminine united. When the storyteller has Baucis request this unity with Philemon, she is letting the listeners know that the union of our internal opposites, the resolution of paradox, is the task of life as we age. Baucis is becoming/has become the woman who, sufficient within herself, does not *need* others to complete her. Because she is free from this need, she is available to relate to others for who they are, with joy and love. Baucis's path is clearly different from the ones taken by the women in the stories of the Snow Maiden and the rolling skull.

Baucis/Philemon, unlike her neighbors, faces her feelings and makes a smooth transition. Her neighbors do not. Once the gods identify themselves, the fate of the neighbors is revealed. These villagers had been caught in the extremes of rational and practical thinking. They had become rigid, stingy, and selfish rather than flexible and caring. "Go away," they said to the strong but unpleasant emotion that knocked at their door. And those feelings often do go away, but it is into our unconscious that they go. Strong feelings, or too many feelings, pushed back into the unconscious will have a reverberating impact. The neighbors in the story drown. In our lives, if we push away the strong, unpleasant feelings, we can grow overwhelmed as the unconscious floods up, and we, too, can drown.

The symbols attached to the fate of Baucis/Philemon reveal the unification of the masculine and feminine. The linden tree repeatedly appears in myth and folktales connected to the feminine. It was sacred to the goddesses Aphrodite and Frigga and was home to the Greek wood nymphs. The linden is known for its honey and the antiseptic nature of its inner bark. It is the feminine aspect of Baucis/Philemon that is transformed into a linden tree.

The oak tree, on the other hand, has always been viewed as masculine, making it an appropriate final symbol for the masculine aspect, Philemon. Oaks are viewed as physically strong with deep roots that anchor them through storms. Indeed the oak has been the symbolic tree of many kings, including King Arthur.

By working both to unite the feminine/masculine aspects of herself, Baucis/Philemon did more than die with duality united. She was transformed into something new and whole. As Baucis/Philemon die, they become a single tree that unites two different kinds of trees. Through this image, we are brought back to the importance in our later years of working to unite the differing aspects of our personalities. The image this story leaves us with is one of dying with duality joined.

There are many ideas within these stories that we can use as we attempt to understand and accept the reality of our own deaths. In each story we are shown that there is sufficient time to do what is needed.

What is needed is the growth of something internal. For one woman it was a question of needing to give up her attachment to her body. Another needed to develop a different type of creativity. A third needed to fill an inner hunger and understand the meaning of her rage. Baucis needed to give up her attachment to the material in order to attend to the spiritual.

What is needed is the finding of one's life spirit—the essence of who we are. One woman experiences this through her dream, that conduit of knowledge and healing from the unconscious. Another woman senses it through a surge of creativity, only to misapply her insight, leading her in a neurotic direction. One has only her rage to guide her and it eventually leads her to her unconscious. The final story woman finds her life spirit in the unity of her disparate parts and in her dedication to the spiritual aspects of her life.

What is needed is the uniting of the various fragmentations and dualities that exist within each of us. For the Inuit woman, living in her tent, the duality is between body/spirit. The Russian woman's duality is an aspect of her neurosis. She is pulled between her need to find fulfillment and her intolerance for ambiguity, which pushes her toward instant gratification. The woman who loses her head is struggling with the duality between the rational/emotional. The duality for Baucis is feminine/masculine and material/spiritual.

What is given to each of us is the creativity necessary to do this task. What is required with this creativity is patience, for it is not possible to see our growth at its beginning, even though it may be sensed. What is also given to us is forgiveness for mistakes—provided we become conscious of what is happening. What is required is that we begin by claiming and holding on to our emotions.

These tasks that we have identified from our stories as necessary if we are to accept the reality of our death just happen to be the same as those required for a fruitful and creative old age. The tasks will present themselves to us unless we are running away from death. If we walk, with courage, toward our own deaths, we find we are in the midst of our lives. We are, indeed, like the marigold, forming seeds for continuing life in the midst of death. That is the paradox.

2

Vinegar and Beans

ACCEPTING LIFE'S LIMITS

The Old Woman pulled herself upright, then began to stretch. She had been sitting far too long, almost all day, and now was stiff from not moving. She began walking toward the river— farther away from the village. She wasn't ready to return. She headed toward another of the shelters on the riverbank, similar to the one she had stayed in these past two days. She needed one more night to allow the meaning of what she had experienced to settle a bit more.

As she walked, she began humming, pleased with her present feeling of contentment. It had been a difficult month.

Cedric had died exactly four days ago, and had been buried the day following his death. Before dying, he lingered for three weeks at death's door, and during that time the Old Woman had sat by his bed, cooling his body, easing his pain with her broth and syrups. It was she who held him as he left for the next journey, and it was she who prepared his body for burial. Others had said the words as he was lowered into the ground, but it was she who placed the first of the cool earth over his now-vacant body.

It had been forty years since they had lived together, and she was surprised when he returned to the village to die.

He had left in anger and she had sent him on his way with bitterness. Each had disappointed the other. For a long time she had worked only to forget.

Eventually she was able to tolerate the thought of Cedric. That was when she began to walk around her memory of their time together until she saw an image of a young girl envisaging the young man a god, and then furiously working with his claylike being, as if she could create what she desired. When she failed, she was filled with anger and then with emptiness.

Finding what needed to grow in that space had taken much more time and much more effort, but she was pleased with what finally came.

He, on his side, had done much the same to her, except where she had wanted a faithful Zeus, he yearned for a mother, the perfect Demeter, devoted always to him as her child.

From the day Cedric left, until that day a month ago, the Old Woman had heard nothing of him. When he walked back into the village, gray and drawn, clearly near death, her heart jumped, and she felt a surge of something, perhaps anxiety. This anxiety quickly disappeared, replaced by her skill and compassion.

An hour or so before he died, she had been sitting by his bed, looking at him while he slept. He opened his eyes, looking back at her. There was a moment then of such intensity that it was as if they melded into a single unit of energy.

She cried out—more an expulsion of air than words—and then it ended. He faded back into that land of foggy sleep and soon passed from his body. She held him silently, being the mother she had never been before.

Then there were the preparations, the work that had to be done. There was no feeling then—only a strange numbness—until she left to be alone in her beloved woods.

She was sad, she realized, not for Cedric's death, since death is only another step in one's journey, but for what they weren't able to have with each other.

But in that one moment four days ago, the magical and divine had happened. It had been a moment of union that left no bare edges open to the harsh winds.

In that moment it began to seem that the work she had done to find the meaning of her individual life had unraveled. All the old pain and injuries were back again just as when she was young.

As the Old Woman and Cedric were joined, in that moment, he had appeared once more to be godlike. She wept again then for the young girl's pain at discovering the reality that humans are not meant to be gods. She wept for the fleeting nature of their intensity. And finally, she wept because she knew in her deepest place that his need for her to be the mother was no different a yearning than what lived in her, and that the two of them, indeed all of humanity, were only different parts of one whole.

And as she wept she began to achieve the comfort that comes from grieving those things that cannot be. It was a grieving that ends in a place where the heart is allowed once again to feel the meaning of reality.

The Old Woman knew when she returned to the village that there would be a gathering. That night the story she would tell would be told for herself, for she was the one who was in need. And what she needed was the reminder that value isn't always found in expected places. The seeds of meaning lie within both what is and what cannot be.

～ The Aged Mother ～

ONCE THERE WAS a woman grown very old who spent much of her time lost in her own thought. Those thoughts circled endlessly around her loneliness. Many years before, her husband and both baby sons had died. Since that terrible time, she had never stopped grieving. She, above all people, understood how unfair her life had been.

One dark night she was sitting with her thoughts when she heard the church bells ring. Thinking she had dozed, she pulled her old body up, wrapped her coat around her, and walked down the hillside to the church for morning prayers. When she arrived, the church shone more brightly than the outside light although no candles burned. She went to her usual pew, only to find it filled with people. In fact, the entire church was filled.

A woman spoke to her. "Look at me," she said. "I am your aunt who died many years ago. Look around you."

As the old woman looked around, she saw that no one from the village was in the church. All those present were relatives of hers who had died over the years. They were all looking toward the altar and the old woman turned to see what they were watching.

She saw two young men, her infant sons now grown into manhood. Both were hanging—punished for some now unknown crime.

The old woman sat, first in shock, and then lost in thought. After a great time, she fell to her knees, giving thanks that those precious babies of hers had been spared this fate.

～

This story from the Grimm's collection, by focusing on the limitations and losses within the old woman's life, highlights a second task in preparing for old age: After accepting our own mortality, each of us needs to face the limitations and losses which have occurred within our lives and to let go of nonpossible goals.

This Aged Mother, like most of us, has encountered loss. The metaphor that the storyteller uses to tell us about these losses is death. It's a metaphor that helps us understand the pain and the finality of loss in later years.

These years are filled with many types of loss, including the diminishment of energy, eyesight, hearing, mobility, general health, and more. Even the amount of available space shrinks when someone moves into a smaller home and becomes more restricted to that home; this restriction may be epitomized by the loss of a driver's license.

In the movie *Driving Miss Daisy*, Jessica Tandy brilliantly portrays a woman struggling with her grief over the loss of her ability to drive. She, like the Aged Mother, mourns with denial and anger, attacking and blaming until she is finally able to accept. Both the Aged Mother and Miss Daisy initially reject loss as unfair, as some terrible mistake.

It is in the nature of loss that it must be mourned. Those who do not recognize this in order to consciously mourn will discover they are mourning in other ways through anger, stress, depression, or aggression. Others, also avoiding a conscious mourning, may internalize the grief and discover it has attacked their bodies through pain such as headache or backache, or disease such as hypertension.

I remember realizing for the first time that a loss—because of my age—would be permanent. I was preparing for a class I was about to teach one evening, when I discovered I was furious. I put the notes down and began to sit with that feeling, and found myself thinking, "It's not fair. At my age I should be cooking dinner with a bunch of grandchildren all around my skirts. There should be a pie cooling on the windowsill, jars of homemade jams on the shelf, and the smell of a roast emanating from the oven. Instead I'm sitting at my desk eating lowfat yogurt, getting ready to go out on a dark, rainy night to teach a class." I tried to think of someone to blame but wasn't successful.

"Where did that come from?" I wondered. I was fond of yogurt, saw my grandchildren often, and enjoyed teaching. But it seemed I also harbored deep inside a vision of myself as a Midwestern farmwife with eight children and countless grandchildren. This vision, a warm earth-mother fantasy filled with crackling fires and laughing children, was one I had always thought I'd have time for. But time had run out. Even though I had consciously chosen my life's direction—at times against what seemed great odds—there was within me anger and sadness over not being able to have the Walton's fantasy life as well.

My awareness of my limitation had this in common with the experience of the Aged Mother: We each were led into awareness through a strong emotion. In my case, the feeling was anger, while for the Aged Mother, sadness arrived. A strong feeling, popping out from the unconscious, is the signal that something within needs attention.

The Aged Mother got up and went to church, a place of contact with something greater than the human ego or conscious mind. I put my notes down and went through meditation into the unconscious, a place where that which is greater than the human ego also resides.

The unconscious is able to provide insight and understanding. But these are the ending points of the process. We must focus first on what must be done to achieve that resolution.

As I explored my farmwife fantasy, I visualized warmth and nurturing and a surplus of love. I waited with the two feelings, the warmth of the fantasy and the anger at its unattainability. What emerged was first a sadness at the realization this would never be. This sadness was very different from the rational understanding I had that my pathway led elsewhere. The understanding and the feeling of sadness rubbed abrasively against each other. To feel like crying because I had chosen another direction—a direction I liked—seems by cultural standards to be acting like a spoiled child.

However, it was a real feeling and as such needed to be accepted without judgment. This unavailability of another lifestyle also needed to be mourned, and I had fallen into the common trap of not letting myself feel bad over something that was illogical. My thinking went something like this:

"The life of a farmwife is hard work. It is not at all like your fantasy. If you were to mourn, you would be crying over an illusion and that is dumb."

And—

"You want your current life more than you wanted a rural life. After all, you can't go in two directions at once. It is nonsense to feel sad about not being in two places at the same time."

And still again—

"You've never met a farmer! How could you be a farmer's wife?"

The point, of course, is that there is nothing rational or logical about the losses or limitations we experience. If we experience a loss or limitation, no matter how silly or illogical or nonsensical it may appear, we must grieve the loss. I had not grieved this loss. But that is not all there is to this issue. The other question that I needed to pay attention to was why the feeling was emerging on this particular rainy evening. I needed to stay with the feeling and see what else emerged.

What did emerge was another feeling—one of fatigue. It was tempting to say, "Oh yes, I am tired. But what else is going on?" Fatigue seemed mundane.

However, I stayed with the feeling of fatigue and realized I wanted to be nurtured. I wanted to sit on a wide front porch, shelling peas and smelling apple blossoms. I wanted to sink into a feather bed underneath cozy handmade quilts.

As I thought about what all this meant, I realized how hard I had been working and how little time in this past two weeks I had spent with family and friends. For a person who counsels other women to take care of themselves, I was doing a terrible job.

I also began to remember other times when I wished for the farm life. These were also times when I was tired or stressed or overwhelmed—in need of care. When my life was smooth, I never thought of a different lifestyle. Now, whenever that fantasy appears, I know I am getting too far away from creating an earth-mother environment for myself. The fantasy is a signal—a type of shorthand. Although there is no way to go back and live out this other life, there are ways to respond more to my own internal needs as they emerge.

Moving from the external to an understanding of inner meaning is crucial. We have been taught, unfortunately, to blame others for so many things that take place in our lives. "I always wanted children but never had them," a woman will tell me. As I begin to question her, the answers come back that "he" didn't want them, or there wasn't enough money, or the company didn't provide maternity leave, or any of a plethora of reasons, all which may be accurate according to external reality.

But the question of internal reality still remains. Why do you imagine you selected that particular "he" or felt the money was so important or wanted to keep that particular job? How did you, unconsciously, carve out this path for yourself, and what does it mean as you try to understand the meaning of your life? Maybe the questioner will learn that her own needs to be nurtured had to be met first and that, if she had that child, she might have been an inadequate mother. Or perhaps she will discover that the research she did or the picture she painted or the elderly she comforted were her offspring.

Many people with illness in their family have grown up to be great healers. Others, experiencing poverty as children, emerge into adulthood as caring social workers. Abandoned children have grown into loving adults who cared for others' children. There are times when what seems like a great injury becomes the fire that forms the beautiful porcelain vase.

One woman I know, Grace, worked on this issue of past injury for over a year. While the Aged Mother was stuck in her feeling that she had been a victim in life, Grace was determined to move on. She had spent her childhood years with an uncaring and verbally abusive mother. When her children were born, she vowed to be nonabusive. She would give her children what she had never had: a loving mother.

At the same time that Grace was fiercely devoted to her children, she was personally searching and unsettled in her own adult life. She was always looking for a partner to love and be loved by in a way she believed was possible.

Grace married and divorced several times during the years when the children were growing. In such turmoil, she was often forced to work several jobs, which limited the time she had to spend with her children. Nonetheless, she provided for them and encouraged her children in their endeavors with none of the belittling she had received from her own mother.

It was true she didn't have time directly for a lot of daily interaction, and she expected her children to be self-sufficient, but she loved and supported them. They always knew she would drop everything if they had a crisis and it was more than once that she left work because a child was ill or hurt.

What Grace thought was that she was struggling with two separate limitations. The first was the loss of a happy childhood and the second, her inability—through no fault of her own but only because of economic necessity—to be as attentive and nurturing a mother as she wanted her children to have. Although she grieved both losses, her feeling of sadness remained. It seemed a wound that did not heal, and so—unlike the Aged Mother who constantly obsessed about her lost children—Grace tried not to think about her loss.

Life went on for Grace and eventually her children produced children of their own. When Grace visited them, she discovered that she easily grew bored and irritated with the grandchildren although they weren't misbehaving. Her feelings were strong. She wasn't simply tired or wanting a change. After a short time of interaction, she wanted to be left alone. She wanted adult conversation. She wanted quiet. She was horrified that she felt this way toward these children whom she loved, and she was even more shocked to recognize that the feelings were not the result of a passing mood or a bad day. This was a part of who she was.

This experience stunned her. She always supposed that during the years her own children were growing up, it was the stress of her life that had been the culprit, blocking her from mothering in the way she wished were possible. She had believed the loss to be the result of external circumstances. Her current experience as a grandmother was providing her with completely different information. The loss was still real, but it was a loss of an internal ability. She had not been prevented from mothering by external forces. She had mothered as much as she had been able. The limit was an internal one. Not having been emotionally nourished herself, she now began to see that she lacked some deep capacity.

Grace's grief over this insight was enormous. She had always felt a commitment to do better than her mother had done and felt harshly judgmental of women who weren't good mothers. And now this judgment extended to herself.

This time, however, Grace sat with her pain without trying to make it go away as she would have in the past. This was a crucial occurrence. And it's one that's hinted at in the story of the Aged Mother.

We are told the Aged Mother sat, lost in thought. It is this external inaction that allows an internal action to take place. What we are awaiting when we sit in thought is an understanding of our internal world. The search begins for the Ancient Mother, and for us, by sitting alone.

Sitting alone means focusing on the limitation. We must quit doing all the millions of things we do to take our minds away from recognizing the limitations which are there. We must overcome the normal pattern, which is to keep ourselves busy with plans for this or that, memories of all the good times, thoughts about others.

Grace, sitting with her pain, began to realize her limitations at mothering others included herself. Indeed, she had probably been the most neglected of all. She began an internal process of getting to know herself in much the same way a mother becomes acquainted with a new baby. She needed to recognize the meaning of the internal squeaks and cries that she had failed to notice all those years. She realized that many of the cries for nurturing were being communicated to her through her body itself, through various aches and pains.

For quite a long period of time Grace gave her full attention to this internal work. She kept the focus of her awareness on herself and on the need she felt to be mothered. As she did so, feelings began to emerge. There was more grief, which surprised her since she was sure she had already finished her grieving. She felt angry, sad, abandoned, and at times quite helpless.

As the feelings occurred, she discovered they often seemed to have counterparts in her body. There was a stiffness in her muscles, probably from holding back the tears for so long. There were other aches and pains as well. She paid attention to what was happening and began to respond, learning when she needed comforting, when to pamper herself, and when it was necessary to give herself a good push to take a walk.

She read books that related to the issue she was struggling with and began to keep a journal. While some people choose to go to a therapist at this point in their lives, Grace didn't. She did attend some lectures, which seemed helpful, and participated in a one-day workshop focused on self-awareness. Perhaps most importantly, whenever a new situation occurred, Grace asked herself, "Is this what you want to do? Is it what you need to do? How does this help you heal?"

To reach our internal truths, we must sit alone with the limitations, think, and allow the feelings, whatever they may be, to surface.

We will find times where we, like Grace, must put the gained insight into action. If our thinking and feeling have led us to a truth, the action we choose will be a correct one for us. If we have arrived at a wrong place or have only taken a "baby step," we will also know that. Our thinking and feeling allow us to know what is true for ourselves.

The combination of thinking and feeling is essential. Too often in our culture, we act without thinking or we stop at intellectual understanding without allowing the feelings to surface.

Thinking comes from the very rational part of ourselves, based on all our years of understanding life in general as well as understanding our own individual lives. Our thinking includes what we've learned from others as well. It comes from our consciousness, what is called the *ego*. Feelings are, by definition, nonrational and— as the storyteller reminds us through her emphasis on the Aged Mother's desolation and sorrow—feelings are an equally important aspect of the process of self-discovery.

What Grace discovered through this process was of great importance to her healing. She learned that even though she wasn't a "milk-and-cookies mom," she had mothered with love to the extent she knew how. She knew from her own childhood how hurtful and crippling verbal attacks were, and she had not duplicated that behavior.

She had worked hard to learn about what children needed and had provided much of that to her children. She had communicated her very real love in a way her children understood.

No matter how much she might wish that she could have done more at the time, she couldn't have, and now she simply had to accept this and forgive herself. Whatever work was left to do belonged to those children as adults.

What Grace experienced as she explored this internal area was similar to what we all experience as we struggle with limitations. Limitations are those boundaries that exist within life. Some are natural—humans can't fly; we can't live someone else's life. Some limitations come from our early family and communal environments. Grace exemplified this as she repeated parts of the pattern she had experienced as a child in her own mothering. Still other limitations are self-imposed—if you believe you can't learn to drive, you won't. Limitations are always connected with a loss of some type.

At first Grace, as most people do, denied any limitation existed. During her mothering years she saw herself as a loving and nurturing mother. Any evidence that contradicted that view was blamed on circumstances outside herself, such as her own heavy work schedule.

But as she had more time to relate to her grandchildren, she developed an awareness that this limitation was a part of who she was. This awareness came through noticing her feelings, even though those feelings were not blatantly visible in her behavior. This awakening was very painful.

Some time later, Grace was back visiting the grandchildren. She had not really thought much about how she would handle future times with them during the time she had been working on herself. However, much to her surprise and delight, she discovered on this next visit that her patience had increased, as had her sense of enjoyment. Her internal work had made a difference in her responses to her outer world.

She also found she was beginning to see her own mother differently. Her past anger and bitterness evolved into a sense that her mother, too, was a woman who had been hurt, perhaps by her own mother who had died young.

The Aged Mother's insight begins with the ringing of church bells and occurs within a church building where she is visited by dead relatives. What the story is telling us is that the Aged Mother enters another realm, the numinous, or spiritual, world of the unconscious where we are able to see and feel aspects of the meaning and the truth of our lives. The doorway to this world is feeling— our emotions. Meaning and insight occur as we process our feelings with our intellects.

Such understanding comes from something wiser than anything that exists in our conscious minds or egos. For the Aged Mother this wisdom is represented as a dead aunt. What occurs for the Aged Mother, and what occurs for all of us at such times, is the placing of the event within a larger context. Pain is then able to receive the healing of meaning.

There are many psychological theories that attempt to explain this process. None of them, however, is able to adequately describe the experience. Some of my clients have described the feeling as "being able to breathe again," or "seeing clearly for the first time," or "having a weight lifted."

When we accept the idea that meaning or truth can be found in our unconscious, we reverse our way of thinking. Most of us have been taught to be rational and to accept only what can be touched and submitted to the rigors of research. Dipping into the unconscious, trailing after a feeling and waiting for something we cannot see to give us an answer seems a bit strange. In fact, it sounds like such a bizarre approach that, if it were not for the experiences of people who have tried it, it would be an idea without a future.

When we do follow our feelings into this realm of the unconscious, we encounter a Jungian archetype called the Self. The Self is the center of the unconscious just as the ego is the center of consciousness. This archetype of the Self is the all-knowing part of ourselves—what Jung calls the subject of our totality. This is the place where the information about meaning and truth is stored. While we may prefer to think that the conscious part of ourselves, called ego, has whatever answer is needed, it simply does not.

The Aged Mother had been stuck within her emotion of sadness for years. Finally she journeys into another place, a place deep within, where she finds a truth. It is only when this deep honesty about meaning occurs that a limitation or loss can be accepted, for that is the time when there will be meaning.

There is something so pure, so awesome about the truth when it is revealed by the Self that to come into its presence does cause one to fall to one's knees. "To fall to one's knees" is to be filled with awe, or reverence, for the purity of the truth. The Aged Mother fell to her knees because of the intensity of this awesome experience. In this instance, the collapse of the conscious position brings one to one's knees because experiencing meaning is such an overwhelming, humbling experience. The ego is humbled by the wisdom of the unconscious.

A client, Joan, came to see me because her husband, after thirty years of marriage, had left her. She grieved the loss but also blamed him as the villain who killed their marriage.

In the initial sessions of therapy she was in the denial phase, maintaining, "It was a good marriage. I don't know how he could do such a thing. We were very happy."

As she sat with this loss, allowing herself the opportunity to think and to feel the pain, she grew aware of many things she had given little thought to as they occurred. She began to see areas in the marriage that were completely superficial.

She began as well to see that the superficiality was put there by both of them to prevent arguments and anger. She saw parts of herself that she hadn't allowed to grow or develop lest they create discord within the marriage.

She felt and thought about all these things, and as she did, she also began to see the subtle ways in which she, too, had pulled back or turned away and how she herself had participated in the creation of the limitations in the marriage.

While she had physically stayed in the marriage, her spirit had left. She had withdrawn small bits and pieces of herself until only the most superficial Joan remained to relate.

She felt pain at this discovery. The relationship was dead and had been so for a long time. She felt pain at seeing that she had also colluded to keep the illness within the marriage a secret as it developed. Although it was disturbing for her to admit to herself, she saw how she had participated in creating this final separation. Once she saw this reality, she was no longer able to see herself as a victim.

As she explored these feelings about the marriage, Joan discovered the connection that was there on an internal level. She had not only hidden parts of herself from her husband but also from herself. She began searching for what had allowed her to avoid herself and him.

What she uncovered was both distressing and, at the same time, liberating. Insight freed her from the lies and limitations. She experienced an epiphany, or the appearance of an inner god of enlightenment, which brought her flashes of understanding. The marriage as well as the divorce now began to take on a meaning in the context of her whole life. While she still felt pain and grief, it was now of a different nature.

As we reach down and grasp hold of our own meaning, we are able to accept our pain as one part of how life is. We find a strength that comes from the knowledge that we are connected to life

itself. We find strength from the realization that we are fully participating in life rather than being "done to" as victims. This experience
frees us to begin the healing process.

We are blocked from reaching such a point of enlightenment
when we convince ourselves that we know all there is to know about
the situation. As humans, we often use all of our accumulated experience to determine what "is" and then stick to our story in just the
way a young child is tempted to stick to the story of not having
touched the cookie jar, although the cookie crumbs down the front
of her dress indicate otherwise.

While it is difficult to sit alone, think, and feel, it helps if one
can accept the possibility that there is more truth to a situation than
we seem to know. An old Eastern tale illustrates this value. I also like
the story because it, like so many old tales, seems as alive and powerful today in my life and the lives of other women facing age as it
was those hundreds of years ago when kings and czars rode into villages searching for soldiers.

ᔐ We'll See ᔐ

A FARMER ONCE had a beautiful stallion, and all the villagers said to
him, "You are fortunate."

The farmer would only reply, "We'll see."

One day the stallion ran away, and the villagers said, "You are
unfortunate."

"We'll see," the farmer replied.

The stallion returned with a dozen wild ponies, and the villagers
all exclaimed, "Oh, how very fortunate you are."

"We'll see," was all the farmer would say.

The farmer's son, in attempting to break one of the ponies, was thrown and broke his leg. "Oh, now he will not be able to help you with the work. How unfortunate."

"We'll see," the farmer calmly replied.

The Czar's men came through the village, gathering up all the able-bodied young men to fight a distant war. The farmer's son was left behind, due to his broken leg. "Oh, how fortunate," the villagers cried.

But the farmer would only reply, "We'll see."

∼

The farmer had lived long enough to understand thoroughly that meaning is not immediately obvious. The ego must be very careful not to jump rapidly to rigid conclusions. We've all fallen into the trap of making a quick judgment only to realize that we were dead wrong. "The world is flat" seemed to make sense once upon a time. Then someone came along and said, "No, the world is round." Many were trapped with what they had always believed, with what their senses told them, and they refused to change their minds.

"The marriage failed because of my husband's betrayal," Joan said and she really believed it. Everything she saw and heard, everything she was aware of experiencing told her it was his fault. But through her own inner work, Joan was able to struggle with her "knowing," to suspend her certainty, just enough to allow an inner voice to speak to her. "Look again, Joan," the voice said. "Notice more of what happened. Notice what feelings you have ignored. Sit with this awhile."

There are many facets to understanding and accepting the limitations that occur in one's life. A story from England, "The Old Woman Who Lived in a Vinegar Bottle," speaks to a different aspect of life's limitations.

⌒ The Old Woman Who Lived in a Vinegar Bottle ⌒

ONCE, LONG AGO, there was an old woman who lived in a vinegar bottle. The old woman was unhappy with this arrangement and so she complained. One day, as she was complaining, a fairy happened to be flying past. The fairy stopped to listen.

"It's a shame. It's a shame. I shouldn't oughta have to live like this."

"What would you like?" the fairy asked her.

"A cottage," the old woman quickly answered. "A cottage with a thatched roof and a lovely garden."

"Very well," answered the fairy. "Tonight before you go to bed, turn around three times. Then go to sleep, and in the morning you will see what you shall see."

The old woman did as she was told. And in the morning when she woke there was a lovely little cottage with a thatched roof and a garden in the front. The woman, however, had not remembered to thank the fairy.

The fairy went off, north, south, east, and west on her own business, but soon decided to come check on how things were going. When she flew past she heard not a happy old woman but one who was again complaining.

"I shouldn't oughta have to live like this," the old woman was saying.

"Well," said the fairy, "what would you like?"

"I would like to be in a larger house in the village with neighbors," the old woman answered.

"Tonight," the fairy said, "before you go to bed, turn around three times. Then go to sleep, and when you wake up in the morning you will see what you shall see."

The old woman did as she was told without so much as a thank-you. The fairy flew off, north, south, east, and west, and, the next morning when the old woman woke, she was in a lovely little house in town with neighbors all around. Still she complained.

When the fairy returned again, the old woman wanted a mansion in the country. The next time it was to be a duchess, and then to be a queen in a palace ruling her own country.

Each time the fairy gave her the same instructions: "Before you go to bed, turn around three times. Then go to sleep, and when you wake in the morning, you will see what you shall see."

Each time the old woman followed the instructions but never was there a thank-you for the fairy as she was flying off to attend to her other business.

When the old woman was a queen, however, the fairy was sure she would be content. She returned one more time to see, and perhaps, to receive a thank-you. When she arrived, she heard once again the familiar sound of complaining.

"What now?" asked the fairy.

"Pope," the old woman answered. "I should be Pope and then I would control the entire world."

With a sigh, the fairy repeated her familiar instructions: "Before you go to bed tonight, turn around three times. Then go to sleep, and when you wake, you will see what you shall see."

Once again the woman followed the fairy's instructions, and once again forgot to thank the fairy. This time, however, when she awoke she found herself back in her vinegar bottle.

∼

The old woman of this story is obviously unhappily living in a small, unusual space. That her unhappiness stems in part from the narrowness of her living space is something we can understand. A narrowing of the world is a reality of aging: Some women sell the family home, downsizing their living conditions out of need. Others lose energy and go out less. Many find the world contracting because of hearing or vision problems.

While the limitations in the story can parallel some outer limitations, we need to look at the specific images within the story in order to understand what these limitations mean.

The vinegar bottle house has several very unusual characteristics, resonant with meaning and symbolism. To begin with, this old woman's home is a *glass bottle,* reminding us of the expression, "People who live in glass houses shouldn't throw stones."

Glass allows others to see what is inside—making us transparent. It also insulates—keeping in warmth and keeping out cold winds. In some way the old woman who is living in this glass bottle is protected from something.

Both heat and cold are symbols for emotion, symbols so clear they pop up in everyday speech. Phrases like "in the heat of the night," "cold as ice," "she froze me out," "in a cold sweat," and "doing a slow burn" all indicate how universally heat and cold are connected to our emotions as symbols.

So here we have an old woman who lives in a world in which she can see things and be seen, yet she is protected from emotion She is able, in other words, to perceive and to understand things intellectually. In this case she understands that the world she lives in is too small, but protected by the glass, she cannot feel a connection and thus lacks any real understanding.

In my own life, I tend to chew on problems. "This is the problem," I will say. "I could do this or this or even that. What should I do?"

And although there are myriad solutions, none seems to feel right, none seems to be the correct solution. Then, suddenly, I spiral around to a place where there is an intense feeling!

"Oh! So that is what this is about!" I find myself saying.

"Yes," a friend will say. "That is what you've been saying all along."

But to me things seem clear for the first time only when they are linked to the strong feeling. It was the emotional connection that led to my understanding of the obvious. I literally could not understand until I arrived at the place where the problem's emotion lay hidden. Until then, I had been behind glass, seeing the problem without really experiencing it.

Insulation from emotions has a severe effect upon relationships. I've seen many couples who are troubled because one member of the partnership intellectually grasps what the other is saying but doesn't get it emotionally.

"You hurt my feelings," she will say.

"Tell me what I did. I didn't mean to, and I won't do it again," he will reply, and then will proceed to avoid the specific offending behavior while missing the overall point.

One woman said, "I feel I don't matter."

"Well, you do matter, so give me an example," her husband replied.

"You forgot my birthday."

So her husband had his secretary write that date on the office calendar and buy a present the next year to send to his wife with his card. The wife knew her husband could not have selected that gift and understandably had the same angry reaction. The husband remained confused.

He had understood the particular, but had missed the point. He was living in a glass bottle.

When, like the husband, we work rationally with situations, while remaining insulated from the feelings behind them, we go in circles. Nothing changes until we can reach the emotions that belong with a particular problem. So when it comes to the limitations we face with aging, we may know intellectually that something must change, and we may even feel angry that things are not right, but we are stuck on a treadmill until we can get to the emotions.

And quite often we don't want to! We can find ourselves caught in a pattern of finding excuses—insurmountable ones!—rather than getting behind the problem.

"I'm exhausted," a client will say. "I need a week by myself."

But when I agree and even suggest a way in which she could have that week, I am met with an immediate barrage of reasons why taking any time off is just impossible.

There is this demand, and that deadline. There is this other person's needs and that relative's problems. Even a weekend off is impossible.

"What about an evening?" I inquire.

"Well, maybe next week."

But then there is a list of things that must be done first. It is a case of the glass bottle again: The person feels trapped but doesn't take the feeling seriously.

But if you take the feelings seriously, you will often find the solution is magically at hand. Consider the woman in the vinegar bottle. Not for nothing is she living in a bottle designed to hold an everyday household item long familiar to the lives of women, a substance that has been a medicine for colds, burns, and memory loss, a substance that has been an aid to healthy longevity, and is also a cleansing agent. Vinegar, as women have known through the millennia, disinfects, kills pain, and restores skin to its appropriate pH balance.

The old woman, it seems, was surrounded by something which would solve her problem. The agent of her cure was literally at her fingertips. But, because she was insulated from her emotions, she was unable to see what it was and that it was there.

What in our lives is the vinegar? Vinegar is the obvious solution that would restore our balance but which we fail to see. Vinegar is the *correct* thing to do that we fail to see or understand because it is not visible to us. Others may see it, but we do not.

For example, in a therapy session I will listen to a client describing in great detail her feelings about something in her relationship with her husband. She is very clear. What is being said is reasonable. I will say to her, "That sounds very clear. Have you said that to your husband?" The thought has never occurred to her although it is a solution that would open dialogue and begin a process of healing.

The story women names her problem as one of restricted space. If only she could have, she thinks, a better, larger living arrangement, she would be happy. The cure, she believes, is external. Better living quarters mean happiness.

One woman I knew behaved so much like the old woman in the vinegar bottle, she could have been the model used by the storyteller.

Originally living in Florida, she complained bitterly to her California son. She was lonely, the weather was too hot, her apartment was not right.

Just when he agreed to help her move to California, she fell and broke her hip. After surgery and convalescence, she was moved to a nursing home near where her California son lived.

There she became depressed, hating the nursing home. The son then found an assisted living home where she could move as soon as she was able to walk. She soon moved in and perked up.

Yet after a few months in this new home, she was again complaining.

Her son took her with him and together they looked at other places to live. She picked one and moved. Again she was chipper and enthusiastic at first. But after a few months in the new place, she was again unhappy. The son, however, didn't move her this time. The problem, he realized, was not with her surroundings.

For both the woman in the vinegar bottle and the moving-around lady from Florida, the problem was not in external conditions, but was internal.

All they consciously knew was that they were unhappy, and they were living in a small space. The fault must be in the small space. Their conclusions remind me of the view taken by a four-year-old friend of mine who ate an ice-cream cone, and then began feeling ill. As it happened, she had come down with measles. But to my friend it was "the ice cream made me sick." It was months before she was willing to try ice cream again.

Let's switch from ice cream to vinegar again, though, and see what the symbolism of vinegar has to say. As we have seen, the fact that the old woman was living in a vinegar bottle means that the cleansing agent was right at hand, if she could connect with the emotions behind her dissatisfaction.

But what the symbolism of vinegar shows as well is another psychological truth. It indicates that if you are ready to deal with your feelings, to discover and feel what is really bothering you, you must expect there to be a sour, bitter, acid quality to what you must then experience.

But if you go through this sourness, you will be relieved of the main pain. You will see clearly. A film will have been dissolved. You will be restored to balance.

The experience of change begins with some type of discontent, disease, dissatisfaction, or sense of uneasiness. But as a result of conscious discontent, energy can appear. In the vinegar woman's story, the energy, prompted by her conscious discontent, appears in a magical manner. The fairy, that creative internal source of ideas, that magical willingness to solve a problem, appears all of a sudden as if from nowhere.

But things do not work out well for the old woman, despite her having followed instructions. She turned three times, and did as she was instructed . . . yet . . . .

There are two ways of going around in a circle. Obsessively going around in circles, getting nowhere, much as a hamster moves on his wheel, is the nonproductive way. Contrasted with that is the idea of ruminating and pondering over and over until a new insight is hatched. The old woman didn't ponder the problem until something new emerged.

The old woman felt the discontent, but she too quickly assumed the solution was external. Her quest was one of external acquisitions to heal what was an internal need.

Most of us seem to start at this concrete level to solve our problems. There really is no difficulty with this until it doesn't work. When we find ourselves, like the old woman, still experiencing the problem after applying our concrete solution, we know we need to move to a deeper level.

We move to this deeper, or symbolic, level by pondering the meaning of the more concrete level. Within the story, the old woman wants a bigger house. Houses are containers, places that keep our belongings, families, and ourselves warm and safe and dry. When we think of being warm, safe, and dry on an emotional or psychic level, we think of feeling cared for or nurtured. Since the original uterine home is common to us all, we associate this type of all-containing nurturing with the image of mother. Even for those who had a poor actual mother, a home is symbolic of the safety and security which the "good" mother provides. By wanting a better home, the storyteller is letting us know that the old woman needs nurturing of some type.

The old woman, instead of examining her present life to see how to meet this need for nurturing, looks outward for an external solution. She tells herself that although something inside is in pain, she will heal through some external salve. This looking outward for a solution is the same dynamic that is operative in the addict, whether that is an alcoholic, a shop-o-holic, or a TV addict. The addict uses something external, in an addictive manner, to ease a pain. But the pain returns whenever the salve wears off, necessitating more and more of the substance. When a pain involves internal issues, no amount of external liniment will suffice.

In all of our lives there are past losses and limitations that have not been accepted, mourned, or understood as meaningful. One piece of our work in preparing for age is to identify and work with these areas.

"The Woman Who Lived in a Vinegar Bottle" tells us that we may be like the story woman, insulated from our feelings about these losses. We may identify the problem, as she does, on a concrete level rather than seeing it as an internal or psychological issue. When we make that mistake, it will follow that we will look outside of ourselves for the solution. It is also true that one cottage, one drink, one hot fudge sundae, one pill does not ease the pain for long, and we, like the story woman, continue to escalate until we return to ourselves.

The story tells us another important truth. There is the necessary vinegar, the necessary energy, to clean, balance, polish, or shine. We have internal resources. They, like the residue of vinegar, may not be immediately obvious. But they are there.

The woman from Florida who moved so often had grown up as an orphan. Her childhood was spent in many homes where she always felt she did not belong. As a child she did not cry. Her energy was focused on how to stay out of trouble. Once she was an adult, she felt those times were behind her. Whenever any memories or feelings came into her mind, she pushed them away. After all, she would tell herself, that was ages ago.

But her feelings of displacement and alienation, with the grief that accompanied them, kept poking through. No current home felt like home because she was behind this glass wall, isolated from her own emotions.

The fairy ordered work to be done: Turn three times before going to bed. The fairy was quite explicit about this. Only after the necessary work of turning around three times is done will the unconscious start to respond with images and insights for us.

In order to understand and reach the emotions of the problem, we must take time to mull and brood. We must begin the process—and introspection and psychological work is a process.

This may have been easier for our grandmothers and great-grandmothers to understand since so much in their daily lives involved a process. The food they ate had to be personally planted, tended, harvested, preserved, and cooked. While we buy a supermarket loaf of bread, their connection with this staff of life was much more involved. After growing and grinding the grain, there was mixing and kneading, rising and baking. To really know something, we must enter into some relationship with it, and this is a process that takes time.

Even though most of us no longer grow and preserve our own food, we, as women, still understand a great deal about processes. It takes nine months to produce a new life and much longer to raise a child. Much of our lives has been spent watching and participating in the process of growth. Now is the time to see that process in terms of our own lives.

"Turn around three times," the fairy instructs. "Keep going around and around until you feel what there is to feel about the discontent within your life."

Again, in fairy tales, no symbol is accidental; nothing is by chance. Why three times? Three in the world of fairy tales is a number that means "as long as necessary." To ancient people, in the Tarot, that old means of divination, the number three speaks of new creation coming from the union of the two. It is the image of the couple with child, a union of opposites that takes nine months to materialize. The third, this child, is not a duplicate of the father or the mother. It is a new creation.

"Turn around three times," the fairy instructs the old woman. "Keep turning around until something new has been created."

Unfortunately, the old woman in the vinegar bottle, though she turns three times, does not turn enough. She runs in circles, like a hamster on its wheel. The point is that the fairy is insisting on some difficult work: If the internal energy is not released, one sees only external answers.

After the fairy grants the old woman's wishes we are told that she "forgot to thank the fairy." Because the storyteller keeps repeating this, we know that there is clearly something more instructive here than a reminder that good manners are important.

The fairy symbolizes internal energy available in what seems a magical way because it is not subject to our conscious control. This life-changing energy is archetypal energy, rising from someplace deep within the stream where we are connected outside ourselves.

Whether this energy is called spiritual or archetypal or divine does not matter in understanding the symbolism we are seeing. This energy is far greater than what a single ego can produce. It is the energy before which one must stand in awe or fall on one's knees. Saying thank you is a symbolic way to express that this energy comes to us as a gift from somewhere beyond ourselves, and if we do not appreciate it, it will not continue to be there for us.

Consider a person with a great talent for music. The talent is there as a gift she was given from somewhere beyond herself. If that talent is cherished, appreciated, and valued, it will then be cultivated by the person and it will grow. However, if the person doesn't value or appreciate the talent, and spends all her time and energy doing other nonmusical things, the talent will erode. One must say thank you for whatever gifts have been given or they will disappear.

Psychologically, thank you means developing on a conscious level the necessary discipline to attend to this energy. This discipline comes from our rational parts. It is the self-responsibility which impels us to set limits, to participate, to pay attention, to stay focused on and conscious of what is important.

Psychologically, thank you also means accepting hospitably the energy that has been given as a gift. This gift is to be treated as tenderly and lovingly as a newborn or a favorite friend who has come from afar.

The old woman's return to the vinegar bottle illustrates that nothing has changed. If she is to grow into her wise old age—making the strong connection between the ego and Self, which isn't possible when we're younger but which is essential if we're to have a satisfying older age—she must face the bitterness of the vinegar bottle. Facing the problem, looking squarely at the bitterness, whatever it may be, is the only way to reach a positive ending. We must give up the insulation of the glass and allow ourselves to feel what needs to be felt. Only then will we know what needs to be done.

One midlife client struggled for a very long time with her bitterness over her relationship with her mother. The mother had been cold and rejecting, favoring the woman's brother. The woman remembered only criticism and sarcasm from her mother during her childhood.

In adulthood she had stayed away from her mother as much as possible. She never wrote and only seldom talked on the phone or visited.

During their once-a-year visits my client always anticipated trouble, and indeed something always occurred that reinforced her feelings of rejection and hurt. She felt she had accepted the reality that her mother was incapable of being the warm and fun mother she wished for. However, there was hope, she felt, in another direction.

My client had one child, a daughter now grown. She had devoted herself to this girl as the child was growing, fearful of repeating any of the hurtful behavior she had experienced with her own mother.

Yet now her daughter was living some distance away, never writing or calling, seldom coming to visit. When they did get together, it seemed inevitably an argument would break out between them, leaving my client feeling rejected and hurt.

"It's like a nightmare," she said at one point. "I think she is meaner to me than I ever thought about being to my mother, and I'm the good mother!"

My client then began a series of running-away behaviors. The first was redecorating the house, followed by volunteering for eight different organizations. Then she began obsessive traveling, leaving time only for occasional appointments. When none of these behaviors provided any relief for her feelings, she came back into therapy, defeated.

She was back in the vinegar bottle with the opportunity now to form some type of relationship with the pain and gain some understanding of it. This was a struggle that took many months, but she was able to do what needed to be done.

What she saw, when it was all said and done, was the feeling that had hidden beneath her anger and bitterness. She faced the vinegar of her own neediness. She saw that, having lacked a relationship with her own mother, she had placed all of those needs onto her relationship with her own daughter. It was too much for the daughter to bear if she herself were to become her own person, and so she pushed her mother away.

It was not what either of them wanted. Once the mother was able to see/feel what she was doing, she could change. When I last saw them, they were finding ways to separate and connect. The woman, in returning to the bitter vinegar within her life, was able to transform the bitterness into something that could heal.

Thus in preparing for our aging, we must face the limitations, mistakes, and failures that have occurred within our lives. In facing these instead of running away, we must work somehow to connect, to pull them close, to allow ourselves to feel whatever pain and bitterness may be present. Only by facing the vinegar and moving through it will we be able to accept what has occurred and transform the pain into some meaning within our lives.

In doing so, we also open ourselves to energy that comes from some source other than our conscious being; a source which some call the unconscious and which some call the divine.

This is work which is internal in the sense that it is about our psyches, our feelings, our spiritual lives. There is a Russian story that gives us more insight into the nature of this internal quest.

⁓ The String Bean That Went Through the Roof of the World ⁓

ONCE AN OLD WOMAN named Eugenia lived with her husband Onuphre in a small hut in Russia. They had very little to their name except for a bed, a table, and a rooster and a hen who lived inside with them.

One day the rooster and hen began making noise, for something unusual had happened. They had each found a seed. The rooster took his seed to Onuphre who, upon seeing it was a string bean seed and not enough for a dinner, tossed it underneath the table. The hen gave her seed to Eugenia who saw it was a lima bean seed. She tossed the lima bean seed underneath the same table.

The two forgot about the seeds, but the next morning, when they awoke, they discovered the two seeds had rooted in the hard dirt floor and had grown into an intertwined vine, which was now pushing against the underside of the tabletop. When they saw this, Onuphre took his saw and cut the table in half so the vines would have room to grow. And grow they did. Within the hour they were up to the ceiling. Once again Onuphre got his saw, but instead of cutting down the beanstalk, he cut a hole in the ceiling. Eugenia and Onuphre stood, watching the beanstalk grow, and then decided they would follow it up to heaven. They began to climb.

They climbed all of the long day and Eugenia had to stop many times to rest—for it was a hard climb for one so old—but finally, by nightfall, they had reached the top of the beanstalk and climbed off, setting their feet into heaven. Who should be standing there, in front of a small cabin, but God himself.

"Hello. I'm old Eugenia and this is my old husband, Onuphre. We've come to visit and are very tired from our climb. Could we rest in your cabin?"

"Yes," God answered, "but there is one rule. I keep cakes in this cabin and you must promise not to touch them."

"We promise," they answered, and went inside to sleep. But as soon as they entered and lay down, Eugenia said, "Those cakes smell so good. I want to see how they taste."

"Go to sleep," Onuphre said to her, and he turned over and began to snore. Eugenia, however, got up and went over to the cakes. She picked up a very small one, moving the others around on the platter so that no one would notice.

Just as she was ready to bite into the cake, there was a great commotion. All the cakes fell apart, turning back into flour and eggs and sugar and vanilla. The platter they had been on broke into a hundred pieces.

The noise woke the old man, and the two of them spent the rest of the night trying to remake the cakes and to repair the platter, but nothing they tried would work, and by morning there was flour and eggs and broken pieces of platter all over the room. Just as the morning light began to come into the room, God entered.

"Did you touch my cakes?" He asked.

"Oh no," the two of them lied. At that point they found themselves sliding down the beanstalk.

The next morning Eugenia and Onuphre decided to visit heaven once more. They spent the day climbing and found God standing at the top of the stalk when they arrived at dusk.

"Hello. Remember us? I'm old Eugenia and this is Onuphre. We've come to visit again and would like to spend the night as we're tired from our climb. Could we sleep outside the cabin?"

"Yes," God answered. "You may sleep in my vineyard, but do not touch any of the grapes tonight."

"Oh, you may be sure that we won't," they answered, and lay down beneath the cool and fragrant vines. The smell of the grapes was very strong, and it wasn't long before Eugenia was sitting back up again.

"Don't touch them," Onuphre warned, and fell asleep. But Eugenia thought to herself, "I'll just taste one little grape. Surely no one will notice."

As soon as she touched the grapes, all the grapes fell off the vines. The entire width and length of the vineyard was covered with grapes. Onuphre woke and the two old people spent the night trying to reattach the grapes, but when morning came, as far as the eye could see there were piles of grapes on the ground. At that very moment, God arrived.

"You haven't touched my grapes, have you?" God asked.

"Oh no. Oh no," the two lied a second time, and once more they found themselves sliding down the beanstalk.

This time they rested for several days, but they could not forget their visit to heaven. They wanted to return, and so early one morning, they began to climb once more. When they arrived that evening, God was waiting for them.

"Here we are again, old Eugenia and Onuphre, come to visit you and spend the night."

"You may sleep tonight in my carriage house, but you must be sure that this time you do not touch anything," God commanded.

"Oh, we do promise," they said, and went in to sleep. Onuphre fell right to sleep, but Eugenia lay there, looking at all the wonderful carriages. "Just to sit in one would be such a treat," she said to herself. "I wouldn't take it anywhere and it couldn't hurt to just sit. After all, I've come a long way and I am a very old woman."

And with that she got up and went over to a carriage. She put her foot on the step to climb in, but as she did, the carriage and every other carriage in the carriage house fell into hundreds of pieces. The noise woke Onuphre.

Although the two worked all night, by morning when God arrived the carriages remained in pieces. God was very sad and very angry.

"Did you touch a carriage?" he asked.

Oh no," they lied once more. At that they ran as fast as they could to the beanstalk and slid down, but before they could reach the bottom, God caused the beanstalk to break. The two tumbled down and rolled to the door of their hut.

They have lived there in the hut for many years since that last climb into heaven because God did not want them back until they had learned a thing or two.

⌢

Eugenia's task, like ours, is to work for wholeness. In the previous story of the vinegar bottle, wholeness was represented by the four directions in which the fairy flew. The vinegar bottle woman's immediate task on her way toward wholeness was to accept some internal loss that was showing itself to her through the external limitation of her house.

Eugenia's story also contains symbols of wholeness such as the bringing together of the pairs of feminine and masculine items. Feminine hen, lima bean, and Eugenia are each paired with the masculine rooster, string bean, and Onuphre. Eugenia, however, is missing all the signals that tell her there is work that she must do. What loss, what limitation must be accepted? What is it that Eugenia must transform in some way into meaning for her life? What does this story have to teach us about this process?

Eugenia is living in meager circumstances. She is given a gift that she does not value—the gift of two beans. Bean seeds are edible, reminding us that there is a potential for nourishment for Eugenia. Beans are a staple in the diet of many people; they are full of healthy amino acids and a good source of energy. The old expression "she's full of beans" means, of course, she's full of energy.

Energy alone is not enough. We begin to understand that truth as the story unfolds. There is a lack of thoughtfulness, an impulsiveness that begins early in the story and portends trouble.

It's troubling to hear that Eugenia begins by carelessly tossing the seeds on the dirt. Any of us who have gardened know that plants, to flourish, must be well planted. When placed deep in the earth, seeds are provided with nourishment, and are given the opportunity to put down deep roots. But those things that are planted carelessly are often stunted or easily blown away. Psychologically, a part of Eugenia that needs to grow was carelessly handled.

The beans are the creative potential that comes in unexpected ways to all, but that requires that we notice and handle it correctly. Potential has come to many aging women, and when planted well in psychic gardens will produce new directions, new relationships, and new creations. Part of the magic of those beans is that the outcome is not predictable. But what can be anticipated is that the Self has in store for each of us something of meaning—if we do our work.

But Eugenia does not do the work. The seeds land underneath the table. We see symbolic tables and tabletops in many instances: the last supper of Jesus with his disciples, the Round Table of King Arthur and his knights, the Thanksgiving table of the Pilgrims, and the family dinner table. Each of these is a place of both physical and emotional nourishment.

But under the table is often linked symbolically to falsehood. When one is paid "under the table" there is a deception of some type. Under the table is a dark, shadowy place. Eugenia is going after plenitude in an unconscious, unintentional way.

"I'd never do such a thing," I tell myself, forgetting how long I tossed the seed of this book under the table. "At least I'd never practice deception," I continue thinking, pushing away any memory of the times I jumped into something believing I'd found a great bargain, only to discover how badly I had deceived myself. In fact, I suspect my initial reaction of seeing Eugenia's behavior as different from mine is itself a self-deception since we are all capable of being unconscious about some aspects of our lives.

Still the beanstalk grows. This creative process, the beanstalk, seems to be a most forgiving and patient process. It forgives having been planted so carelessly, without light or water. It continues to grow. Later in the story, the stalk remains in place despite Eugenia's repeated attempts to steal from God. It is certainly good to hear that our bumbling mistakes, our carelessness and unconsciousness will not immediately cause our creative energy to disappear.

There is an un-thought-through quality to Eugenia/Onuphre's behavior. She seems consistently to do the first thing that pops into her mind: Cut the table, cut the roof, climb the beanstalk, taste and touch things. She seems unable to hold still long enough to think through any plan. In this she reminds me of my grandchild at about fourteen months. If something was pretty and attracted her attention, she felt she should taste and touch it. She, at that age, had no ability to discriminate between what was hers or not, what was safe or not, what would feel good or bad. Glass, ice, strange dogs, fire, electrical cords were all as appealing as blocks and teddy bears. If she thought she could get to it, off she went. Eugenia's behavior has the same innocent, unconscious impulsiveness. She is immature, rather than malicious. She is just unable to restrain herself.

"Why did you go out with him?" I asked a client one day. "He's not only twenty years younger than you, but you describe him as boring. What on earth made you say yes to his invitation?"

She looked blankly at me. It was clear she had no idea why she had said yes. Apparently it was one of those things that seemed like a good idea at the time, but was not thought through.

The client and Eugenia were needy. What created the problem in each case was that neither knew what the neediness was about. Eugenia cannot find what she needs unless and until she is able to slow down and find out what loss or what limitation is at the root of all this energy.

I have a friend who is so tuned into her own body that she immediately knows which type of food her body needs at any given moment. While most of us experience hunger, my friend experiences a need for potassium and will grab a banana to eat. She tells me that with discipline anyone can learn to be this body-wise. The secret is in slowing down and tuning in because the body always gives the correct message if we know how to hear.

Eugenia must slow down and learn how to hear what message is coming from her psyche. She is hungry (needy) for something. We know this because she keeps grabbing for whatever is placed in front of her. She is completely unconscious of the inappropriateness of her behavior.

Eugenia is unconscious, but she also feels entitled. She falls into the trap of hubris or arrogance. "Don't do this," God says. "I can if I want to," answers Eugenia through her behavior—she says nothing actually, but just does what she wants. "If I just take a very little," she thinks, "God won't notice." It doesn't matter what God's rules are. Eugenia makes the rules for herself.

There are others who have also broken the rules. There was Eve, tasting of the tree of knowledge in the garden in Eden. In the story of Psyche and Eros, the beautiful maiden Psyche disobeys her god/husband, Eros. Eros in this story had forbidden her to look at him, but Psyche, while he sleeps, lights the lamp to see him.

Both Eve and Psyche disobey, but by so doing each set into motion a journey toward consciousness or greater awareness. There are times, it seems, when to do only what one is told is to remain in a state of childishness and dependence, to remain in an unseeing, unconscious state without knowledge.

But there is an important difference between Eve and Psyche on the one hand, and Eugenia on the other.

The consequence of Eve's disobedience was that she would, from that point on, bear children in pain. Symbolically, creation— the bringing forth of the new, whether this new thing is a baby or part of one's own consciousness—is like birth, a long and at times painful process.

Psyche also had to pay a price for leaving her childish dependence. She loses contact with her beloved husband, and must, before she can get him back, perform a series of difficult tasks.

Eugenia, like the others, is filled with arrogance, but she doesn't pay. She never changes or grows from the experience.

We see the seriousness of her naïveté when Eugenia repeats the behavior—without having increased her insight or awareness. She speaks directly to God, seemingly aware of where she is, yet she is unable to accept the limits or learn from the first or second mistake.

Eugenia is like my client who dated the man twenty years younger than herself, or the clients who appeared to have recog nized that something they were about to do was a mistake, but went ahead anyway,

They are people who look as if they know what they're doing, but they don't. They are childlike in the way that a child may be able to verbalize that fire is hot, but simultaneously does not comprehend the consequences of touching the flame.

We see the same type of problem in ourselves when we use a charge card for something we really can't afford, eat something in conflict with our healthy intent, or unrealistically overextend ourselves at work or at home. There are countless temptations to behave as if we were entitled to do as we please without consequence. This behavior is promoted by merchants, merchandisers, and advertisers and is acquiesced to eagerly by the immature, entitled child within.

In the story, we are reminded of overeating, alcoholism, and traveling in the fast lane by images of cakes, grapes, and carriages. Eugenia is striving for self-satisfaction in an instant way. But there is no instant gratification.

When you try for that, it will fall apart in your hands. If you forget that finding the truth about yourself and your life is a process, you will get nowhere.

Part of the task of facing and accepting our limitations and losses in life is to recognize their relationship to our limits and boundaries. Did we go too far, like Eugenia, and do we need to understand why we crossed those lines? Did the loss or limit seem to come from outside? Looking back, was it good that the loss was there or did we have too weak a boundary which let in things which shouldn't have been allowed in? What sense can we make of all of this? What needs to be reopened? What needs to be seen differently?

The truth and meaning of Eugenia's life was on the ground. Her life had limits. She was given a gift of something very small but very powerful: two beans. The beans held great potential. They showed her a part of herself that was exceedingly needy. Now it was up to her.

The message of this last story is simple: Stay grounded in your life as you have lived it. Notice and come to terms with what is there. Just as the woman was returned to the vinegar bottle and Eugenia to her cabin, we must continue to return to what our lives have been. We cannot gain meaning by only remembering the good parts or fantasizing about the future.

When we become aware of the limitations that have occurred—symbolized in these stories by vinegar bottles, undone cakes, fallen grapes, and broken carriages—we realize that an instant or external solution will not heal or resolve the issue. Nothing will really help but to stop and focus on attempting to find meaning in whatever is happening.

There is also the message that we will find ourselves where we need to be. The vinegar bottle woman had a reprieve for a time, but she was returned to the vinegar bottle in the end. Eugenia had several forays into heaven, but she was eventually plunked back down on earth to get on with the work she needed to do.

The stories we have looked at so far have told us of the need to face our losses and limitations and have pointed to some aspects of that process. Our final story, from England, tells of a woman who has managed to work through some of these issues. She is clear about who she is and what things have value in her life.

⌣ The Hedley Kow ⌣

ONCE UPON A TIME, a woman lived in a village with her neighbors. Although she was poor, life was good and she was happy. She did errands for her neighbors, helping where help was needed. They in turn shared their food with her so that she was never hungry.

One night as she was returning home, she spied a large black pot sitting in the middle of the road. She looked around to see who might have put it there. Seeing no one, she went up to look more closely at the pot. "Perhaps," she thought, "it has a hole in it and is no longer useful. Well, I could use it as a flower pot, so I think I'll take it home."

As she bent down to pick up the pot, she decided to look inside to see if she could see the hole. But when she lifted the lid, the pot was filled with pieces of gold.

"Oh my," the old woman exclaimed, quite taken aback at the sight of so much gold. "Won't this just take care of me for the rest of my days." And, since the pot with all that gold was too heavy to carry, she tied her scarf through the handle and began to drag it toward her house. After a short time, she felt out of breath and stopped to rest for a moment. As she was resting, she lifted the lid to look once more at the gold. What she saw instead was a great shining lump of silver.

The old woman blinked and rubbed her eyes to be sure she was seeing what she was seeing. When she was sure it was indeed silver, she sighed once more. "If truth be told," she said aloud, "I'm please it's a great lump of silver. I was beginning to worry about how to keep all those pieces of gold from getting lost or stolen. This lump will be safer and easier to keep up with." And she once again began to drag the pot.

In another short time, she tired again and stopped. She lifted the lid to look at the silver, for she was beginning to worry about how to care for it. The silver, however, was no longer there, and in its place was a lump of iron. "Oh my," the old woman cried. "How very fortunate I am, for if truth be known, I was worried about the silver. Iron is easy to sell in the village, and it will give me enough money for this winter yet to come." And she continued on her way, dragging the pot behind.

By now she had come to the gate leading to her cottage. She turned to look at the pot. Behind her attached to her scarf in the place where the black pot had been was now a stone. "Oh my," she said. "What a beautiful stone and what a perfect size, for if truth be known, I have been searching for just such a stone for a long time to prop my front door open these fine balmy days."

The old woman turned to pick up the stone. As she did so, the stone changed into a creature as large as a horse with two long ears, a tail, and four lanky legs. It let out a squeal, and then, kicking its legs high in the air and laughing, off it ran.

The old woman watched it until it was quite out of sight. Then she went inside to sit and think about her good fortune. "To have seen the Hedley Kow," she said over and over to herself. "I am very lucky to have seen the Hedley Kow. Imagine. Just imagine. I saw the Hedley Kow and it was just this close. If truth be known, I must be luckiest old woman around."

～

The old woman in "The Hedley Kow" lacks many of life's external things. Yet we are meeting her at a time when she appears to have accepted the limitations of her external life.

Indeed in folktales old women are usually portrayed in humble or meager circumstances, unlike young woman in folktales or fairy tales such as Cinderella, Sleeping Beauty, and Molly Whuppie, who usually end up in a castle. Putting older women in meager surroundings is another device used by storytellers to reinforce the idea that when one ages, meaning is not found in the external.

Each woman in the stories in this chapter has received a gift. The Aged Mother's gift of insight and awareness of meaning comes through her vision. The woman in the vinegar bottle and Eugenia each experience inappropriate solutions for poorly understood problems. Their gifts are the experiences, from which learning may occur, and the opportunity for another chance.

Now in "The Hedley Kow" we meet a woman who has reached a level of self-contentment and security that comes when life has been accepted for what it is rather than what we want it to be. She, like Ulysses in Tennyson's poem of the same name, can say:

Tho' much is taken, much abides; and tho
We are not now that strength which in old days
Moved earth and heaven; that which we are, we are.

Indeed, "The Hedley Kow" woman does not worry much about her meager conditions; she brings to her situation a level of practicality and realism which is also a gift of old age. "This pot would be just the thing," she says, "if I had anything to put into it!" And she looks around to see if the pot has an owner; she has lived long enough not to take things that are not legitimately available to her. The replication of this idea on an internal level is an important part of achieving a healthy aging.

Some things belong elsewhere, the story tells us, and some things belong to us. Sorting out which is which is a process that goes along with accepting the limitations of one's life. For my friend Grace, who felt such conflict over discovering her own feelings toward children, to have continued to see herself in glowing terms as a mother would have meant taking something that didn't belong to her. She would have been equally guilty of taking something that didn't belong to her if she had remained stuck in those feelings in which she felt, having discovered irritation with her grandchildren, that she was "worse than her own mother." A certain amount of feelings and perception belong. It is part of our job to sort what does and what does not rightly belong to us.

The ability to sort accurately allows us to determine where the boundaries of "self" occur. Sorting, in folktales, symbolizes the ability to differentiate one feeling, description, characteristic, or truth from another. Without this ability, we are vulnerable. We will not be sure of who we are. Most of us have met people who are one way with some people and different with others. They are like chameleons, changing their colors to blend in where they are. They have not developed a sufficient ability to sort.

This task of sorting is a repeated theme in myths and folktales. Psyche was given sorting as one of the tasks she needed to accomplish in order to be reunited with her husband, Eros. Cinderella was twice told to sort grain and seed from the ashes by her stepmother.

Vasalisa, a Russian Cinderella, was required to sort good from bad grains by the witch Baba Yaga.

Developing the ability to sort means being able to see the difference between good and bad. Cinderella had to put the good lentils into one pile and the bad into another. The old woman in "The Hedley Kow" sees that gold will ease everyday financial hardships but will create a security problem for her.

When we sort, we get below our surface reactions. That everyday response of "fine" when asked how you are is an unsorted response. While some things aren't worth the energy to sort, much in our inner life is very important. We all, as we age, need to begin to sort our events into the real laundry piles!

"Into this pile goes my temper. With it I can put both the times it was used inappropriately and hurt someone with all the sadness I still carry about some of those experiences. In that same pile I will also put the times my temper gave me the energy and strength to stand up for someone or some cause that was important. Into another pile go the times I pretended I had no bad temper; the times I blamed my temper on someone else; and the times I lied, to myself or to others, saying I wasn't really angry at all. In a third pile go all the attempts I've made over the years to understand and set appropriate limits on my temper. Maybe I'll divide this pile into successful and unsuccessful attempts."

On and on we go, looking at ourselves with our own personal limitations and losses as we work to connect with the Self which gives meaning to what has occurred.

My friend Mary is a mother who has learned to sort the grain of life. She sets limits for her young children whenever necessary with a gentle ease. "No," she will say to the four-year-old. "It's too close to dinner for ice cream." When the four-year-old puts up a fuss, which happens at times, Mary is firm and at the same time understanding of the disappointment. It's a wonderful and amazing combination that she is also able to apply with the older children. She has four happy, well-adjusted, and rambunctious children. What Mary is able to sort is the child's "want" from his or her "need." She is also able to sort her desire to have peace or be liked from her responsibility to be a parent who does what is right for a child and her ultimate faith that those relationships will be solid.

As women, we have thousands of feelings and thoughts and realities which must be sorted. A woman with an ability to sort has developed patience. She is assured and confident. She, like the old woman, understands where she will find value in her life.

"Sort," this old woman on the road is telling us, "so that you will increase your understanding of what is yours and what is not. Sort so that you will continue to increase your understanding of what has value in your life. If you do, you, too, may be privileged to experience something beyond the material world."

Moses saw God in the burning bush. The Aged Mother had a vision. This old woman saw the Hedley Kow. What awaits each of us will appear only when we have learned how to sort, to locate the true value of what we find in our lives

Ode to Menopause

The stream of my womanhood flows through me
tugged by tides, moons, the seasons and the stars
I am awed by its power, felled by its demands
forced to acknowledge a sovereignty I conveniently ignored

My body speaks its memories, in pain, in joy
it tolls my years in secret calendar, calling from its cells
from bone, gland and organ, from most clandestine recess

belittling my ignorance of its language
my body winds its clocks
they pulse in the night in the rain's respite
when the birds are still
in the small, clear hours before the dawning

I am delivered to the cliff-face of my mortality
and death herself brushes me with soft wings
reminding me that the angelic, the soul, the mind are but
    a part
and my clay pulls toward its enduring earth
and now I take count of my days, and reckon their worth
for their tally is not infinite after all
and I mourn those creations
stillborn within my womb, never to sniff sunlight
I mourn those acts my body never can fulfill
for the clocks have ticked too loud
frailty has proscribed its fences, set signposts on my path

This time is truly a time for pause
for contemplation, meditation, inward turning
for numbering the grains
considering their harvest and weighing their bounty
be still and listen sings my body,
take care, step slow and gentle on the earth, forgive now
for life has limit and ending and boundary stone
and soon, you will sleep sweet in the dust

And I wonder if I have left footprints in the sand
scratches on the rock
If my works will be marked in lives given and lives changed
    in deeds remembered

and whether I've made meaning, collaborated with god and
    the angels
for if not, the tocsin cries and reveille is sounded
I must wake, catch time, now, quickly, by her passing tails.

But I know transformation has been wrought on me
and the lines on my face and my body's aging
have been most dearly bought
wise woman, crone, elder of the people, is come to being
birthed by song, touched by time's magic
It is not too late
not too late, not too late at all.

—SHOSHANA KOBRIN
Poem 91
3/12/95 ©

3

Snakes, Worms, and Rice Cakes

AN INTERNAL SHADOW

The Old Woman was uneasy. The evening air was muggy and still. Indeed, the entire day had been overcast, and now, in the distance, she could hear thunder.

Someone had lit a lamp—there would be no moon that night—and a faint glow spread across the faces of the people sitting expectantly in front of her.

This uneasy feeling, she knew, was coming from some source other than the impending storm. She looked around the gathered group.

Her gaze moved from one person to another, not picking up any pain or distress, until finally her eyes came to an erect figure sitting on the edge of the crowd.

This was Elizabeth, one of the other elder women, who was always addressed as Mother.

The Old Woman continued her survey of the gathering, then she returned and settled her gaze on Elizabeth. It was Elizabeth whose pain was causing this uneasiness.

Elizabeth was alone in the group.

No child had chosen to lean against her legs or snuggle into her breast. The small ones, wanting softness and warmth, would not find Mother Elizabeth's hard boniness inviting.

They came to her later in childhood when they were in need of the honing and polishing that would enable them to adapt to village life. Elizabeth's strength was as a teacher. In this she excelled. Hence she was given that title of respect: Mother. But tonight her distance from the group was great; her sense of aloneness, severe.

The Old Woman saw a dark grayness surrounding Elizabeth, darker even than the evening's overcast sky. Elizabeth's face was taut and her body was drawn tightly, tighter than ever, as if somehow to strengthen a boundary.

The Old Woman closed her eyes for a moment, allowing her spirit to leave and enter the circumference around Elizabeth. She needed to know, and she could know only if she allowed herself to feel.

Once she felt and came to know, she would be able to choose her story for the evening. This would be a story for Elizabeth, for it was clear that the healing tonight belonged to Elizabeth. A story came into the Old Woman's mind. It was one she had heard years ago from a traveler. Perhaps within this story lay the healing Elizabeth needed. The Old Woman blessed herself and began.

∾ What the Snake Had in Mind ∾

ONCE UPON A TIME, **long ago in Japan, an older woman decided to go from her village to the next to visit a temple.**

As she walked along, she noticed a young woman in front of her. Although they appeared to be walking in the same direction, the older woman followed quietly, choosing to say nothing. Soon they arrived at a stream. At first the older woman wondered how they would cross without getting wet. The younger woman, however, stepped directly onto a small stone, the first of many that provided a pathway. Before the older woman could follow, she noticed that the first rock had tipped and from underneath had slithered a small spotted snake. The younger woman did not notice the snake who had begun to follow along by her side.

The older woman continued to follow and watch, but it appeared the snake meant no harm. The snake followed all the way to the temple. It sat quietly during the service and then followed when the woman left.

The young woman and the snake stopped in the town at a guesthouse for the night. The older woman, unable to leave this drama without seeing how it would end, secured sleeping space in the same house. The woman watched late into the night, even asking the very old woman who was their host for a light in order to spin. Still the snake sat quietly and even the very old woman appeared not to notice. When the woman woke the next morning, the snake was gone and the young woman told of the following dream.

"A woman came to me," she said. "In the beginning of my dream she was part snake and as she talked she took on more and more of a human form. She told me she had once been a woman, but that her feelings of hate had transformed her into a snake. For many years she had to live beneath one of the river rocks, but yesterday I freed her when I tipped the stone by stepping on it. By the time she had finished talking to me she had completely transformed into a woman. Then she smiled and told me I would have a good life. And with that she disappeared."

The older woman looked around the room. There was no snake anywhere in sight. She and the young woman became friends during the ensuing years and it seemed that the snake's blessing came true because life did go well for the young woman.

~

In the process of growing and maturing we learn to tame many of those undisciplined impulses that exist within each one of us, female or male, at birth: We no longer cry when hungry; we learn not to grab for something we want; we learn not to bite someone who gets in our way. To fit into the fabric of family and society, we become socialized, learning to pull back on impulse and to handle problems with rationality and a degree of diplomacy.

In women, encouraged to become nurturing, peacemaking, sensitive, and thoughtful, it is anger and aggression especially that are repressed. We are taught to transform contentious and aggressive qualities into "sugar and spice and everything nice."

As a child, whenever I left the house I was told, "Be sweet." While those uniquely southern words may never have been uttered to you, probably you were told as a girl to "be good," "act like a lady," and "to remember you are the reflection of your parents."

As adults, we are told by one and all to "have a nice day."

But what happens to all the other feelings, attributes, tendencies, and aspects of one's personality under such a regime? While we would like to believe they simply disappear, they don't. The human psyche doesn't work that way. In reality, these other feelings, attributes, tendencies, and aspects remain; but they are repressed. And in an embarrassing or disconcerting manner, repressed aspects of ourselves may pop out in slips of the tongue, cutting remarks, or unexpected feelings.

A major task for us as we prepare for old age is to understand some of those repressed parts of ourselves, to form a conscious relationship with them. In this way we can come to terms with some previously unknown parts of our personalities that are now beginning to surface.

Everyone has repressed aspects; repression is a natural part of maturing. We repress some parts of our personalities to eliminate aspects that seem unpleasant or in conflict with how we wish to view ourselves.

Consider a woman who has developed her thinking ability to a superior degree. Because she cannot be many things at once, she has not developed those functions which are opposite. The modern-day Athena, the Greek goddess who was rational, assertive, logical, skilled at decision making, organizing, and thinking things through, makes decisions with her head, not her heart. Her feeling function, which is opposite her thinking function, remains in her unconscious, in a less fully developed state.

There are many modern-day Athenas. In this era we call them efficient or busy or cold or calculating. They manage and direct because they have great strength within their thinking ability. It is more difficult for these women to know or honor their heart-decisions.

These undeveloped or repressed aspects, like the snake, are inviting consideration by their appearance. It's better to achieve a conscious relationship with these aspects of ourselves, lest they declare themselves in monstrous, shocking, upsetting, or even destructive form. When a relationship is developed, the opportunity opens for new, appropriate behavior. When we ignore the snakes, they are free to behave badly.

As it happens, this process of coming to a conscious relationship with our repressed aspects can be either a positive or a difficult experience. But even a difficult experience, once integrated into our conscious awareness, becomes positive.

Betty had a comparatively positive experience. In her family, it just was not ladylike to work machinery or even to understand how machines operated. So from childhood on, she saw herself as unmechanical.

Her children, however, grew up in another era, and her daughter, living in Alaska, had become a skilled airplane pilot and an adroit mechanic, able to handle engine mishaps in the wilderness.

When Betty and her husband retired to Alaska, she began flying with her pilot daughter. It didn't take long before Betty was helping with the airplane maintenance. Shortly after that her daughter convinced Betty to work for her own pilot's license. "It's important," the daughter said, "if we want to have frequent family visits."

To her own surprise, the unmechanical Betty discovered she in fact had quite a good mechanical aptitude. She worked on developing it and now is a licensed pilot, qualified to handle the workings of a plane. No longer is the mechanical side of Betty's personality undeveloped.

But uncovering aspects of the unconscious is not always enjoyable. We may find material from painful, traumatic episodes, or from an infantile, impulsive, self-centered part of ourselves that we thought no longer existed. Why look back? It's a question women frequently raise.

Here's a report of a conversation that often happens in my office between a client and myself:

"I'm a nice person."

"I agree."

"I'm kind and thoughtful, cheerful, and fun-loving."

"I've noticed that about you."

"Then why on earth should I go digging around for some painful stuff, which, it sounds like, may make me unkind and grumpy?"

"There's probably no reason, unless you find you need to do so."

"Why would I need to do that?"

"I don't know. This is a question every person must answer on her own. Everyone's answer, everyone's reason is different. I can't answer the question for you. What I can tell you, though, is what I've experienced and what some other women, as they begin to get older, have experienced."

"And what is that?"

"A realization comes that one is living out a life that isn't entirely one's own, that isn't mine. There is a sense of putting on an act and wondering, 'Why am I doing this?' With the realization comes a strong revulsion or anger or sorrow. The combination of the feeling and the awareness provides a strong motivation."

We all have repressed a great deal, and it's fine if some of it stays repressed forever. It is what calls to us that demands attention. These calls come not just through our slips and emotional eruptions—although these are great clues—but also through what we project onto others. When we have a particularly strong reaction to behaviors that seem completely like them and not at all like us, we may be projecting. That is a major clue that something has been repressed. Calls come through not being able to move from Point A to Point B—"I can't get myself to . . . , even though I want to or think I should." And calls come when we realize that we're being inauthentic.

Gert experienced this recognition of inauthenticity. She was involved in a relationship that was very destructive, and as we talked, she said, "I've always thought it was better to be miserable together than risk what would happen if I were alone.

"Now I know I can't keep living like that and that I have to find the strength somewhere to look at how I can reclaim my life. I don't have that many more years, and I don't want the rest of my life to be this way."

This perception of being inauthentic is a powerful one and often signifies that it would be worthwhile to take on the task of discovering what is authentic. And although this process of self discovery is hard work and sometimes painful, there is an encouraging thought to consider: the pain of discovering what is repressed is temporary while the discomfort of continuing to keep something repressed is lifelong. On the other side of pain is a marvelous sense of relief and freedom.

There are other forceful reasons for tending to the task of bringing unconscious matter to the fore. We can put an end to emotional upsets, repetitions of dark moods that seem to come out of nowhere, and annoyances apparently provoked by others pushing our buttons.

"Button-pushing" is something that family members seem especially skilled at. Have you ever found yourself saying something like, "Why do you do that when you know it upsets me?" or "If I've told you once, I've told you a hundred times . . . ."

If you have, then you know what it is like to have an emotional button pushed. It's always a strong, uncomfortable feeling. You find yourself angry, sad, self-righteous, or victimized. And you use a lot of energy reacting or trying not to react.

Your emotional response is intense and stronger than the situation warrants. With me, the button was whining. Whining children, whining adults, it didn't matter—they all annoyed me. I would change, at the first whine, from an understanding, caring, compassionate person into someone who immediately wanted to strangle anyone around me who was whining.

I was ready to kill a flea with a cannon. As this continued over the years, it grew difficult to escape the insight that the only constant in these situations was my reaction. The problem I began to realize, wasn't with whoever was whining. I needed to assume responsibility in these situations. And to do this, I needed to learn more about my personal sore spot. My healing had to come from within.

Because what I discovered was that whining for me brought me right to the door of horrible feelings of incompetence.

To move from anger at whining people to my own feelings of incompetence was a complicated succession of steps. This sequence, common to us all, begins with an unpleasant or unacceptable feeling that occurs in response to an event. In my case, it was old feelings of inadequacy in response to times when I mumbled in the school play, stumbled at the school dance, or fumbled at introducing my parents to school friends.

Feelings this unpleasant are pushed away for protection. They are pushed down or repressed into the unconscious, and if they emerge, they do so switched into another feeling. Like the snake, these feelings are hidden from view although still alive.

Some event will occur that wiggles the rock or defense. The feeling is in danger of being exposed. I believed that people who whined were people who felt inadequate. After all, I had felt inadequate and had wanted to whine. But for various reasons I had pushed those feelings down. Now, the whining of others wiggled my rock. I was in danger of identifying with their inadequacy and having my old feelings resurface. To stop this from happening, I would automatically switch the feeling into anger and the rock would settle down.

I did all this switching unconsciously, which is the way it works. Most of us, nice people that we are, would not be so conniving as to intentionally turn one feeling into another. That is too much of a conflict with our need to keep a positive self-image.

The unconscious, however, has other needs and little concern for the ego's needs to think well of itself. The unconscious accepts the original feeling. When something wiggles the rock, the unconscious feels it is going to lose something and so it sends anger. The anger serves both to keep the feeling protected within the unconscious and to keep at bay anyone who is getting too close. A second thing will happen with this feeling. The unconscious likes to use it and so will send it up from time to time. These are the clues we talked about earlier—the slips of the tongue, the eruptions, the inappropriate reactions.

Even though the unconscious is able to develop and implement such a creative plan, this process is both an exhausting and usually a temporary solution. The problem continues until solved, and a solution is possible only when one is aware of what keeps those buttons active.

These days when people whine, I often fail to notice or I see them as experiencing vulnerability. I don't waste energy judging them. And when I do feel irritation, I know that I need to go inward and find out what I need to do for myself to take care of myself.

Our older years provide us with the opportunity to do the work of looking into these sore spots. The opportunity arrives, like the snake, when we least expect it. At first we may not notice. No matter! The snake follows. Still we may not notice. The snake sticks close. Finally, as we continue our inattentiveness, the snake becomes more active, appearing in a dream to tell us a very relevant story from our own life. The task has presented itself to us from our unconscious. "It is time to notice this part of you," we are told. "Don't push this back under a rock for it is important that you resolve these issues. This is part of your work to prepare for your old age."

Once we reach midlife, we have accomplished many of the outer events and goals from the first half of life such as developing relationships, raising a family, and attaining a career. Now there is time for our attention to turn to those tasks that form the second half of life, tasks of integration and internal wholeness. The ancient folktales were built around life issues that people faced and reassured them that if someone was telling a story about their "problem," then they were not alone. It's terrible to feel isolated with a problem. No one wants to feel flawed in that way. Today in our splintered and fast-paced world, we need to know that we are part of life's flow. The stories allow us to feel the connection.

The stories speak directly to our unconscious as well as to our conscious mind. Like a poem, a sunset, or a winter storm, the folktale communicates on this deeper level, sending its meaning. It jars us, disturbs us, soothes or energizes us. When a tale is ours and has spoken to us, we remember it. It has stirred something within.

The ancient ones who shaped these tales did so from their knowledge of humans and nature. These comprised their world. They understood both human nature and the character of the natural world. We have traveled great distances from our ancestral homes, learning much along the way. These old folktales provide us with an opportunity to retrieve some of the important truths we have forgotten. We have left the earth-based wisdom too far behind.

Consider Elizabeth, the old woman sitting erect on the edge of the circle. Elizabeth had "overlearned" what was socially acceptable. Within her were repressed aspects that needed to be found to humanize and soften her.

By the time the Old Woman came to tell the healing story, Elizabeth was experiencing depression—the dark grayness surrounding her, the mood which came up and caught her—signaling that all was not well.

In Elizabeth we see the woman who needs to get in touch with the parts of her personality she has repressed. Seized by moods, cutting herself off from people, feeling her life stale and flat, Elizabeth benefited from the tale of the snake, a story about the shadow.

The part of the unconscious where we put repressed ideas, feelings, and impulses is the shadow. The *shadow* is a term developed by psychologists that provides us with rich images.

Picture yourself outdoors, the sun warming your face. Your shadow is there, but you must turn to see it. Formed just as you are, it is yet different.

Your shadow is you made shorter, or longer, by the way you move and what you do in relation to light—and light is a helpful image for your own personal insight. As you move in connection with your own insight, your own light, your shadow changes.

Shadows cast their own influence. Unlike a reflection, which will give a clear image, a shadow is different from that which it represents. Shadows communicate a darkness in which things, while not impossible to discern, are difficult to make out clearly. A "shadowy figure," as we know, is someone who is unclear.

What's in the psychological shadow? The shadow contains those aspects of our personalities that we want to deny, disown, reject. But they don't disappear. They just seem to. In fact, the more we reject these qualities, the deeper into the shadow they go and the more trouble they are able to create. "Everyone carries a shadow, and the less it is embodied in the individual's conscious life," writes Carl Jung, "the blacker and denser it is. At all counts, it forms an unconscious snag, thwarting our most well-meant intentions."

Your shadow is active as well without your conscious intent. It will, as we've discussed, send a feeling up in a slip or eruption. It is a dynamic source of energy and should not be viewed as a musty closet seldom disturbed or opened.

The young woman in our story was thwarted. Something had happened in her life to produce an extreme amount of anger, which the storyteller characterizes as a snake. Why did the storyteller choose to describe the woman's hate as a snake, and how does such a story help us understand the process of the shadow?

To begin with, a snake is a cold-blooded creature, and the hate it symbolizes is cold, far different from hot, passionate hate. The hate symbolized by a snake is cut off from emotion and feelings and is difficult to grasp.

The slithering snake is a primitive creature, undeveloped, barred from a higher consciousness. In this way it symbolizes repressed aspects, which, by being repressed, are barred from consciousness. Repressed material remains developmentally immature because of its insulation from conscious life.

Yet as we can intuit from the story, the snake, while a symbol of immature, cold-blooded feelings, also has very positive qualities.

Snakes shed their skin in a whole and obvious manner. One can walk through the woods and find, on a rock, an entire snake-skin, minus the snake who has gone on its way.

Early peoples believed snakes were immortal, shedding skin and returning to youth with each shedding. Thus the snake, symbolizes regeneration and rebirth.

In humans, such shedding does not occur in a physical way by producing a youthful complexion or appearance, but in a psychic or psychological sense. When we shed the weight of our shadow material, we are transformed, no longer bent over with the burden of that material. Our bodies may grow old, but our souls, our psyches grow vibrant, alive with energy. With each shedding of the skin that has been used to keep aspects of ourselves repressed, we experience transformation. This is the same idea my grandmother expressed when she would say, "My heart is heavy," or on another day, "I feel much lighter today."

In ancient times the snake was already a prominent symbol. The ouroboros, an old symbol, is a serpent biting its tail, forming an unbroken circle.

The ouroboros is also depicted as half dark, half light, reminiscent of the Chinese yin-yang symbol. In this portrayal the snake allows us to see that the nature of life is really in the balance of dark and light. And even more importantly, we see from the symbol that the dark is natural. When we allow ourselves to be what we are, that is, both dark and light—an ouroboros—we are free to discover the energy that resides within. Only then can we release the energy that we've been using to keep the shadow from consciousness and use it for healing. The serpent biting its tail is the symbol of balance and the cycle of life.

Consider what happens when we don't come to terms with our shadow or haven't discovered how to do the work of shedding the skin. Consider what life is like when we don't know to do that.

"That child has a terrible temper," my grandmother's friend Aunt Essie would say of me.

"She's working on it," Grandmother would reply calmly.

My temper made Aunt Essie quite angry, but instead of saying she was angry, she would glare, scowl, tighten her lips into a thin line. Her reply to Grandmother's assurance that I was trying to learn to control my temper would be something like, "I hope so. I'm sure one won't get far in life being angry."

Later I would ask, "Why does Aunt Essie get so angry at me?"— it was obvious to a child that what Aunt Essie was, was angry. And Grandmother would smile and answer, "It's because she doesn't think she's angry. Anger is on her disapproved list."

This was a conversation that made no sense at the time, but it stayed with me and I grew to understand it. Grandmother almost certainly didn't know much about Jungian terms like the "shadow" and "repression," but she certainly understood the process.

Because Aunt Essie disliked her own anger so much, she had to repress it. She wouldn't and couldn't see anger as part of herself. Yet because it was one aspect of who she was, it couldn't be denied. Her anger was apparent to everyone. The only one who didn't see Aunt Essie as irritable and angry was Aunt Essie.

When she saw my temper, her own anger slipped out from the rock, but rather than face her own temper, she denounced mine in an angry fit, which must have made her very uncomfortable, but which she saw as justified anger over an objectionable trait in another.

In therapy sessions, I often find myself asking a client, "Why do you suppose that made you angry?"

Generally the client will look at me, as if I hadn't been listening, and then retell the tale of how the other person acted, often with additional examples of the other person's obnoxiousness.

I listen, and then often reply, "Yes, I understand all of that. That person was very mean to do that.

"But I wonder why you didn't feel sorry for them because they are so limited. I wonder why you didn't perhaps feel bored given that you have seen this behavior repeated so many times. I wonder perhaps why you weren't, say, frightened. Given the range of possible responses, I wonder why your response was one of anger?"

"I always get angry at that," clients will often then say.

I answer, "Yes, I can see that you do, but I still think it might be helpful if we were to wonder why. It is possible to react differently, but something is being touched within you in a way which is unique to you."

The rigidity of an "always angry" response indicates the anger is a rock—covering some repressed feeling or event. Intense feeling and rigidity are clues that shadow feelings are being stimulated to pop out and must be tightly covered.

It is important that we don't begin to feel that anger is wrong. The anger is a gift to us, telling us that there is something we need to investigate. While we may not enjoy the feeling, it is important to see it for its helpfulness just as we know that a fever, unwelcome as it may be, serves to alert us to something that needs attention within the body.

I had a fifty-five-year-old client whose husband had left her. When she came to my office talking about feeling frightened, confused, and exhausted, I sensed a great deal of anger. As we talked about the possibility that what she was feeling was really anger, we began to explore why she was responding with anger, an anger so deep it was hard to recognize even under the welters of fear, confusion, and exhaustion.

She soon began to recognize the anger. At first, it was diffuse, immature anger much like that of a young child who becomes angry with every part of her being.

It was an anger as primitive as the snake, slithering here and there, striking at whatever came near. She was angry not just at her husband, but also at the dry cleaner who was too slow, the commuters on the highway who were too fast, the people sitting in front of her at the theater who were too tall. She was angry at whatever she encountered.

It wasn't enough, of course, for her to recognize that she was angry. We needed to work together to provide her with some relief from these feelings that often were so strong she felt they were too much to bear.

Gradually, we managed gently to set limits and to help her focus on where her feelings were truly directed. She learned that it wasn't necessary or even helpful to be angry at everything, because everything wasn't hurting her.

As she began to learn ways to limit her reactions and to find relief from the unbearable feelings, she learned something which surprises people. It's a possibility that has never occurred to them, but it provides the chance of real relief and mastery. She learned that she could form a relationship with her own repressed anger.

We are able to form a relationship with repressed feelings in exactly the manner we have learned to relate to feelings of loss. We must focus on that feeling. To ignore the feeling would be the same as ignoring a person you've just met. If the feeling is anger, as we focus, we will notice whether the anger is cold-blooded, intent on a calculated striking out like the snake, or hot-blooded, exploding and spewing forth like the volcano. What is this anger about? How long has it lived within? What does the anger want?

We must not only learn about our repressed feelings, we must learn to accept the reality that emotions, even those we've been taught to dislike, are valid. We live as naturally in the dark as the light, and the world needs the lion as well as the lamb.

Further we need to view all the emotions with compassion. It is very common for a client to say, "Well, something like that shouldn't make me angry." I also hear, "My parents did the best they could," meaning it's unkind for the adult child to feel angry or hurt. Or "That was years ago. Whatever I felt then is over and done with and, if it's not, it should be."

These are just a few examples of ways we've learned how not to be compassionate. "Yes," I may reply. "Your parents did the best they knew how to do. And the little child felt hurt. Both were true. It is not necessary to call your parents and scream at them. It is necessary, however, that we give some comfort to the feelings which are still inside."

While we may not want to pat a lion, we need to accept that the lion must be lionlike in its nature. Accepting this allows us to provide space away from our towns for the lion to be who it will be. While we may not want to encourage a rage, we need to accept that the rage is there for some reason and learn what space the rage could occupy.

My client explored both her anger and the other feelings which began to emerge. As she formed relationships with these emotions, her energy increased, her helplessness slowly gave way to the belief that she would be able to take charge of her own life. She found she could work with the dry cleaner, requesting overnight service when hurried. She found she could change her seat at the theater if she couldn't see.

Although she was angry about feeling powerless to keep her husband, she discovered she was not powerless in other areas of her life. She began to be able to separate the issues, and she grew stronger.

As odd as it may seem, when shadow elements are brought into the light of consciousness, we discover they contain great energy and healing power. When Gandhi brought to consciousness all his repressed rage at the unfairness of the colonial system, he was filled with energy to become a great leader in his country.

My client discovered, as she formed a relationship with her anger, that there was a long history of anger she needed to face, extending back to a time when she was encouraged by her mother to marry this man. Unsure and unable to trust her own instincts, she complied and had harbored anger at her mother ever since.

Once she became aware of that aspect of her anger, she felt a great deal of energy to sort through what all of this meant. Without the elements in consciousness, she and we are functioning as half complete, subject always to the harmful slip of behavior toward another person, subject to the overwhelming surge of an unexplained emotion, subject to the exposure of a seemingly shameful self. But when we own our shadow, life is somehow enhanced.

The story of the snake, while it is seemingly about three women—a younger woman, a midlife woman, and an older woman—really shows the varying responses to shadow material in one woman, who represents every woman, at three phases of life. And it shows us that although the years pass, we maintain all three phases within ourselves. We are who we are, and who we always have been.

The young woman in the story doesn't apprehend what happened when she accidentally tips the rock, revealing the snake. Intent on heading where she's going, the young woman doesn't notice the appearance of something important. In our own lives, feelings and moods often aren't tied to what we consciously intend—they just show up!

That younger portion of ourselves, too intent on heading somewhere, is unable to notice that these moods signal something within our shadow calling for attention.

The midlife woman notices both the overturned rock and the snake. She is the conscious ego; the part that has matured enough to say, "Whatever is going on here has some personal meaning or internal connection. I've lived long enough to have learned I must be patient and focus on whatever has emerged for whatever period of time is needed for the meaning to become clear."

We in midlife have completed the years when children must be borne and raised, a living earned, and we must nurture people and feed them.

We have reached the stage in life when there is time to search for who we may be in the larger reality that some call the spiritual world. This is a time to search for a meaning beyond our external goals and to relate to that other world, which lies just beyond our sight. The relationship of the midlife woman to the snake is a metaphor for the ability we each possess to attend to this task of searching and relating.

And then there is the very elderly woman in the story, the owner of the guesthouse, who represents our wise and spiritual aspects, who is able to provide the house in which insight can be gained. She is that part of us who releases courage or reassurance, faith or confidence, food or rest or light at just the right time.

While the young woman doesn't notice the snake, the old woman doesn't concern herself with its meaning: She understands that task belongs to other parts of the self. The old woman does what she can do: She provides us with whatever we may need to shelter us as we do this work. This sheltering is physical in the sense of reminding us to eat and sleep. It is also emotional in the sense that it encourages and comforts.

The real value for women our age in the story is in the way the midlife woman handles the appearance of the snake. She does not look the other way or make excuses for it. Compare this to the way we behave in our own modern lives when we ignore something, hoping it will go away, or when we excuse or deny the truth of our behavior. "No, I didn't mean it that way," or "Who me? Angry? Of course not?"—these are some of the ways our unconscious tries to distract us or deceive others from seeing the true shape of the shadow material

In the tale, the midlife woman does not run away nor does she try to destroy the snake. She does not pick up a rock to smash it as many of us do when confronted with a bad feeling. We often try to smash bad feelings back down and cover them with a happy face: "Oh sure, I was feeling a little upset or depressed, but I got busy or went shopping or . . . ." At these times we indulge in any of the hundred other things we've learned to do in order to convince ourselves of the insignificance of a feeling that is, in fact, signaling that something important is trying to come to consciousness.

The midlife woman does not run from the snake. Instead she focuses relentlessly on its presence, knowing that only the snake can inform her as to its meaning. And she knows that meaning will only emerge through patient observation and listening.

Shadow material emerges independent of our own will and ego. In an era when we like to be goal-oriented, results-directed, and to solve problems quickly and then move on to the next thing, discovering the nature of something in our shadow can be a difficult process indeed.

A friend, Connie, sent her last child off to college, only to discover a feeling of restlessness growing in her life. A competent professional who still had healthy ongoing contact with her children, she, notwithstanding this, didn't feel right. Something was missing.

"There is a little depression, too," she told me. "Though primarily the feeling I'm experiencing is one of being restless and bored. My work isn't as satisfying as it used to be."

There was no noticeable drop in the quality of her work during this time. She put in the hours, won the usual accolades from others, yet continued to feel internally upset. "I know I'm supposed to change directions," she said, "but I can't imagine what else I'd do."

Connie remained alert and took several retreats from her home base. She took extra time to rest, making sure she paid attention to proper nourishment since she had a history of either eating too much or too poorly, feasting on junk food when going through transitions. In short, she summoned her internal wise woman. She let this old woman care for the midlife woman during this period of watching, waiting, listening, and observing.

After almost a year, a phone call came from a totally unexpected source, offering a new opportunity. As Connie listened to the offer, something deep inside opened up. She was being invited to work for a project that was international in scope. Her old wanderlust surfaced from where she had buried it years before along with other immature and irresponsible aspects of herself. Here was her next step, yet it was one Connie never would have thought of on her own. Her love of wandering had been buried too deep. She took some time before answering in order to sort through all this and to determine why what seemed to be so simple a solution had eluded her for so long.

Although in retrospect it seems as if Connie had only to wait calmly for a time before insight and new direction would emerge, she didn't experience the waiting with tranquillity. There were times of impatience, of anger, and of dejection. She frequently paced back and forth in my living room, railing against the fates that led her to and through such a good life, only to dump her, seemingly, in a spot of total confusion.

Connie was often baffled about which direction to take. And before the phone call came, there were many other offers of new directions. Fortunately she trusted her instincts enough to know that none of them felt right. Connie knew in her head that the process would work and lead her to where she needed to be. That intellectual knowledge didn't make it any easier, though, when she did hit those days of frustration.

When something emerges from your shadow, the only way you will understand its meaning in your life is to form a relationship with what has emerged, to put yourself in a position where you can pay close attention. You have no control and cannot force the issue, but if you are attentive and patient, eventually you will understand.

Remember in the story of the snake, the woman watched late into the night and still received no information. Finally, when there was no more light, she slept. She endured a dark night of dreams. This is when the information comes. To those of us who are goal-oriented, this is frustrating. And it is especially frustrating when you realize that the night described in the story could, like many nights in fairy tales, last a very long time.

Within my own life, I've seen this long darkness as a time to begin to understand that many things are outside my control and that I must wait for the gifts or insight to be given. It is a hard lesson that I've had to learn many times and will probably have to face again in the future.

What the story tells us by representing insight through sleep is that the final insight, the ultimate authority, the final source of what is meaningful in a true sense comes from the dialogue we create between the unconscious and our egos, a dialogue similar to that of the world of dreams when the veil between the conscious and unconscious is thin and porous, allowing messages from our unconscious to be told through the symbols of our dreams.

In the young woman's dream in the story, the dream says the hate you once felt made you similar to a snake, capturing you under a rock. Keeping the hate repressed meant you were moving through the world with a rock-heavy weight on you. But by recognizing and releasing your anger, you are no longer in danger of being snakelike, striking and scaring people around yourself, scaring even yourself. By releasing your anger, your anger becomes a human anger instead of the cold and dangerous thing it was before.

The tale is a story which tells us that when we form a relationship with repressed shadow material we will move toward a more complete knowledge of who we are. It is a story that identifies this task as important as we prepare for old age; important, that is, if we want a satisfying old age.

To ignore the task is to become vulnerable to outbursts of shadow material. Recently when I was in the city, I encountered such a shadow outburst. The sidewalk was crowded. An old, rather decrepit-looking woman bumped into me. As I turned toward her she said, "What's your problem, bitch?" While most of us don't become quite so aggressive with strangers, we hear a lot of anger and recriminations ventilated on family members by elderly women.

"What the Snake Had in Mind" tells us that the feeling from the shadow will show up as the snake did and will allow us many opportunities to form that relationship. We do not need to go on a snake hunt to find these starting places. At a certain stage of life, the snake comes to us. The choice available to us is how we will deal with this snake. Our answer can make all the difference. Understanding repressed shadow material can humanize us, keeping us from erupting spontaneously toward friends or associates.

The story of the snake is a story of direction and hope. But it is not always so with shadow images. Our next story tells of a woman who saw a shadow image but formed a very different relationship with it.

This woman emotionally merged with the shadow material instead of forming a relationship to something "other." She is the codependent wife, or the woman who becomes one with her victimization. While we may not know an old woman on the shore of an Eskimo village, we have all met old women who have merged with negativity.

∾ How a Worm Destroyed a Tribe ∾

ONCE UPON A TIME, far to the north, lived a tribe of Eskimo. Each spring they left their village to hunt for the meat they would need to

survive the following winter. As the warmer breezes came and the
heavy ice began melting, they packed their provisions and summer
tents to make the long hunting trek.

One spring, however, they left behind an old grandmother.
Whether they did this on purpose or whether she was simply forgotten, I don't know. But they left no provisions for her. So she was quite
alone and destitute. However, she was not ready to die and so the old
woman began to go down to the beach each day to pick up whatever
had washed ashore to use for her supper. It wasn't the best of food, but
it did keep her from starving.

One day as she was walking, she found a small worm. She thought
he was too small to eat, and besides, by now she was feeling lonely.
She decided he would make a fine companion for her. She took him
home and whatever food she found from that time forth, she gave half
to the worm.

Because of all this attention and nourishment, the worm began to
grow quite large; in fact, he grew larger than was really quite normal
for a worm. Soon he was large enough to hunt and began to bring
home small birds and land creatures for their supper. The old woman
made sure the worm got as much as he wanted to eat of this food, and
he continued to grow until finally he was so large and strong that he
could hunt the largest animals on both land and sea. He had become
a monster.

By now it was autumn and one day the boats of the tribe could
be seen approaching. The old woman was glad to see them, but the
worm was not. When the old woman realized the worm was angry at
the return of the villagers, she tried to warn them. But the tribe mistook her shouting and waving for a sign she was welcoming them,
so they continued to approach until they were close enough for the
worm monster to attack. A terrible fight followed, but all of the villagers were killed.

As she saw how the battle was going, the old woman became terrified and ran away to escape the wrath of the monster worm. When the

battle was over, the worm went into the village to resume his life with the old woman, only to find she was gone. He easily followed her tracks, however, and when he caught up with her, he was so angry, he killed her.

That was the end of the people in the village. As for the worm, I do not know, but perhaps he still lives in that village by the side of the sea.

～

Among the Inuit people of the Arctic, whose story this is, life is organized around survival. People band together in food-sharing groups in which the rule is simple but serious: If one within the group eats, all eat. Life in this harsh Arctic clime has fostered a level of concern unknown in our society.

So any listener to this tale would immediately recognize that a serious split, a true division, was occurring between this woman and the others in her group.

The people of this story are a migratory people, moving in a circular fashion from place to place as food gives out and as the change of seasons brings new opportunity elsewhere. At the moment of this story, the Inuit, to eat, would be moving on to summer villages, where the ice had broken, making the whales and seals, migrating on their paths, accessible. In these villages, they would hope to catch enough food to last them not only for the summer, but through the next frozen winter at the village where the old woman remained alone.

The old woman, who as the central human figure symbolizes the ego or the conscious aspect of a person, was, from our point of view, losing touch with parts of herself. These parts are the young, vital parts, capable of pursuing nourishment. In a psychological sense, she was losing touch with the parts of her psyche that would provide the energy to desire life.

The villagers, who left seeking nourishment, represent the instincts, the compilation of that inner unconscious energy that sends birds flying southward in winter and that moves us, as well, toward our own survival.

Feeling abandoned, finding the instinctual energy to nourish herself out of sight, beyond the horizon—that is, deep within the unconscious and thus not available—the old woman faces dangers, many of which are familiar to us.

One of the grave dangers in this situation is that of fooling ourselves by staying in motion. We do this, we do that, we run here and there convinced that by being busy we are continuing to live.

The other extreme of doing nothing is just as dangerous. We must begin somewhere, and if a seashore or garbage and a worm is all we have, then that is the place to begin. The old woman's mistake is twofold, and we can learn from her errors.

Finding and eating garbage is better than nothing until she can learn to hunt. She needs to grow, to expand, to develop, and to mature. She needs to learn how to find healthy food for herself, to grow beyond her childish dependency. Instead she chooses to ignore this opportunity and to remain dependent on what the sea tosses up for her . . . until the worm appears, that is.

When she finds the worm, the old woman realizes that in addition to hunger, she also feels loneliness. The worm, tossed on the beach from the sea, is accepted. He meets her needs for companionship and, in time, he also provides her with food. She transfers her dependency from what the sea provided to what the worm provides. They become codependent. She takes care of and focuses exclusively on him, and in return, he feeds her.

Their codependent relationship is as inappropriate and unhealthy as any modern-day human one. Many of us have known someone in such a relationship. Beth is an example. She was married to Paul, a man who "blew up easily." "It's just that he works so hard and is always so tired," she would say. "He never hits the children—he just wouldn't do such a thing, but things still become unpleasant when he gets angry. There is a tension."

Her life was busily spent trying to get the children to be quieter. She filled days avoiding controversial subjects or behaviors when Paul was at home. She developed an almost separate life with the children and her friends that sprang forth when he wasn't around. She and the children had many secrets from Dad.

Cut off from her feelings, Beth was starving to death in the separate life she and the children had developed to cope with the tension. Eventually she came to realize she needed to be honest with herself about what was happening. Once she was able to do that, she could see the work she needed to do; work that was very risky because Paul might be unable or unwilling to do the work he needed to do to change along with her.

Although Beth was very frightened of anger, hers and everyone else's, she was able to begin to face what was going on. She saw that her own timidity and dependency fed and encouraged the tyranny in Paul. She needed to learn to speak out, to allow herself and the children to live normally, and to protect them from Paul's unreasonable anger. She needed to risk confronting this unhealthiness in the hope that the marriage and family could heal and become a viable place in which to live.

In this case, it turned out her husband also was feeling alienated and wanted change. The two of them went together into counseling. The last I heard, things were going well.

The worm, in Beth's case, was the codependency she had developed in her family system. Once she began to see and say things that were the truth, particularly about her own anger, she felt great relief and a sense of strength. It is this strength that allows us to continue to develop necessary "hunting" skills.

When we befriend our worm, we are actually getting stuck on something that needs a different sort of handling if we're not to die from the relationship.

I've met many people in recent years who have become stuck on what a miserable childhood they've had. They originally recognized this by reading one of the popular books on the market or by attending a lecture or self-help group.

A whole world began to open for these people, and they felt, for perhaps the first time, a great relief. The great relief occurs with the sense of recognition when truth is told. They met others who had gone through similar painful childhood experiences, and felt nourished from the support. There was even a name for the source of the pain—the dysfunctional family.

From that point of relief and recognition, many have moved on. But some haven't. There are those who feed the childhood victimization. It grows larger and larger until it begins to feed them. The "love" and "understanding" found in the new community has unfortunately kept some from learning that life need no longer be halted. Instead of continuing to discover what they have internalized and repressed, they have become stuck on blame and the newfound sympathy and love they receive because of their injury. They are stuck in a codependent relationship, feeding victimization and self-pity. Their group of new friends becomes the worm.

Eventually the worm will kill the internal instincts or life-giving energy, just as it killed the returning villagers. If we stay with our worm long enough, feeding it and allowing it to grow, it will turn on us, killing first our instinctual selves and finally us as well.

In every geriatric facility in which I've ever worked, I've seen at least one old woman cut off from the nourishment of her own unconscious. These women have become bitter, blaming, one-dimensional. Any attempt to reach out to them is rebuffed. Any inquiry into their lives or interests invites only a tirade as to what's wrong. They have simply left life. They have merged with the worm.

Janet was a woman who had merged with her shadow material. She complained each time I visited about how lonely she was.

"There is nothing to do and no one comes to see me," she would say, looking at me with large, albeit watery, eyes.

"You told me you wanted to play bridge. Did you go down to the bridge room any day this past week? They were expecting you."

"My daughter didn't even phone me. I could die and she wouldn't care."

"Did you call her?"

"I expected that at least one of the grandchildren would come by, but no one did."

"I thought your son and his wife were here last night."

And on and on we would go for as long as I would play the game with her. She was completely merged with her disagreeable obstinate shadow material and wasn't to be budged. Her daughter told me that the family had always seen some of that throughout the years, especially when Janet's attempts to control family members didn't succeed, but that this phenomenon seemed to grow and grow until now it was all there was. The "her" had been killed, and now she and the worm were one and the same.

The image of the old woman walking the shore alone is powerful. In my own journey, there have been various times when I have felt akin to that old woman, abandoned and alone on a cold, windy shore. At those moments, something important is at stake, and it's clear that to lie down would bring the death of something that should live. There's only one thing to do then: persevere! Those are the times when one knows, or learns, not to abandon oneself.

We all catch glimpses of worms from our own shadow from time to time, often triggered or brought to the surface by some event in daily life:

Old age comes too soon and we become angry or frightened about what that may mean.

Children move away or become too busy or fail to fulfill our dreams for them.

Retirement plans prove less than what we had hoped for.

Our partner lets us down somehow.

In short, there can be as many difficulties and disappointments toward the end of life as before. But in these later disappointments we can find the slipping rocks, from under which some snake or worm may escape. As we age, our current disappointing or frightening events make it difficult to maintain our facade. Out from under the rock of disappointment slithers something like a need to control or some other long-buried trait. Whenever the "outer" breaks down from what we expect, the "inner" has the opportunity to come forth.

A worm is both a symbol of death, because it destroys everything it feeds on, and an aid to growth, because it aerates soil, allowing plants to grow.

When a worm appears on our soil, announcing itself in small or great ways, it signals that something could open up within the unconscious, allowing insight which, like oxygen, is necessary for life itself. But it is difficult to gain the objectivity to see parts of ourselves for what they truly are, so it's easy to understand how the old woman in the story got herself into such a bad situation. She was hungry, then lonely, and she took the first things that came along.

The old woman's behavior, befriending the worm that would kill her and her instincts, seems so familiar. We live in a culture that teaches us to take the easy way. We like instant gratification. We are in a hurry and stop for fast food, without any consciousness of the connection between poor diet and the quality of life. If bothered by a headache or backache, we simply take a pill as if the headache or backache were merely the result of aspirin deficiency.

We cure the hunger and pain of our spirits with television, which is junk food or aspirin for the spirit. Or we identify with our feelings of victimization, self-pity, or abandonment. These become worms.

This woman's worm is named "Take the Easy Way." While the easy way is better than no way, she fails to form an appropriate enough relationship with the worm to be able to see him for what he is.

The easy way may be all right for those things that don't matter, but one's life, health, and integrity do matter and deserve more. When the old woman met "Take the Easy Way," she should have then begun to learn what the next steps were toward competence and independence. It was an opportunity missed.

While it is difficult to recognize an aspect of our shadow directly, there is a way. We see our own shadow first in those to whom we have a particularly strong emotional reaction. Most of us experience this as a reaction to some quality about the other person—we seldom miss seeing it, but at the same time, it seems almost impossible to believe that whatever is causing the reaction has anything to do with our own personality.

That's because we have so effectively pushed it out of our consciousness that we are being quite honest in saying, "I just don't see that anywhere in me." Essie, my grandmother's friend, who was so upset by my childish anger and yet never saw it in herself, is an example of this phenomenon. My former aversion to people who whine is another example. I have discovered, over the years, that I do whine, although for a very long time, I disguised it by never using a whining tone of voice so that my whining came out as simply relating a problem—or so I thought until I took the time to look at the worm.

There are only a few worms who are harmless. When a worm is tossed up from the sea of our unconscious, we must examine it seriously. Worms feed off of whatever they are attached to—whether vegetables in a garden or human hosts—eventually killing those that feed or pamper them. In that regard, the worm is a symbol of death.

We have now seen two opposite ways of dealing with the personal shadow. In the first story, the woman did the work of watching and waiting until the element revealed itself and its meaning through a dream that the unconscious sent.

Because of her patient work, the hate from the unconscious became humanized, meaning the woman was able to relate to it, and then it went on its way—a separate way.

By humanizing the hate she reduced it to a size that a human being could handle. She did what my client did who was enraged at everyone. The client humanized the rage by separating her anger at her husband from the anger at dry cleaners and others in her environment.

Once an emotion has been humanized, it can no longer be a snake to pop up and strike. If she sees it again in the future, it will have a human form that she will recognize.

In the second story, the old woman continues in a passive mode, growing dependent on the worm, and doing nothing of the work to transform the dependence. The worm is not humanized. It grows monstrous instead through the woman's reliance on it in her life.

The difference lies in the responses of the two women. In the snake story, the woman did not run, but stopped to watch and observe. In the worm story, the woman did not run, but entered into a mutually dependent relationship with the worm, in which she essentially identified with the worm's needs.

The lesson is that when faced with something emerging from the shadow, we must study it and learn from it, but not merge with it.

That's part of the hard work.

In the next story, the old woman shows a third way of relating to shadow material.

～ The Old Woman and the Rice Cakes ～

ONCE UPON A TIME an old woman lived in a small village in Japan. Although she was very poor, she had a tiny house on the side of a hill in which to live and she had rice to make her supper each evening.

One night as she was fashioning her evening supper, a cake slipped from her hands and rolled out the door and down the hill. At the bottom it was grabbed by an Oni, a type of monster or night creature who lives in Japan.

The old woman chased the rice cake and the Oni through an opening in the hillside, through a maze of tunnels. All the while she hollered at him to return her supper, but the Oni kept eating. Finally, just when the old woman was quite out of breath and ready to turn back, they emerged in a large cave. The room was filled with huge pots, a stream for water, a cooking fire, and a lot of Oni.

"Here," said the Oni to the woman. "Take this paddle and this grain of rice and cook more rice cakes."

The woman put the grain of rice into a pot of water and began to stir. Soon the pot was filled with good rice, and the woman made rice cakes for all the Oni. That was a lot of rice cakes, for Oni are very hungry creatures.

Things continued in this way for many days. Although the woman wanted to leave, she was unsure how to find her way back through the maze of tunnels, and so she cooked for the Oni each day while they slept and then slept each night while the Oni ate. Then, one day she had a plan.

"I think," said the old woman to herself, "that this stream must lead out from under the mountain." She dragged the large pot across the floor to the water, took the paddle to use as an oar, and jumped in. Swiftly she began to paddle away, knowing that even if the noise from dragging the pot woke the Oni, they would not follow her because Oni dislike water and will not get wet.

She had managed to get quite a distance downstream when a peculiar thing happened. The pot began to scrape on the bottom and all around her fish were flapping and floundering on the dry sand. The water was disappearing.

She looked back toward where she had left the Oni and a strange sight greeted her. The Oni were awake now and standing by the side of the stream. Each Oni had grown enormous from sucking up all the water so they could walk across the dry streambed to bring her back.

It is impossible to outrun Oni and the woman had little time to think. It is not clear exactly what she did. Some say she made such faces and gestures that the Oni burst out in laughter. Others say she threw the floundering fish to them. Whichever way it was does not matter for this much we know: The Oni opened their mouths and the water poured forth. The stream was once again full. The old woman paddled as fast as she could and was soon out in the sunlight where she knew she would be safe—for Oni only come into our world in the dark of night.

Back at her own home, the old woman began to cook rice. With the magic paddle, there was always enough for her and the neighbors to eat, and so none of them were ever hungry again.

⌒

In fairy tales told of a young heroine or hero, you will have noticed, that these young people often resolve their problems with violence: Gretel kills the witch; St. George slays the dragon; Jack kills the giant.

But in tales built around older heroines only infrequently do they kill. This reflects psychological reality. When one is young, it is necessary to strengthen the ego or the conscious self and to separate strongly from the unconscious self. When a fairy tale describes a killing, what the story is advocating is a pushing away from conscious awareness so that one can act in strong, proactive ways. Whatever is pushed away or repressed is then as good as dead as far as daily life is concerned.

As one ages, however, a different need emerges. The task, now that we have already developed those skills and accumulated that wisdom that allow us to live within the world, is to reclaim those buried parts of ourselves to reach wholeness. Instead of pushing away, we must come to recognize our buried impulses and feelings.

That's not easy. We've been killing dragons for so long, we think that we must continue to do so by battling with our Oni. Just yesterday I heard three different women, each in her middle years, express this admittedly valiant viewpoint in three pertinent ways:

> "Beginning today, I am going to deal with this weight problem. No matter how hungry I get, I'm going to stay on a strict diet."
>
> "Even though Mother B—— drives me crazy, I'm going to force myself to be nicer to her."
>
> "I just won't give in to this silly backache. There is just too much to do."

The backache, the feelings in response to Mother B——, and the need to eat are being resisted by these three women. "Kill the Oni," they are saying, unaware that these "bad" things may be appearing with helpful messages or that some of what we've learned to call bad may not be bad at all.

The story of the rice cakes tells its hearers to assess a situation but not necessarily to assault it. To assess something you must first have a relationship with it. Whether our own Oni is anger at Mother B——, or a backache, or hunger, the approach is the same:

Form a relationship with the feeling so that you will know what needs to be done. To assault something would mean to approach it with anger, attacking and lashing out. It is an action that invites an immediate retaliation.

The old woman forms a relationship with the Oni, but she does not merge with them. She neither attacks nor melds. Instead she assesses things. Her view is, "There are a lot of them and I know little of their strength or of their true nature. Besides, I'm in need of some nourishment. I will do as they ask, giving them sustenance as well. That will give me time to understand what needs to be done."

In this way she is similar to the midlife woman in the snake story who follows the serpent attached to the younger woman.

But the old woman who made rice cakes had to do more to relate to her shadow material, to her Oni. Her food, her insight, had been repressed on a deeper level. It was under the ground—down a maze of tunnels. The snake in our other story popped up from under a single rock next to a shore in bright sunlight. The worm was waiting on the shore. While the Oni came out of the cave to snatch the rice cake, he didn't remain there. He scurried right back down to the cave, and the old woman followed.

This old woman would or could be a modern woman who is overwhelmed by depression and needs to follow through one memory and emotion after another into the unconscious. She would be the modern woman who begins the journey to unravel what her lifetime of needing to be in control has been about. That type of information is not available on the shore, but demands a trip to the unconscious. When any of us find we need to journey into the unconscious, we are on a perilous journey.

We may see many strange, frightening things in our unconscious and can easily get lost there. I remember watching rock climbers in Yosemite Park. They were carefully tied to each other. In the event one slipped, this lifeline would save her from a deadly fall.

In the same way, travelers into the unconscious need to be linked with a lifeline. A therapist is one useful modern lifeline. Continuing to function responsibly within the reality of everyday life is another.

What we're doing, psychologically, is attempting to form a relationship with this unconscious material. But not all material in the unconscious is relevant. Because the unconscious is itself dynamic, there is sometimes a pull that can occur, much like quicksand. Psychotic people have been pulled into the unconscious. This doesn't happen often or with permanence for most people; what is more likely to happen is that a person will feel enough of a tug that she reacts with fear and wants to avoid all future growth. Staying grounded in the everyday and staying connected to others becomes the lifeline that provides assurance.

In the story, the old woman stays connected by continuing to do what she knows how to do: cook. When Carl Jung was laboring intensely with his own unconscious, he continued to perform as a therapist in order to support his family. By maintaining contact with his external reality, he later wrote, he was able to stay connected, able to keep himself from getting lost.

Few, if any of us, are going to be able to chase a rice cake to arrive at our unconscious, so how do we in fact access this part of ourselves? This is a question that many women wonder about. There really is no one recipe that will work for all women.

But the key is to engage in something that will allow the conscious ego to let go and allow a flow from within to begin.

Some find a way by reacting thoughtfully to the material provided by dreams. Others utilize their imaginations, their fantasies, their daydreams. They meditate or engage in stream-of-consciousness writing. They paint or dance or sing, and they behold what emerges.

Physical activity also assists unconscious material to float up to consciousness. I have noticed the defense many people use to keep unconscious material down is held in their bodies. I call this *muscle memory.* Active body work such as creative dancing and receptive forms of body work such as massage, chiropractic techniques, or Rolfing often serve to release some of the energy held in the muscles, allowing repressed material to surface.

Repressed material takes time to surface. The great temptation, once we see an Oni face to face, is to turn and run, telling ourselves we now have what we need. "There, I did it," we're tempted to say. "I stayed with the feeling all the way down to the cave, and I can see that Mother B—— does things which remind me of . . . ."

But to stop there is to halt before anything has really happened. If the old woman had merely gone into the cave, observed that there were many Oni there, then turned and left, all she would have known was that Oni lived under the hill. But nothing would have happened. The storyteller's wisdom is greater. She has the old woman stay long enough for some wisdom, some transformation, some magic to happen. In our own journeys, we must stay long enough to see clearly what unknown part of ourselves needs to be understood.

Bess is a good example of someone who left too soon. She came into therapy because of depression and discovered she was angry at her husband. In fact, she was in a rage. It seems he was a man who was never available to her. He played golf, came home late from work, volunteered with the scouts, sang in the church choir, and was active in their home owners' association. "He's always too busy to do anything I ask," she complained. "He has time for the children—baseball, scouts, camping. But if I want a faucet fixed or the lawn cut, he'll say, 'I'll get to it,' and then I have to wait and wait and wait."

Bess began to confront her husband, telling him of her needs, but nothing improved and she quit therapy, saying, "This has been helpful because I'm no longer depressed. The problem is his attitude, and I'll just have to keep working on that or else leave him."

Bess had found the Oni who lived underground, but that was all. Nothing really had changed. She needed to stay with the anger.

She did come back into therapy a year later with the marriage still a mess. This time she was able to stay in the cave long enough to make the necessary internal connections, and as she understood more about herself she was able to create change.

Our old woman stays and continues on. And once she is in the kitchen, where the heat is, she encounters magic—a magic paddle that, when it is used to stir, creates more of the thing it is stirring. This gift, like any of the gifts we receive from working with our shadow, is impossible previously to imagine. It is completely unexpected.

The magic instrument is a cooking utensil, an everyday tool, and one of the many marvelous images from the lives of women, and although it is magic, it requires a kitchen fire to unleash its power.

The point is not that women must stay in the kitchen. The point is that in the ordinary, in the familiar, we will find the tools we need and in the humble, we find transformation. A kitchen fire, as ordinary a tool as history has ever provided, has always been an agent of transformation. With fire, raw eggs become an omelet. With fire, flour, sugar, eggs, and milk become cake. Choose ingredients skillfully and blend them, apply heat, and you can have a masterpiece.

And just what is the kitchen fire in our own psyche? Our emotions! A little emotional heat can always cause something to bubble.

Too much or too little feeling won't work. The right amount creates the process of transformation. And the transformed substance becomes nourishment.

The old woman was given the magic paddle. With the paddle she could reach farther. With the paddle she could tolerate the necessary amount of heat. And with the paddle she could continue to keep things stirred up so that nothing became stuck. Finally, with the paddle she was able to leave the underground place of the unconscious and return to her everyday life in the world.

In our own lives, we can give ourselves the magic paddle we need. Not for nothing does the storyteller choose a wooden paddle, another common object, as the means of magic. She knows this will resonate with her listeners' experience and sense of the charms of the world.

"Touch wood and it's sure to come good" is an old saying reflecting the belief that wood protects, and the old woman by touching her wooden paddle certainly seems to be able to protect herself, nourish herself, and move away from the underground.

A magic wooden paddle seems like something we'd all like to have around. Perhaps we already do.

What is the magic paddle we all have? It is our accumulated experience in the world of reality, our wisdom, our common sense, all those aspects of our thinking or rational self. The paddle represents the thinking conscious self that invites us into hard work and self-reliance. The paddle is our thinking self that says, "You can't just sit here. Do something!"

But the paddle is useless without the heat and the rice, each of which is part of the emotional unconscious. And the emotions are useless without the pot—that ability to contain or keep the emotions within limits.

In our society, we place great stock in intellectual solutions, but this story seems to suggest that to stir the paddle around without the pot is to try to solve problems on a strictly intellectual level. And many of us have experienced how that really doesn't work.

And yet to have the heated pot without the paddle is also useless: No nourishment comes without the paddle to cook with.

Together though, the water, the rice, and the kitchen fire (our emotions), and the paddle (our common sense) and the pot (our container) work magic, and also enable us to return from our unconscious to the everyday world.

A woman named Rose made an appointment to see me. She had been struggling with feelings of depression for a long time. To combat these, her physician had put her on an antidepressant medication, which unfortunately created side effects but did not relieve her depression. She tried a second and then a third drug with similar results: harmful side effects and just a minute diminution in the intensity of the pain she was feeling.

Rose also tried various forms of therapy: hypnosis, biofeedback, and sessions with a counselor from her church who taught her techniques for positive thinking. She found temporary relief with these approaches, but her depression always returned. When she came to see me, she was discouraged and skeptical. She doubted anything could work. Her first question to me was, "Can you cure my depression?"

"No," I answered. "I'm not even sure I can help you to cure it, but that might be a possibility."

As we talked through the session, I began to see a woman of great courage whose enormous strength had borne the weight of depression over many exhausting years. She needed, I thought, to learn to refocus that energy. If she could use her strength and courage to hunt down the feelings which fed her depression, and then to stir them around, she would be able to form a relationship with the depression itself.

I thought she might indeed have the strength for that task. Tracking down and forming a relationship with the depression would be the first major step of our work. Once she had done this work with her unconscious, she and I would be able to see clearly what the next step would be.

The content of the sorrow, trauma, or injustice will be different for each person, but the next steps will be the same. Each person must understand clearly and in detail what occurred *and* each person must feel the accompanying emotions about her own experience. These two next steps are the paddle (the intellectual understanding) and the fire (the emotions). From these two will come meaning, and from meaning comes transformation.

Rose decided to "try" therapy with me. Our work together lasted three years. Many were the times she wandered down side tunnels in her effort to find her way to her feelings or her insight. And many were the times when she appeared to be so deeply within a cave that she and I both wondered if she would ever find a stream or tunnel that would connect her back to the world. She would find herself for weeks at a time sinking in her feelings of depression with no new insight or feeling. When she seemed close to despair, a memory with all its attendant feeling would emerge and a new insight would put her back into the right tunnel. These were exciting moments, each one leaving her stronger and wiser than before.

Rose's early traumas had been serious, and her journey—to transform her resulting depression—was long. Each victory left her more able to continue. Yet all the while she needed the boundaries, the link—the pot—to keep her from burning in the fire. She used me as her therapist, the routine of a schedule, and the necessity of continuing her daily job as her lifelines.

In our story the old woman, like all of us, needed to find some way to link that inner world with the everyday world. She did so via the stream. The stream flowed from the inner world outward as do our emotions, dreams, and fantasies.

In order for the stream to be there for us, we have to value the internal life and value increasing our connection to it. The stream, connecting inner and outer, is our ability to form a relationship between our unconscious and our ego, or conscious self. Otherwise, the internal strength from our shadow will not be there for us in our conscious lives.

When the Oni discovered the woman was leaving, they shouted in rage. They, like the worm, wanted the woman in their service. And they were very powerful. They began sucking up all the water, the emotional energy the old woman was utilizing.

Anyone who has suffered from depression can identify with this image. Depression, when it strikes, results in a feeling that all emotional energy has been drained from deep within. When we are depressed, we have no energy to do anything, even when we know we must do something. We become stuck in the mud of our own apathy.

Obviously unconscious shadow material is very powerful if it can suck away energy. Its power must be given a great deal of respect. At the same time we must not feel powerless when faced with the Oni. There will be setbacks and times of slowing down, but there will always be something that can be done.

There are two endings told with this story. One is that the old woman threw the Oni fish. In the second she made lewd faces and gestures, thereby producing laughter in the Oni. Both are symbolic of moving away from the fear of the moment to a more spiritual level. Both imply the need to see the Oni and the situation within a larger context of meaning.

Fish are symbols of the sacred. Within the Christian religion, Jesus was called icthys or fish, and He promised to make his followers fishers of men.

There is also an old belief that throwing a fish's bones back into the sea allows the fish to be reborn.

The fish symbolizes the need to transform primitive Oni material by understanding it in a larger or spiritual context. This is the quest for transformation into a place of meaning.

The alternative ending, one of making lewd faces and gestures is the gift of humor, which also transforms. When Demeter, the Greek harvest goddess lost her daughter Persephone, she went into a deep grief. Once she was in the depth of depression, it appeared that nothing would cheer her until Baubo, an old goddess, made lewd gestures. Once more Demeter laughed.

Most of us have been in that cave where the feeling of heaviness or fear or anger or despair appeared so large we could see or imagine no relief from the pain. At those moments the Oni are draining the stream and only one thing will help. We must find some way to see the larger picture, which will then return the water to the stream. This is "putting things into perspective" or seeing the meaning. This is the transformation.

The old woman's relationship with the Oni was an appropriate one. She fed them but didn't become "best friends" with them as our other old woman did with the worm. She learned their nature and received the gift they had to give. Then she left, feeding them on her way out. This old woman continued to be the person she was. She approached the unconscious using all of her thinking and feeling skills.

During my young adulthood I remember crying about something. Grandmother was there, solid as ever in my eyes. After listening and comforting, she looked at me and said, "You're right to feel that way. It's a terrible situation, but it's not just cleaning that requires elbow grease. Living life the way it's meant to be lived takes a lot of elbow grease, too. Someday you won't remember this, but if you learn how to handle it, you will always be stronger."

This was a powerful image Grandmother gave me that day. Feelings are important, she was saying, but one must also pick up the paddle and then get out into the light of day. And she obviously was right because I cannot remember what I was crying about.

Following our own individual Oni down into that place where the repressed darker parts of us reside cannot be done with only halfhearted attempts. It takes both the feelings and the understanding to produce the magic that transforms.

We are told in the story that the old woman was never hungry again, meaning she felt full, she had an internal feeling of fullness. She also had enough left over to share with her neighbors when they were in need. It would appear that she became one of the wise elders, connected within the spiritual or internal realm and well-nourished enough so that she no longer needed to worry about the external. The journey to the unconscious provided her with the opportunity for transformation.

And as aging women, when our bodies begin to change, we should recognize we are being invited to explore our internal world where the magic of transformation resides.

Our first woman met an aspect of the personal shadow by accident. But not until she received insight during a dream did she really notice the presence of this shadow aspect of herself.

The second woman saw something from her shadow and cultivated it, allowing it to grow monstrous and destructive.

Our third woman met the shadow by accident, but noticed it right away, and interacted with it. She formed an appropriate relationship using her own cleverness and common sense.

Each of us has filled her own personal shadow with the help of our parents, teachers, and the culture in which we grew. It is filled with all those parts of ourselves we believed were bad or wrong or dangerous, hurtful even. And guess what? From the standpoint of society and adapting to the standards of the group, many of those parts are useless or worse. However, in order to be complete as individuals, we must often face traits in ourselves that society, in order to run smoothly, must ignore.

The storyteller does not advise us to become one with the Oni, although there are many old women to whom it seems that has happened. They have not grown simply eccentric, which can be delightful: They have grown unpleasant and nasty. These are the women who, in one way or another, have fed the worm, and it has killed their humanness.

The danger in life for most of us, especially those of us who are women past forty, is not in having learned rules. The danger is in believing, as Elizabeth began to believe, that these rules, and our adherence to them, define who we are. We are those people who obey the rules, who are good, nice, clever, and bright, but we are also the opposite—in our shadows.

To continue to deny that our personal shadow is an aspect of ourselves turns us into stiff, rigid old women who are unforgiving of the faults of others. Or we become shallow, superficial old women who cannot afford to consider anything of substance out of a fear that such a journey might awaken the Oni.

And who knows? It might. While we might meet Oni and worms along the way, this is also the place that contains the magic paddles that allow for our transformation.

As we look around and see the unhappy, contrary, and complaining women, we need to see them as women who were unable to explore, bring to consciousness, and form a relationship with their shadow material. As a result, this negativity overtook them. Perhaps they, like Elizabeth, believed shadow aspects must be always attacked and fought, promoting only the "good." To continue to believe that is to miss the paradox that there must be dirt and manure in order for a beautiful garden to grow.

4

Which Witch?

The storm had been raging for days—it was difficult to believe that the heavens could have any more rain to send, but still it poured down on them. The Old Woman had heard stories of a great flood and wondered, "Did it begin like this?"

Much of her time in these rainy, worrying days had been spent with Cerina. There had been little enough she could do, but she was the only one Cerina allowed near. Perhaps Cerina allowed her to approach because the Old Woman wasn't afraid of what possessed Cerina.

A few others, summoning up courage, had tried to approach Cerina. But whenever someone else had ventured close, offering food, comfort, or attempting to apologize, Cerina had spit and clawed, hissing terrible curses. And so now, for the last two days, she had been left alone, except for the Old Woman.

Now as they sat, Cerina rocked and moaned. Cerina's hair was matted, her face encrusted with dirt and bloody scabs from the times when she had torn her own flesh.

Her moans were so deep they seemed to be coming from a place deep within the earth itself. The moans moved on the air with the rhythm of her breathing, broken only by sequences of screams and curses. She had gone on this way for three days.

Cerina had never been a well-loved elder.

People talked behind her back. Young people taunted her with name-calling.

Indeed she was unsociable, had never had a partner, and took part in community life only to the extent necessary to fulfill her obligation of tending the shared garden. Between Cerina and the people, until recently, there existed only a mutual toleration, but that had been sufficient for coexistence.

But then things changed, though at the beginning, no one had thought to blame Cerina. The first incident was the accident that had killed Mava's husband.

Next came the sickness of Benni's little boy.

After that it was the babies: one after another born dead, until the village could count four who had never taken a first breath.

It was when that third baby was stillborn the talk began. At first it was only a whisper here and there, but it grew, the way such things do, until the name Cerina and words like *witch* and *spell, potion,* and *magic,* came together, rising like the morning pond mist swirling on the northern wind.

Then, after an agonizing two-day labor, the last baby was delivered. The cord was twisted and wrapped tightly around his darkened neck. At that point, the baby's father and a group of his friends collected knives and left their homes.

The Old Woman didn't see what happened for she was with the stillborn's mother, applying all her skill to bring that life back from the twilight. She was told Cerina's animals had been killed, each cut into two pieces.

That deed finished, the men had dragged Cerina through the mud between the animal halves, making her swear she would forsake her evil ways. She had been left, dazed, on the edge of the woods all night while the coyotes came seeking the warm meat around her.

Sometime during that night, the rains began. The next morning Cerina was found, moaning as she lay in the mud between what was left of the animal halves. The Old Woman was summoned, and she had not left Cerina's side since.

The Old Woman was deeply troubled. The community was in need and she was to tell stories tonight but what could she tell? What healing could she bring?

It wasn't Cerina's deep needs that troubled her: Cerina's grieving would heal her soul, and everything possible was being done for her body.

It was about the others that the Old Woman was vexed. A great evil had been and was still in their midst. Perhaps, the Old Woman mused, this evil is always under the surface, waiting for some great grief or fear to summon its face, its presence, to visibility.

She at first thought she would tell stories of illness and death, but she rejected that idea. It was not death which needed the speaking, for everyone knew that must be grieved. No. Not the deaths. It was the evil that had been done by those of good heart that must be talked about. This was the poison that was lingering unspoken in their midst.

The Old Woman knew that good people did evil. So her stories tonight would be told to ease people into that understanding. And there was more they needed to know. They needed to know that the witch was not Cerina; the millions she had heard about being killed on the continent were not witches, either. The people needed to know that there is a piece of the witch in each and every person alive. They needed to see that the witch was inside.

That was the situation of our Old Woman. What of today? By the twentieth century the idea that old women cast spells on their neighbors was old-fashioned.

The change did not occur because of an increased respect for the universality of this dark power or because we realized it was wrong to project. Rather it occurred because of the rise of a rational scientific atmosphere in which a witch is believed to be simply magic, and magic is believed not to exist.

When the dominant culture decides on a new paradigm, that paradigm does not alter the reality of what is, only what is spoken of and taught. The archetype itself when denied doesn't disappear but continues underground. For all the "nice" people, the witch remains repressed, continuing to be projected, although it now goes by altered names such as *enemy* or *bitch*. Some religious people continue to rail against the presence of this dark power calling it "the devil" or Satan, while C. G. Jung gave it the name of the Dark Feminine.

Over years of living, each of us has buried this dark energy deep within the unconscious. When she emerges in a nasty comment or a cruel act, we push her back.

This energy remains though, existing within ourselves. And deeply repressed, it often attacks our bodies. "You will have to fortify yourself to keep me in," the witch whispers. Many of us have shoulders or backs that have turned into stone. We have become the fortress. Our youthful bodies may have easily accepted the strain of repressing the witch's energy, but as we age, our bodies become more vulnerable. Vulnerable bodies complain. Vulnerable bodies refuse to do what they did easily in the past. The nasty side is able to sneak past the vulnerable, expressing itself in the body.

The witch energy also expresses itself through sarcasm, unfair criticism, tantrums, biting remarks, and petulance: these are a few of the many guises in which this Dark Feminine is able to emerge, guises not possible in younger years when we were more concerned with the impression we made on others.

Anger, often over losses and the defeats of aging, usually summons the Dark Feminine from her hiding place. And she can be quite destructive. One of the tasks of aging is to learn about this internal witch, to understand the ways in which she might be able to ride into our conscious life, create some damage, and ride back out again.

She cannot be told, like a bogeyman, to go away, and it is impossible to ignore her without peril. One thing that happens to those who try to avoid the Dark Feminine within themselves is that they lose energy. The witch torments them so. These women appear to deflate much like a balloon with a slow leak. They talk, but they say nothing of interest to themselves or anyone else. They become walking ghosts of their former selves.

Other women, unable to block the witch's energy as effectively as those collapsing ones, discover the witch popping out. She snaps and bites with her words. These women become feared or hated because they're so hateful, so full of poison. Eventually for these old women, the malicious witch energy becomes dominant. Others, including family members, avoid them. They lead lonely lives.

Most of us who have experienced in our own lives the popping out of the spiteful witch can understand the importance of learning ways to keep her from taking over. When we find where this energy resides, and can form an appropriate relationship with it, we are able to keep her in our sight. This is the way to avoid an ambush.

As we begin to meet this dark aspect of ourselves, though, an amazing surprise awaits. We find that the dangerous witch, the Dark Feminine, has a positive contribution to make. She is the source of great energy and creativity.

During the mid-sixties I attended a conference at which the atmosphere was one of peace and love. Everyone at the conference that first night was enthusing about the wonderful power of love. Well, almost everyone! Sitting next to me, badly crippled with arthritis, was an elderly woman. She had been a psychologist during her working days, and although now retired, felt it was important to keep up with the latest research in her field. So she continued, despite her physical pain, to attend meetings.

As one young woman finished expounding on how empowered she had become by tapping into her love, the elderly woman smiled.

"I'm glad that's so helpful for you," she said. "I find at my age that I need quite a bit more energy to get me through my days, and anger is the feeling that will do that for me. I'm very grateful for my dark place where the adrenaline is made."

This elderly woman understood that the dark energy, the witch, the Dark Feminine, inside has power for good as well as for evil. She had learned how to safely connect with her witch. People who do not connect with their own witch energy see that energy only as a part of other people.

Today we call this projection. Much as a movie projects its images onto a screen, we project our internal psychic energy onto others. The projection of this dark energy always goes toward someone who has some quality that allows a "hook."

Perhaps this insight into others wouldn't be such a bad thing if any of us had godlike insight and could see clearly. The problem is that, although we may see great faults in others, these faults are always colored by our own prejudices and blind spots. The wise church fathers of the past were sure they accurately perceived the evil of Joan of Arc and others, while believing themselves to be above reproach.

Cerina provided hooks for the villagers. She kept herself isolated from others, which made it appear, in this close village, that she had something to hide. She was abrupt, offending many, so they labeled her as mean.

When this great tragedy came to the families within the village, they felt the destructiveness that exists in life. They experienced the dark energy within themselves first as helplessness, but their helplessness quickly turned into rage. Unable to tolerate the rage, they looked for a place to project. Cerina had the necessary hooks. Cerina's need for solitude became secretiveness in which the others saw witchcraft, and her unpleasant demeanor became, in their eyes, a cruel and malicious nature.

As people gathered that night in front of the fire, the rain was still dripping from their hats and down their faces, leaving tearlike streaks. There was nervousness in the room. The father of the sick boy sat hollow-eyed at the edge of the crowd. A woman, weak from childbirth and grief, leaned against her husband. He sat, his large beefy hands twisting back and forth against each other, as if he were wringing some pain deep within the bone.

The woman who was feeding Cerina's chickens—spared in the blood ritual—sat nervously in the back, her eyes darting from one person to another. Even the children were silent tonight. The Old Woman raised her head and began.

~ The Owl ~

ONCE UPON A TIME in a village perhaps not too far from where we ꞏꞏꞏꞏ ꞏꞏ, ꞏ ꞏꞏꞏꞏꞏ ꞏꞏꞏꞏꞏ to a day which proved to be not at all like any other day. He and his wife and children and his farmhand were all busy about their morning chores. The farmhand had no sooner gone into the barn to fetch hay then he came running out again, quite pale and out of breath.

"Help, oh help, oh help," cried the farmhand. "I've seen a monster in the barn."

"Nonsense," replied the farmer. "You are always looking for some excuse to get out of doing your chores. I'll fetch the hay from the barn to prove to you there is no monster." And the farmer went boldly into the barn.

Now during the night while everyone slept, a great horned owl had flown into the barn through a door that had been left ajar. The wind had blown the door shut and so the owl was trapped. Once the farmhand entered, letting sunlight into the barn, the owl had flown up to a rafter to wait for the darkness to come so that she could safely fly away.

When the farmer entered and looked at the rafter, he found himself staring directly into the unblinking eyes of the owl, who was sitting still as a stone. The farmer paled and ran out, shouting, "Get help. Go to the village and get help. It is indeed a terrible monster."

Soon all the men from the village were gathered. One after another went into the barn, only to exit pale and trembling with fear. Everyone was in agreement that a more fearsome monster had never been seen. At that point, the bravest man in those parts arrived and agreed to enter the barn to vanquish the monster.

He entered, his chest puffed out in front of him, muttering words of courage to himself while the villagers offered prayers for his safety. When the owl saw him, she puffed out her chest, ruffling her feathers, and she spoke words of her own: "To-who, to-who." At this sight and sound, the man knew that he must be encountering something of a nature other than human, and he turned and ran from the barn.

"There is nothing to be done," he said. "The monster is indeed too terrible to fight, for it began to cast a spell from which I narrowly escaped. We must burn the barn."

And so together they lit fire to the barn, burning it with all its contents, including the owl. Afterward the village returned to its normal routine, which included the building of a new barn for the farmer and his family. But for many a year after that time the men of the village sat around at night and told the story of how they had all banded together to rid the village of the fearsome monster.

～

"The Owl" is a Grimm's tale about witch burning. In this story, the villagers turn fear into aggression against something external and go after an owl, a night bird, that is not only a traditional companion to witches, but a frequent story symbol for a witch.

The choice of an owl as a symbol for witchlike old women is apt. The owl's eyes, placed as they are in the front of its head, are immediately noticeable. They stare with directness and intensity. The owl looks back, eye to eye, meeting the onlooker's gaze on an equal basis.

I remember a game we played as children. Two children would stare directly into each other's eyes. Each hoped the other would be the first to blink, to look away. It was a game about power. The one who blinked first was defeated.

There is in some old women the same direct, no-nonsense assumption of equality. They are outspoken, saying what they think without beating around the bush. These women are no longer interested in being coy or deferential or in creating a favorable impression with a man. They have no investment any longer in such behavior. They see things "as they are." And often such women are perceived as threatening, their directness experienced as a challenge.

The internal Dark Feminine has a similar quality. She stares out at us with a directness we often find threatening. She glares in ways devoid of subtlety or gentleness.

"You've gotten fat," she spits out in my inner ear. Or, "You're wearing that to the retirement party? How dowdy!" Is there truth in her message or is she busy spreading poison?

To learn to listen and evaluate her messages is very important: She may have information I need. By listening and evaluating, I may come to her know her better. And she does have gifts.

Witches and owls are not only direct, they are wise—wise not only from experience, but also from emotions and what used to be disparaged as "intuition." And women who utilize these tools—

emotional and intuitive information that defies logic—are often threatening to people who operate solely from logic or in their rational minds.

The grandmother of a friend knows an amazing amount of information about her six children and twenty grandchildren. For example, she has known every time one of them became pregnant long before an announcement was made.

In two cases, she knew before the mother-to-be. Indeed one of these two believed she had finished her family. There were to be no more children—and she had no symptoms of early pregnancy so when Grandma told her of her condition, she was convinced this old woman was wrong. The baby turned out to be a boy, which Grandma also seemed to know.

Through much of history, this unconscious, nonrational way of knowing was considered evil enough to warrant the labeling of women who exercised it as witches. During more recent times, including my own young adulthood, intelligence of this type was defamed as "women's intuition," dismissed as frivolous and silly. Anyone who admitted to this way of knowing was viewed as a "lesser" person.

The individual Dark Feminine within us has this quality of intuition. With a flash, we know things that may appear to be illogical. Long before any external information is available, a mother may know when a child is ill or in trouble. One may know a partner's mood long before anything is said. This intuitive knowledge emanates from the inner reaches of the Dark Feminine.

To date, no one has been able to identify definitively how this happens, and so skeptics abound, declaring that in spite of the evidence, intuitive knowledge doesn't exist.

In spite of not understanding the mechanism of intuitive knowing, psychologists and physicists are now validating its existence. That is reassuring but not of much practical help.

While school trains and hones our minds to be rational and analytical, no one teaches us how to recognize or sort through our intuitions. We arrive at adulthood, possessing this gift of great gold still intermingled with the base ore of the earth. Our intuitive potential is so enmeshed with logic, so buried under rationality, that it is difficult to even recognize. Worse yet, many of us discount or distrust the gold itself.

That intuitive message, delivered as a hissing commentary in my ear by the Dark Feminine, the witch within, about the dowdiness of my dress for the retirement party wasn't mere poison—it was accurate.

My friend's retirement came during a busy time for me and as a result I was viewing my friend's party as just one more obligation. I had put little energy into preparing for that evening and had unconsciously selected a dress that was a match for my attitude and energy level.

When I realized what was happening, I was able to refocus. The party marked an important milestone for my friend and I wanted to be able to join the festivities with enthusiasm. Perhaps she wouldn't really notice if I showed up in body, but not in spirit. I would have noticed, however. And that low energy was not what I wanted to experience for myself or to put into our relationship.

So I canceled a social event the evening before her party and slept in the next morning. The right dress was in my closet all along, a fact I was able to notice when I was more rested and enthused.

This time the witch's message was gold, but I needed to sort through it in order to be sure. There is always a lot of base ore and fool's gold around.

My alternative, which would have been a trap, would have been to ignore the message and drag myself to the party in my dowdy dress. This would have created a perfect setup for the witch energy to pop out at someone there who irritated me, or for me to interpret any look or comment on my attire as the other person's "witchiness."

When the witch inside is saying something, listen—an explosion may otherwise result. We can see the witch in these types of eruptions. What is more difficult is to see another's witch as somehow connected to ourselves.

Accepting the idea that another's apparently witchy behavior may be actually reflective of something within us is a huge first step toward recognizing our own personal witch. And it's a difficult step, because we believe that the problem is the other person and not us. Few of us initially can feel the internal Dark Feminine.

We have seen how each of us places our individual anger, contrariness, and other unpleasantness into the shadow part of the unconscious. Archetypes are different. An archetype is inherited and will be similar for everyone because the qualities attributed to each archetype are universal qualities.

The Dark Feminine, one of the archetypes, is part of the unconscious of all of us, female and male. It is not the result of having had a "bad" personal mother or a traumatic childhood. This Dark Feminine archetype entails or speaks to certain traits like a devouring, regressive quality, a prehuman animalism. The witch, a personification of the Dark Feminine, lives in a deep part of the unconscious.

Although residing at such an inaccessible level, this energy does surface, and after a time of focusing, we begin to recognize the witch. The witch has the power to make us unconscious of those things we should be noticing. We see this in stories like "Sleeping Beauty" or "Snow White" in which the witch puts the heroine to sleep. The witch poisons with nastiness and resentments—remember the apple in "Snow White"? The witch is that part of us that eats children, something we literally do when we pull our children so close they cannot breathe or live their own lives. We eat their independence. The witch bewitches us and is underneath our confusion about what is apparent within our lives.

Our Western culture has attempted to eliminate images of the Dark Feminine while other cultures have remained more open. In India she is currently worshiped as the goddess Kali, while in Hawaii, she is Pele. For most Westerners, however, she has fallen out of fashion and so has become repressed. But she, like other repressed material, hasn't gone away; she continues to lie buried within the unconscious, personal and collective, private and cultural.

Becoming aware of our unconscious and its role in whatever is occurring ultimately has a positive effect. Awareness helps us to avoid the traits that are specific to a given archetype, in this case the devouring qualities of the Dark Feminine. Without awareness we are in danger of acting out these cruel behaviors toward ourselves and others.

We have been taught, and most of us agree, that certain of these traits, at least as they first appear, are to be avoided, but as we prepare to move into our older years, we need to ask ourselves, "Where did that part go?" And we also need to ask the equally important question, "What consequence have I experienced as a result of having buried and repressed this archetypal energy?"

Introverted women will be more likely to feel the effects of this repression in a physical or internal way. As these women age, they neglect themselves, going along with what husband, children, or coworkers want. And when they do begin to focus on themselves, they may discover a large part seems to be missing. They have sacrificed or devoured aspects of their unique selves.

Introverted women may eventually collapse under the weight of sickness or exhaustion. As a result of their overcontrol of themselves—and the witch is controlling—they have worn themselves down to the point where they no longer have sufficient defenses against attack. While there are variations, it is the essence of the introverted woman that is attacked and devoured by this terrible energy.

Women who are extroverted find that this witch, this personification of the Dark Feminine, besets others. Perhaps an extroverted
woman is a controller, sure she knows how to live someone else's
life. In the process of trying to do this, she not only steals the life of
another or others, but manages to lose her own since no one can live
two lives. Some women find they are caught in this scenario with
children. Daughters quite frequently see that this is so, long before
controlling mothers do.

Extroverted women possessed by this Dark Feminine energy
may also find themselves assailing others. An extroverted woman
may strike without thought because she is convinced that what she
is saying is for the other's good or is what they deserve.

One woman I knew lost five jobs and most of her friends
because of such behavior. Although her jobs usually began well,
she quickly saw the behavior of others as hurtful to her. Whatever
her coworkers did was a personal affront that caused her to retaliate.
She saw herself as victimized. Until she could form a relationship
with her own Dark Feminine, nothing would change.

We must find a way to relate. There really is no other way. Unless the Dark Feminine is acknowledged, the witch within will manifest itself with increasing energy as we age. But as we approach this
energy there are dangers to be aware of and to plan for as drama-
tized in the following Grimm's story.

～ Frau Trude ～

ONCE UPON A TIME there lived in a deep wood a terrible witch whose
name was Frau Trude. Parents taught their children never to go near
that part of the woods for fear Frau Trude would catch them.

There was one little girl, however, who would not listen to her parents. No matter what they tried to teach her, she would do the opposite, and she always found herself in trouble because of her disagreeable nature. One day she said to her parents, "I am quite curious and I am going to visit Frau Trude and see for myself what she is like."

Her parents forbade her to go, and when they saw that wouldn't alter her determination, they began to beg, plead, even to threaten; but the girl ignored it all and set off to the woods. Soon she arrived at the clearing around Frau Trude's house.

On the steps was a man, black from head to toe. The girl began to tremble, and the man disappeared only to be replaced by a green man. He, too, soon vanished, and a man as red as blood itself appeared for a moment. By now the girl was feeling quite weak with fright, but she continued on, looking through the window of Frau Trude's house. She pulled away and knocked at the door.

"Why are you so pale and trembling," Frau Trude asked, as she let the girl in. "What have you seen that has frightened you so?"

"A black man."

"A collier."

"A green man."

"A hunter."

"A man as red as blood."

"A butcher."

"And when I looked through the window, I saw the devil with his head all fire."

"Then you have seen too much," replied Frau Trude, and she changed the girl into a log, which she tossed on her fire. Then she sat down to warm herself.

～

This is a story in which everything goes wrong. The protagonist, who represents the young girl part of ourselves, is undeveloped, lacking the ability either to understand danger or set realistic limits. She is "unconscious" about what is really going on. She reminds me of a client I once saw in therapy who worked alone from 11:00 P.M. to 6:00 A.M. in a convenience store in an inner-city neighborhood known for its high crime rate. Although familiar with the cautions and warnings expressed by others, this young, attractive woman was oblivious to any sense of personal danger. Then, at work at 4:00 A.M., she was robbed by two armed men. She had to undergo this experience before she realized the import of what others were telling her about the dangers. This young woman had been bewitched, so to speak. She was unconscious of the realities of the danger around her. She, like the girl in "Frau Trude," assumed she could do whatever she chose to do—without any personal danger.

Unlike the girl in "Frau Trude," she escaped harm. That was luck, and neither she nor the witch who had rendered her unconscious could claim any credit.

I see this same attitude frequently in teens who feel that drinking and driving or engaging in unprotected sex are dangerous only for someone else. As we age, most of us give up such thoughtless physical risks simply because we grow more conscious of our mortality and are more aware of those things that constitute a danger to ourselves.

"Frau Trude" suggests that there are also internal risks in any encounter with our own witch. The girl's approach to Frau Trude warns us that some ways of approaching the Dark Feminine are dangerous. By understanding the errors the girl in the story made, we will be able to form guidelines for ourselves about appropriate approaches to our own internal Dark Feminine.

The girl in "Frau Trude" does as she wants to do instead of what she should do, and what she wants to do includes barging into Frau Trude's home. She goes without having the sufficient awareness that would protect her. It is possible to survive very dangerous situations if sufficiently armed and if you are alert and lucky. Without these safeguards, there is grave danger.

The story makes it quickly apparent that seeking to satisfy curiosity is not an appropriate adult motivation. The girl's desire to satisfy her curiosity causes her first of all to disobey her parents. It is parents, externally in childhood or internally in our adulthood, who understand that all behavior has consequences. When we disobey our parents, we are living for the present joy or thrill or fun without thought of what an action may produce.

But how could it be that we, as older women, might disobey our internal sense of knowing what is appropriate and fall pray to what psychologists call feelings of *entitlement* and *inflation*? And when we do, in what ways might our own Frau Trude show herself?

Some women eat without regard to what their bodies need. Most of us grew up on diets of questionable merit, rich in red meat, fried food, butter, whole milk, and sweet deserts. The good housewife was one who knew how to make biscuits, roll a tender pie crust and keep a full cookie jar. And although we know these old ways of eating are unhealthy, many of us either maintain or return frequently to this pattern. It's comforting; it's familiar.

"I've lived fifty-nine years on this type of food," one woman said to me. "Why should I change now?"

Her attitude is an example of entitlement, which is the outlook that believes "I deserve" to have whatever I want. She, like the girl in "Frau Trude" and the young woman at the convenience store, has had her judgment put to sleep by the witch. There are always consequences, and seldom are they harmless.

The aftereffects of unhealthy eating literally are an attack on our bodies. Our arteries become lined with fat. Our internal organs are stressed. Our immune system is weakened from the lack of appropriate nutrients.

What most people tell themselves when caught in this entitled behavior is that this is freedom. "No one can tell me what to eat or what not to eat. Those days ended with my childhood," one will say.

The reality, of course, is that we are never completely free, and that refusing to look at what comes next, which in this case is illness, is to be a prisoner of the consequences.

At those moments when we allow ourselves to drink too much or to sit without exercising or permit ourselves to say whatever pops into mind without consideration, we are caught in a cycle with no awareness of the consequences. We are like the toddler who reaches for the "pretty" fire or the lion who kills whatever it sees when hungry. Maturity demands more consciousness.

The young girl in our story follows her curiosity and arrives at Frau Trude's house. Once there, she sees three aspects of the witch in the form of three men: a collier or coal miner, a huntsman, and a butcher. What does the symbolism of each of these figures tell us about what we might expect to find in the domain of our Dark Feminine?

A miner digs deep into the earth for riches. This miner digs for coal, a lump of energy created over time deep within the earth. Once mined, it becomes fuel, producing both heat and light.

The Dark Feminine provides us with an energy to go deep into our unconscious; to mine in order to find buried feelings and insights that will provide us with heat and light.

The warmth that comes from reaching emotions is powerful, compelling. And with those feelings comes the light that allows for psychological insight. Comic-strip artists have often drawn the moment of insight as a person with a lightbulb above his or her head. Joseph Campbell, the late mythologist, called behavior in response to such enlightenment "following your bliss."

This witch or Dark Feminine embodies a deep knowledge that is often more "true" than anything known by the conscious ego.

The hissing in my ear about the party dress was a minor example; often her knowledge is more profound. The witch doesn't really care whether we want to hear, whether the truth will hurt or damage, or whether it is even useful to us. She likes to pop out with the information she has.

There are many times in therapy sessions when I will have a flash of knowing or intuition. Once when this happened I suddenly knew that my teenage client's mother was having an affair. Nothing had been said by the client, who had been talking about school and friends—the usual teen concerns. She was also, I was sure, unaware that she possessed this information in her unconscious although it had been sent to me by her Dark Feminine. It was information sent by the witch in the form of intuition. For her to have these facts at this time would do great harm, and I did what I could to strengthen her defenses against the witch.

About three years later I saw this same young woman in the grocery store. At that time she told me things were still going well for her. She was in college, living away most of the year. Her mother, to her surprise, had divorced her dad and married this other man whom mom had "known for a long time," she said with a knowing wink. "He seems very nice, and Mom is happy, which is what counts." I was glad the witch had kept the information to herself three years before. My former client now seemed comfortable with the information.

There are times, however, when the information is more valuable than even coal, and we need to listen to what the witch has to say. Her words have the power to give us great perspective, insight, and wisdom about who we are. She does not sugarcoat her messages and so we can count on her to "tell it like it is."

We must have enough maturity to be able to profit from the coal that the collier brings. Any mined substance will emerge in a crude form that must be made ready for use. We refine our crude knowledge or gift from the Dark Feminine through the use of our rational or conscious mind. We form a relationship with this aspect, watching, thinking about, noticing, and ruminating on what we hear, and then making a judgment. As we put energy into this process, we will develop a high level of skill. The lump will become refined coal, able to give necessary heat.

The second great aspect of the Dark Feminine the girl meets is the hunter, the part that tracks down our instincts. Our instincts or animal nature have both positive and negative aspects. Negatively, our instincts can obviously harm us when they turn nasty. This happens when our instincts operate without the taming influence of our experience and rationality. Positively, however, this part of our animal nature is filled with an energy that operates to aid our survival in mind and spirit as well as body. It drives us to eat, take in, consume, and savor it all physically, intellectually, emotionally, and spiritually.

"It's not until you're tested that you know what you're capable of," Grandmother used to say whenever adversity or tragedy would strike. As a young person I had concluded that I would willingly exchange self-knowledge of what I was capable of for a fun and smooth life. But I now know that it matters a great deal to me that I find within myself the resources to face life's dragons.

It is my deep instinctual nature that often helps me, allowing me to know where the "meat" of my life is hiding. Without this way of knowing, I might be able to feed myself only on the weak and easily caught. Perhaps, more likely, I would have been killed by one of the dragons I've encountered. The hunter within the landscape of the Dark Feminine seeks out deeper instinctual capacities and brings us closer to them, especially when life, which is uncontrollable, presents some terrifying things.

My friend Marie, during her sixty-five years, had buried her husband and two of three children. Her first child died at the age of six, killed by a hit-and-run driver on the way home from school. Her husband died of a heart attack when Marie was just fifty, and when she was sixty, she nursed her daughter through the final stages of cancer. Each time she grieved but never did she emerge bitter or filled with self-pity.

Once when we were talking, I said to her, "I can't imagine anything worse than having any of my children die. I don't know how you've managed to keep going."

She was quiet before she answered.

"It was pretty awful. I thought my son's death was the most painful thing in the world, and I wasn't sure I'd survive. I did though. When George and then Kate died, it was equally horrible. But in some strange way there was a blessing buried in each of their deaths.

"I don't think I would have been able to know that death wasn't an ending if these things hadn't happened. It's hard to explain. I'd always been taught about life after death and heaven and all that, but somehow there was also a distance between that concept and my feelings.

"With the deaths of Bobby and George and Kate, something happened. Nothing as dramatic as a voice from beyond, but just a knowing, deep inside, that death was like a birth into whatever comes next."

Although Marie had no control over what life presented her, she was not killed by her dragons, but instead was able to hunt to find the meaning. Marie, during her life, had come to understand the importance of the hunter energy. She had developed the hunter skills of patience, tracking and capturing what she pursued.

After the miner and the hunter, the little girl met a third aspect of the witch in the form of a butcher. The animal the hunter catches is unusable until it is skinned and cut into pieces of meat. A butcher breaks down the large unusable material into smaller, usable pieces that will fit in the pot or can be cooked on the fire.

Our internal butcher cuts and trims at the event or the issue to arrive at the essence of what is true. Remember the sayings "This is the meat of the issue" and "Let me chew on it for a while"?

The woman who kept on getting herself fired from one job after another was in desperate need of contact with her butcher. Her animal, that enormous amount of untrimmed meat called anger, needed cutting down.

What emerged for this client after the two of us worked for long months was a picture of a little girl, adopted at birth by parents who thought they were unable to have children of their own. Yet nine months later, a daughter was born.

My client felt this second child was favored. The younger sister was prettier, smarter, more personable, and more talented. As a result, the young sister was given all the advantages. She was sent to one type of activity or lesson after another as they grew up. Finally when the time for college came, this sister chose an expensive eastern school while my client went to the state university.

"What did your parents say when you would ask for those things you wanted?" I asked her.

"I never asked," she said. "There was a problem with money, and I always knew they couldn't afford to send me. My selfish sister didn't care, and she kept taking and taking from them, and it ended up they loved her the best anyway."

The client was living with all the pain and fury of feeling a distant second to her sister. She spent her childhood attempting to please her parents through her thoughtfulness, hoping against hope her virtues would be rewarded by them with appreciation, praise, and love. They, however, seemed not to notice. It appeared they gave to each child what the child requested. Since my client requested little while her sister solicited much, she was given what seemed to her an insufficient amount. Her sister asked for and received the parents' favoritism.

Now my client saw exclusion and favoritism everywhere she went. She experienced a business-oriented boss with poor personal relationship skills as intentionally rude. She thought that coworkers who didn't go out of their way to include her in every conversation were gossiping about her.

She raged inside at all these slights, her anger leaking from every pore, causing others to back away. Their withdrawal further convinced her that people were against her. What this client needed was a good internal butcher to help her chop and trim.

Most of what would happen when she began a new job had little to do with her. What did happen was a reflection of the personalities of the people there, of the group dynamics already in place. My client needed to be able to slice off each of these other behaviors, separating them from her own early experience. She needed to be able to cut off what didn't belong to her.

When this client began her work, she was exhausted and overwhelmed from dragging an entire raging lion around day after day. As she worked to separate each piece from the other, cutting away at what didn't belong appropriately to her, she began to find those things that were hers and that would nourish her.

I find it very reassuring to know the ability and energy to dig deeply, to hunt, and to cut things down to manageable portions lie within each of us. For the child in our story, however, these abilities are of little use, for she is too headstrong and inflated to stop and consider what the images she encounters mean.

This child lives within all of us. She is that part of us who says, "I don't need to obey the speed limit; there's no policeman around," or "I'll just slip the magazine from the doctor's office into my purse—everyone does it."

This is the child who quiets our better selves. This is the child who doesn't know that there are consequences. This is the self-indulgence that comes from wandering into the land of the Dark Feminine unprepared.

The little girl's final and fatal mistake is, by way of extension, a final lack of discrimination. When the witch asks what else she has seen, the little girl replies that she has indeed seen the witch's evil nature. She tells of the devil's head. Had she had the butcher with her, perhaps that inappropriate comment could have been trimmed, and she would have known how to discriminate. In failing to do so, she reminds me of almost all small children who say freely such things as "Mama, look at the fat lady."

The little girl, too naive, too inexperienced, too undeveloped to handle the interrogation, ends up in a disaster. The witch, Frau Trude, turns her into a block of wood and throws her on the fire.

To burn something is to change it from one form into another, but the process is irreversible. A piece of wood becomes ashes—the symbol of humility and penitence, which is exactly what the little girl in our story needs. But ashes cannot become wood.

"I really got burned that time" is a familiar expression that indicates we got hurt. To get burned is to get a strong invitation to change.

When we continue to ignore our internal witch, we are granting her the power to live and work her poison. She continues to whisper. When we listen to her whispering, believing her poison is truth, we remain, like the girl, naive. In fact, the naïveté spreads and we find ourselves justifying entitled behavior in a number of areas:

> *Government graft:* "The lobbyists will only give it to someone else if I don't take it."
>
> *Shoplifting:* "Stores charge too much anyway."
>
> *Cheating in school:* "Everyone does it and I have to get good grades to get anywhere in life."
>
> *Armed robbery:* "Society is set up to keep me from getting my share unless I take it."

What our story suggests, though, is that we must be conscious that the whispering is from the Dark Feminine or else we will be burned.

Going into the land of the Dark Feminine is a descent into the unconscious. It can be hell, a place of burning. But there are those who can make the descent and survive. We have examples of those who faced the witch in her darkest guise. From Greek mythology, there is Persephone is abducted by Hades, god of the underworld, but returns after six months. There is beautiful Psyche from the Greek myth, who descends to hell—also called Hades—to get a special box to win back her husband, Eros. Each descended to a dark world of chaos.

There are also modern examples. The psychiatrist Viktor Frankl is one of the better known of those who survived Auschwitz and other Nazi death camps. More recently, we've followed the stories of Terry Waite, lengthily imprisoned by terrorists in the Middle East. There is Mother Teresa, working daily within an urban hell.

These people, unlike the little girl in "Frau Trude," have learned to live within limits, tolerating strong feelings of frustration at not being able immediately to have what they want. In so doing they have built an internal strength and wisdom that sees them through hell.

The second lesson of the story is to stop along the way, slow down when you encounter an aspect of your Dark Feminine. See what it is about. See what it has to offer you. Form a conscious relationship with it. When you do this, you will know what to do next, how to behave.

The girl in the story, already alone, encounters the three men, aspects of the Dark Feminine or witch, at the home of Frau Trude. She does not communicate with or observe any of them long enough to reach an understanding of who or what they might be or what they might mean to her. She does not associate with or watch long enough to develop any respect for them or their natures. She develops no knowledge of them, no compassion for their essence, nor is she able to name any of the three.

Only when you learn to tolerate the frustration of delaying your gratification and forming a relationship with the Dark Feminine will you be given gifts of truth or insight, which are invaluable.

Once early in my career, I had a memorable encounter with my own witch. At the time I was supporting my two small children by directing a school. When I found I needed to take a six-week leave, I hired the wife of a graduate student to fill in for me. Within a few days of her beginning as my fill-in, I received a call telling me my services were no longer needed. I was being permanently replaced by the woman I had hired.

I was understandably devastated. My first reaction was that the other woman was a witch. "How could she do this to me?" I cried. "We were friends. She knew how political the situation was, and she manipulated things the minute my back was turned." I then went through a very long list of things I would have liked to have done to her, all of which had the flavor of witch burning.

I, like the girl in "Frau Trude," saw the situation as something external to me. I wanted my job back, and so, after I had quit crying and calling her names, I confronted both her and my employer.

At that point things went from bad to worse, and my ego and self-esteem ended up badly burned. There were no friendly faces for me. Instead of slowing down and attempting to tolerate my frustration long enough to try and understand what was happening and what my options were, perhaps even learning something, I ran off to a lawyer. He advised me to be quiet, to make no further contact with anyone at the organization, and to let him try to negotiate a settlement based on my contract.

What finally emerged was partial settlement for my salary for the remainder of the contract. It was grossly unfair. I was both burned by the experience and burned up over it. I carried an ongoing fury for months. Although the intensity finally faded, it took

my getting older for me to be able to go back and begin to understand the situation in a different light.

What I realized when I returned to that place where the memory with its feelings was stored was that I, too, had been an active
participant in the political manipulation. From the time I first knew
I would need the leave, I recognized there would be opposition to
my taking off such a long period of time.

I finessed the political opposition by arranging the leave
"through the back door." I, like our story girl, had gone after what I
wanted without regard to the complete reality. While my replacement and my employer were not completely honest and direct, I
was not straightforward myself. I was burned with my own match,
although at the time I was too young and naive to understand.

The Greek myth of Perseus fits here. Perseus, a young hero was
set the task of killing a horrible gorgon named Medusa. Because
Medusa had the power to turn into stone anyone who gazed at her,
Perseus used a shield borrowed from the goddess Athena. He was
able to use this shield as a mirror, thereby gaining a clear view of the
gorgon without the danger of looking at her directly. The shield
provided the necessary reflection that must always precede an encounter with the Dark Feminine.

When I was fired from my job, I rushed in blindly and I was
turned to stone. Because I was reacting from a strong emotion without benefit of reflection, I rushed around creating a lot of motion but
not really gaining anything. Not only had I failed to figure out how to
proceed in this instance, but I immobilized my own future growth. I
was literally "petrified," meaning that I was stuck with the old way of
understanding. No new awareness or growth or self-knowledge was
coming to me from the experience. As a result, I repeated the indirect
way of dealing with situations several more times before I began to
catch on to what I was doing. Reflection is indeed a shield.

Athena had also given her sword to Perseus. With this sword
he was then able to cut off Medusa's head. In addition to taking the

time for reflection, we need to discriminate. This is the symbol of the sword.

When we reach this internal place where we can see the reflection of our own Dark Feminine or witch, we, too, must use the sword of discrimination to separate the "head" or academic understanding from the instinctive or emotional understanding of the body. It's not that intellectual understanding is either wrong or useless—to the contrary, rational understanding is necessary. But it is also true that knowledge that exists on a deeper, unconscious level must be brought up, as was the lifeblood of Medusa.

As the blood flowed from Medusa's neck, Perseus collected two vials. One vial of blood had the power to give life; the other, death. Additionally, from her blood came Pegasus, the winged horse of creativity, and Chrysaor, his brother in human form. Medusa's own head was placed in a bag and taken back to the goddess Athena who wore it on her shield.

Pegasus was a perfectly formed horse who was able to soar birdlike with the aid of wings. Chrysaor, his brother, was a giantlike man who had a golden sword. Pegasus went on in his life to release the fountain of poetic inspiration, while his brother Chrysaor married a water creature, fathered a monster, and was never heard of again. These children parallel the two vials of blood—one life-giving and the other destructive. This is the Dark Feminine in all its potential.

I have done much work as a therapist with artists, as they have confronted their own Medusas. Some of the energy that comes forward from these reflections seems to be like Chrysaor, never really forming into consciousness, but emerging, producing a bit of something, and then sinking back below the surface of awareness. Some births are not meant to be.

At other times, Pegasus emerges. Paintings, play scripts, sculptures, poems, stories, and performances have all "emerged." From their deep internal source have come creations capable of soaring skyward.

By placing Medusa's head on her shield, Athena is sending an important symbolic message. A shield is that part of the warrior's paraphernalia that both protects from attack and is seen first by those approaching. The goddess is notifying all who come into her domain that the Dark Feminine has a dual function. It can be dangerous and kill, but it can also protect and provide elements necessary to life. This information illuminates an aspect of our own shields. We know that our own Dark Feminine is not simply a destructive part of ourselves that we must fear. Indeed, she is that, but she is more. If we reflect and discriminate, she also provides us with a shield.

So far, our stories have presented us with the Dark Feminine, or witch, as a part of the unconscious that has the ability to spring forth. If we approach too closely we may be burned or petrified. In this next story from Scandinavia, we see some of the different ways she manifests herself.

⌁ The Witch's Shoes ⌁

A WET, BEDRAGGLED old woman was walking. The day had grown dark and a mist was falling. There had been no purpose to the old woman's day; she had just wandered through the woods. As the day grew late, she noticed that she was feeling tired and hungry, and she wondered if she had energy to return to her home. She was about to sit down on a rock to think about what she wanted to do when she noticed a small cottage through the trees. "Perhaps I'll spend the night there," she said to herself.

Now the cottage belonged to an old witch who was planning to go out for the night. In preparation for her evening, the witch had greased her shoes and placed them in front of the fireplace to dry. She wasn't happy to hear the knock at her door and discover the old woman there, but she opened the door anyway.

"I'm tired and wet and hungry," the old woman said. "I'd like to come in and spend the night."

"I'm going out tonight so you can't stay," the witch replied. "However, you may sit in front of the fire to dry off if you'd like. When you are dry, you must leave."

So the old woman came in and sat in front of the fire, taking off her shoes and placing them close to the coals. It seemed to her a very short time passed before the other woman said, "I am planning to leave soon. You must go."

The old woman sighed and reached over for her shoes. She put them on without noticing that she had picked up the wrong ones. Her shoes remained on the hearth while on her feet were the witch's shoes. She thanked the woman for allowing her to rest and went outside.

As soon as she stepped on the pathway she began to fly upward. The shoes wouldn't stay on the ground, and she bounced this way and that, first head up and then feet up, for she had no broom to keep her level.

"Oh my, oh me, oh deary me!" she cried as she flipped around, grabbing for branches as she passed. "Oh help, oh help, oh mercy me!"

A man who was passing saw her predicament. He waited until the old woman bounced down again, then grabbed at one of the shoes. The shoe came off and the old woman was able to land on that foot and pull off the other shoe.

Meanwhile the witch was unaware of what had happened. She put on the remaining shoes, thinking they were her own, and grabbing her broom, went outside to begin her night of fun. She jumped up, but the shoes had no power, and she landed back on the ground. Once again she jumped but did not fly. The witch tried again and again and again, refusing to believe that she could not get off the ground.

She jumped and landed so many times that she dug a very deep hole in the earth. Finally, she fell into this hole and the ground caved in on top of her. She was buried quite securely. At least for the time being.

~

The two sides of the protagonist, the witch and the wandering woman, stand in strong contrast to each other. The wanderer's conscious ego aspect has grown weak. She is functioning on little energy, walking around unaware. She, at the end of the day, finds herself tired, hungry, far from home. She has lost the necessary strength and fortitude to set a goal, to plan ahead.

Her arrival at the witch's cottage is accidental. She had not set out to find this part of herself. Indeed, once she makes contact with the witch, she doesn't recognize her as someone possessing special powers. However, she is able to summon enough initiative to knock at the door and to seek shelter.

This witch, the symbol for the old woman's Dark Feminine, is very different from the previous witches we have met. She is active, full of energy, planning to go out on the town. When the old woman knocks, the witch is not welcoming—she has her own business to attend to that night. But she does allow the woman to enter for a short time, to dry off and warm herself.

The Dark Feminine has more to offer, and it surprises us that this witch appears to offer little. That there might be more, say an accidental enrichment because of the contact, is left unspoken.

Indeed the gift from this encounter is not offered but is received because of the accidental exchange of shoes. The old woman doesn't intend to take the shoes. The witch doesn't offer the shoes. The exchange happens through no one's conscious intention.

The shoes do not even appear to be a positive gift: The old woman, wearing them, is tossed here and there screaming all the while.

We see this dynamic when something bounces us from a comfortable rut, forcing a change we don't want and don't like. Years later, we may look back and understand that in the change there was great value. At the time it occurs, however, we feel tossed on our heads.

The story raises another issue for us, however, and that is the issue of possession. Once the woman puts on the witch's shoes, she is possessed by the energy. For her there is no clear reflection and discrimination.

Recently I attended a conference on geriatrics. One of the speakers, discussing the survival rates in care facilities of various elderly women, found elements of the Dark Feminine or witch running like a common thread among those women who survived best. "These are not docile old women," she said. "They dislike being told what to do. They generally are uncooperative. There is a feisty, quarrelsome tone to them." I recalled the other conference, back in the sixties, where an elderly doctor preferred her anger to the power of the then much-touted love.

The elderly doctor, however, was very aware of her dark side. She went there consciously and was able to gain insight or energy and integrate it into her consciousness. This is a process which had occurred over time for this doctor and one in which she had clearly developed skills.

The feisty old women being described by the lecturer, on the other hand, sound as if they are possessed by the Dark Feminine. Many of the rather disagreeable women I've met in long-term care facilities have been placed there because there is no other place for them to go.

These women are enraged because their power has been taken from them. Instead of forming a relationship with their internal witch, they have merged with her. They do not integrate or use her energy, they become her. Perhaps, as the conference speaker suggested, this energy keeps these women alive, but it is a life that I believe lacks quality.

Every story, including this one, reminds us that there is, or there ought to be, both contact and distance between the witch and the conscious self. We do need to know her, to relate to her. We will interact with her, and we need to understand what these interactions mean. But we should not get too close, and we cannot live together, for she is much too dangerous. She will need to return over and over again to her home in the unconscious.

An accidental encounter with the witch, albeit upsetting when it turns our lives upside down, is filled with potential. We need only to keep the perspective that there can be something useful for us in these encounters. The wandering old woman's state is familiar. She is any one of us when we enter a time of feeling listless, depressed, or caught in a superficial rut.

My friend Gwen found her active, busy life interrupted by a heart attack. After her return from the hospital she went through a period of wandering around. Little seemed to interest her. "I make myself get up and do something," she told me, "but I don't really seem to care."

That was five years ago. Now Gwen describes her heart attack as the best thing that could have happened. "It was a wake-up call which changed my life," she said. "Since the heart attack I do things differently. I want my life to have meaning. I want to be able to say I really lived the life I was meant to live and that I was who I was meant to be. I thought I was wandering without purpose after my heart attack, but I was wrong. My wandering was before. My life then was busy and active, but it was going nowhere. It was spinning without substance."

Gwen's story is echoed in thousands of women who met the witch in the dramatic form of a life-threatening illness. When one has a major illness it is as if someone or something has turned you or turned your world upside down. There is no firm ground on which to stand—at least for a while.

In a similar manner, an idea, a mood, an urge, or a yearning may appear in our lives. We recognize these in a similar way to the way the old woman recognizes the cottage through the trees. It is a "Well, I never saw that before. I wonder what it is doing here" kind of recognition. This is the threshold, the pivotal point.

If the wandering old woman had not approached the cottage, there would have been a very different outcome. She might have made it home and no transformation would have taken place. Or she might have died in the woods.

When we see that cottage, mood, urge, yearning, or idea, we need to stop and evaluate. We need to consider that there may be potential there. That belief will allow us to move forward.

"But what if I'm wrong?" a little voice whispers. The answer this story provides is, "It doesn't matter." The woman receives a little of what she sought, what she thought she wanted. She is allowed to rest and dry off, but she is not offered food or a bed. However, she is given something she never could have imagined: She is given energy and a different perspective on life.

What the story does not tell us is what she did with this new perspective. The gift is there, but it is up to her to do the work. If the work is not done, then the first gift does not amount to a great deal, and nothing will change. However, without that first gift of energy and the fresh way of viewing things, she would not have "gotten off the ground" to work on her own transformation.

In this story we can see the witch energy within our unconscious as a great benefactor. Our next story from the Sudan warns us that it is still necessary to maintain distance, separateness.

⌒ Nyanbol ⌒

THERE ONCE WAS a young man whose father urged him to marry. The young man did as his father bid, choosing a beautiful young woman. Some days after the wedding, the young man's mother asked for the bride to come to her hut. The wife was sent, and the mother ate her.

Some months later, the son married again. After a week, the mother asked for the new wife to come to her hut. This wife was sent to her, and once again, the mother ate her.

This time the son waited longer to remarry, but the same thing happened. After a period of time, the son had married, one after another, all the eligible girls in the village except for Nyanbol, and his mother had eaten each and every one.

The father decided that Nyanbol would be the next wife, but the son refused to marry. The father pleaded and threatened, threatened and pleaded, until the son finally agreed.

The day after the wedding, the mother asked to see the bride. Nyanbol went to her hut, taking her younger sister with her. The sister cooked supper and they all talked. When it was time for bed, the mother said, "Nyanbol, come and sleep with me."

Nyanbol had heard the stories of all the other brides and saw the skulls around the hut. "No," she answered. "I will sleep on this side of the room with my sister." The two sisters lay down together, but it was difficult to sleep.

During the night they heard the mother stirring around, checking to see if they were asleep. As soon as the morning light began to show, they got up and began to run for their home. Soon they heard the mother's footsteps running behind.

"Quick, climb this palm tree," the sister said to Nyanbol. The tree, sacred to her family, bent low for Nyanbol to climb onto its top. Then the tree straightened. At that moment, the mother caught up to the sisters.

"Go away," the mother said to the sister. "I don't want you. I want Nyanbol." The sister began to run toward her home, calling to the husband to come and help.

The old mother commanded the tree to bend low for her, but the tree remained straight and tall with Nyanbol safely at the top. Then the old mother took out an ax and began cutting away at the trunk of the tree. She had not cut long, however, when her son arrived.

"Your wife has gone to the top of the tree, and now she is stuck there. I am cutting down the tree to save her."

The tree, seeing the husband, bent low once more so that Nyanbol could climb down. The three of them left together, returning to the mother's house. That night the son said to the mother, "You sleep in the hut, and Nyanbol and I will sleep outside."

Once the mother was inside, the son blocked the door with heavy logs. Then he set the hut on fire and in this way killed the mother.

～

In this story there appears to be no gift. What we are shown is a mother with a proclivity for killing her son's wives. Her voracious appetite marks her as a witch. Enormous appetites are characteristic of witches, in fairy tales, myths, and our internal psychological lives.

Remember the witch who caged Hansel, intending to fatten him for dinner? That tale is from Germany, but all cultures have witches with similar properties. In Russian folktales, there is a very ugly witch named Baba Yaga, who lives in a forest hut surrounded by a fence topped with the skulls of her victims. India's goddess Kali, the personification of the Dark Feminine, is often pictured with the blood of her victims dripping from her body or mouth. She also wears a necklace of skulls.

When the witch is portrayed as evil, she often is spoken of as being able to transform herself into a wolf, another ravenous creature. This is the instinctual energy, turned nasty. The wolf was chosen almost certainly because of its untamed nature. It's also worth noting that the wolf was sacred to early goddesses. As wolf, the witch is also known to eat her victims.

While in some tales, like "Frau Trude" or the tales of Baba Yaga, nothing bad happens to the witch; in other stories, such as the story of Hansel and Gretel, the witch is destroyed. There are times, the story seems to suggest, when the only appropriate approach to a facet of one's Dark Feminine is to kill it. Send it back down to the unconscious.

Kali, as a goddess, is above destruction. She is the symbol of the Dark Feminine archetype. As an archetype she is universal, existing in the deep collective unconscious of all humans past, present, and future. Kali, the Dark Feminine archetype (and indeed all archetypes) can never be fully understood. They are constantly unfolding. Like a diamond, many faceted, the archetype shows first one face, then another.

Thus we meet, in the story of Nyanbol, a flesh-eating aspect of the Dark Feminine, which we have met before.

Considering that all persons in a tale are aspects of the central character, what this story is suggesting is that as various new elements emerge in our psyche, they are vulnerable—like a bride at the beginning of marriage, they are inexperienced and inconclusive. When they seem to emerge into our consciousness, only to disappear, we must suspect the carnivorous portion of our internal Dark Feminine. We see and hear this phenomenon in remarks like:

"I always wanted to but . . . "

"I always thought about, however . . . "

"Once I almost . . . "

"But something came up . . . I wasn't really talented enough. I don't really know."

Women have been encouraged within our culture to believe the witch's message that they are unable and inept in very many ways. These are the teeth that chew up the innocent potential when it emerges. The witch lies behind the silly girlish voice that says, "Who me? Oh, I never could do . . . or be . . . or accomplish that!"

The encouraging part of this message is that there is always another young bride—another maturing part of us to try again. The brides keep appearing. We also hold the ability to continue to show up, each time a little wiser and a little stronger until we become Nyanbol.

In other words, our unconscious continues to provide new opportunities for us to join with previously unknown parts of ourselves.

It took the son-portion a very long time to catch on to the fact that a witch was at work. We are tempted to think we would respond in a very different manner. Well, maybe, but maybe not. A friend from childhood told me this story: "When I would finish drawing a picture, mother would always take it and give me a clean piece of paper. Don't draw on the back she would say. You can never tell when one of your pictures will be a masterpiece and you certainly wouldn't want anything on the back of a masterpiece."

My friend was always open to the idea of a masterpiece, whereas the rest of us in elementary school were convinced we couldn't draw because we were continually asked, "What is it?" and "Why did you make the horse a purple color?" We saw ourselves as "not artistic." It never occurred to any of us that a witch was at work in our lives, spreading poison. These types of messages about our inadequacies and shortcomings are still familiar.

The other major symbol in "Nyanbol" is the palm tree. Trees reach down into the underground of the unconscious and up through the air of our conscious reality into the heavens above. The palm itself is a symbol of victory, of self-renewal, and of righteousness. The palm is the tree that never sheds its leaves and continues to bear fruit until it dies. The palm is our ability to connect with and draw strength from our unconscious below and the spiritual or transpersonal above. This connection with life provides us with the ability to remain fruitful and creative.

The union of the husband and wife is a metaphor for individual wholeness. This union occurs and lasts because the husband or masculine part of the personality has become conscious about what is happening. He has matured enough to see that there is no place in their lives for this destructive energy, and he is able to destroy it. Often insight and action are lacking because of fear, but when this fear is overcome, the individual is free to experience his or her potential or wholeness.

Nyanbol has also matured enough to set limits. "No I will not sleep with you. No I will not stay beyond daybreak. I will run away. I will call forth the magic of the palm tree, and I will not come down until it's safe to do so." She, with the support she gains from her clever, assertive shadow sister, is able to face the Dark Feminine.

The Dark Feminine is transformed by fire, meaning she is sent back to the unconscious. However, she, like the other witches we are meeting, will be back again.

That we must set limits is a constant theme through these stories. There must be some distance. The Dark Feminine must not be allowed too close and we must not invade her private space. A beautiful woman doesn't really belong working in an all-night store in a high crime city without incurring terrible risks.

In "Frau Trude," the girl is destroyed because she speaks to the witch about the witch's true nature before the girl is able to comprehend what that means. This is invasive and is thus disrespectful.

There is a parallel story from Russia in which a girl asks the witch, Baba Yaga, the meaning of three riders whom she has seen approaching the witch's house. But she refrains from asking about Baba Yaga herself, even when invited to do so by the witch. Although Baba Yaga says the girl can ask more questions, the girl is silent. She then says to the girl, "It is well you ask only about what you have seen outside my house, not inside my house. I do not like to have my dirty linen washed in public, and I eat the overcurious."

Many people in therapy try to force the Dark Feminine to reveal her secrets. They find themselves in the grips of an aspect of this internal witch. It may be rage or depression or some other terrible mood, but the Frau Trude inside has a grip on them. "I can't shake it," they will say. "I want to get to the bottom of this. Why am I feeling this way?"

They search, talk, analyze, go 'round in circles. They find themselves angry at themselves, then at me as the therapist, at their own unconscious. Their teeth are out and they are beginning to bite themselves.

"She will let you know when she is ready," I tell them. "She will decide."

The witch is neither a fortune cookie nor a crystal ball ready to tell all for a price. The witch is the symbol of all the energy of the archetypal Dark Feminine in the collective unconscious. This, as all unconscious material is, is dynamic. It speaks to us. It sends its information as it deems important or necessary.

Any one of us may want our hair to turn from gray to brown or from brown to blond. Short of using a coloring agent, simple wanting will not make it so, for the cells have their own mind and their own pathway.

The unconscious, in a similar way, has its own intelligence, which is far greater than that of the conscious mind alone and resists being controlled. The only possibility is to form relationships with aspects that emerge and, as in any relationship, exercise respect, restraint, and an attitude open to learning.

Besides trying to force the witch to reveal what she is about, we often try to discount the importance of her message when it does arrive. "In a bad mood? Well get over it!" is a common attitude. Many a witch has been known to give a headache or backache or other pain to the conscious ego who treats her disrespectfully. The arrival of depression or anger or some other mood is a message. The witch is saying, "Stay tuned. Pay attention. Something is about to be broadcast."

What we can see from these stories about the witch is that there are scores of different ways for her to show up in our lives. We can also see how many variations exist regarding appropriate responses.

The key is to form a relationship with our own Dark Feminine. If it is a relationship of respect for who she is, and if we are able to be patient and keep an appropriate distance, we will come to know something about her. We will also discover that our lives are richer because of this relationship—she has many gifts to give. She holds the key to our creativity and a great deal of energy.

5

Spindles and Spiders

THE GOOD MOTHER

The Old Woman's thoughts this day were on Nona, a child of only eleven summers. Two weeks ago Nona had wandered into the village, exhausted and heavy with child. Her story of betrayal and abandonment had quickened the hearts of the villagers, and she was taken in and sheltered.

Within days a miraculously healthy baby was born. Although Nona recovered almost immediately, she had no idea of a baby's needs and often would leave him under a tree while she slept or flirted with village men. In spite of reminders, she neglected to check the soft moss between the baby's legs and his skin became burned from the continual acid dampness. When his insistent cries summoned her to nurse, she held the child much like a toy in which she'd lost interest.

The baby, given no name by the mother, was called Colin by the villagers. There were those in the village who talked of taking the baby to raise. It was an idea Nona would surely accept for it would leave her free to flirt and attach herself to another man. The Old Woman, however, hoped for a better solution. When she looked at Nona, she saw a lonely, frightened child pretending to be grown. Nona needed mothering as much as she needed to learn how to mother Colin. A way must be found.

Discovering how to be our own Good Mother is another task of aging. Today many older women wear emotional scars. Injuries, sustained during childhood and buried deep within the unconscious, wait for healing.

Other older women had caring mothers. These women, in turn, are able to mother others, but many of them have never learned to apply this mothering to themselves. We have lived for generations with the mistaken idea that for a woman to do for herself was selfish and indulgent. This mistaken value of selflessness has caused great harm to women, limiting them severely in preparing for healthy aging. When women are ignorant of their own needs, they are unable to mother themselves and they become helpless as they age. Before a woman reaches old age is the time to discover the Good Mother archetype. We all need her on this journey.

According to D. W. Winnicott a psychologist, there is no necessity for a mother to be perfect. He coined the expression "good enough mother" to describe a loving, competent mother who, in spite of some mistakes, raises a healthy child. It is when a mother falls below the standard of "good enough" that trouble occurs. The not good enough mother is either emotionally too close or too far away. A too close mother is clinging and dependent or omnipresent and controlling. Distant mothers are excessively indulgent, lenient, or disinterested, neglecting through permissiveness or absence. A good enough mother nurtures with limitations. It is that balance of limiting and nurturing that children need. So do mature women as we journey through the second half of our lives. While children find the source externally, adult women must search within.

An injury resulting from childhood deprivation lingers until healed. A woman living with this unhealed injury longs for the perfect love she imagines others received as children. There is a fantasy that good mothers are *all* loving and giving. She often goes through several marriages and countless friendships over the years looking for this type of love. She enters each relationship hopefully, believing that this person is and will be all loving, giving, sensitive, or caring— the answer to her lifelong search. As the relationship progresses and the other person's flaws emerge, the woman feels betrayed. She has no internal image of what is "good enough" to guide her. Even the expression "good enough" angers her. She has no experience of a loving mother who sets limits and sometimes lets her down.

Jean was a woman with this problem. She arrived in my office looking a very attractive thirty-something. She admitted her age was fifty-two only after asking me several times about confidentiality. Jean was ready to leave her fourth husband, George. They had married only fourteen months before this visit.

"Did you live together before you married?" I asked.

"We didn't, but I wish we had. Then I would have known. He can be very grumpy and selfish."

"What have you done to try to work it out?"

"I've told him and told him but he doesn't change. He just makes excuses like, 'I'm tired' or 'I'm too busy.'"

"Can you give me an example?"

"Well, just last night, he was sitting with his martini, and I said, 'Why don't we go out tonight. We never go anywhere. We could go into the city and have dinner.' He just gave me a look. So I got mad. I've seen that look before. Then I said something—I can't remember exactly what—and he got really mean."

"What do you mean by mean?"

"He says I'm impossible. Then he refuses to talk to me. He won't comfort me even when I cry. He just says, 'Grow up.' But this is all the time. He never gives me anything I want. We never do anything fun. He doesn't even want to be with me. I hate him."

"Why are you here? How can I help you?"

"I want him to come to see you so he will understand what he's doing. I can't take much more of this. I'm unhappy all the time. He said if I came, he would come with me the next time. I'm willing to come if it takes that for him to hear what he needs to do to change."

Jean and I talked about how both people in a relationship needed to change for a relationship to heal. Although she agreed, I suspected she wasn't able to understand.

As we talked during the remainder of that hour, I began to hear a terrible tale of childhood abandonment. Jean's mother had been *unwell,* spending most days in her nightclothes in bed or on the living-room sofa. From the age of three, Jean remembers finding her own food and putting herself to bed, usually on the floor in front of the television. She had to take responsibility way beyond her years. Her father worked two jobs, and Jean saw him only occasionally. He came home tired with little patience for either a sick wife or a needy child. It was a neighbor in the projects where they lived who took Jean to school for the first time, but after that first time Jean has no memory of the neighbor. By the time she was twelve she had dropped out of school and moved out of the house. From then on she lived wherever she could find a place.

Jean was aware that a better life was possible, and she began looking for wealthy young men to date. It seemed to her young mind that money made the difference. She learned grooming and discovered ways to appeal to men. By seventeen she had her first wealthy husband and felt she had put all those painful years behind her.

Husband number four, George, arrived for the next appointment fifteen minutes late. "Things seem fine to me," he said. "I have no idea what gets into Jean."

As George told his story, it became clear that he, too, had been the product of a self-absorbed and abandoning mom during his childhood. He was being entirely truthful when he said he had no idea what Jean wanted or needed because what she needed was something he had never experienced.

If Jean and George were to stay together and heal, they needed to share their individual childhood deprivations. Knowing that the other had lived through a similar lack might have provided each with enough understanding to tolerate the pain. By seeing the similarities, they would have been able to empathize with each other. Doing so could have helped their healing. Perhaps it would have also created closeness between them. However, neither was able nor willing, wanting instead to cling to the belief that only the other had a problem. After a third session, Jean decided to file for divorce.

"At least you're rich," she told him, "and I'll get something from this fiasco of a marriage. I'm going to the spa to try and release the stress of you and this marriage. If you have anything more to say, tell it to my lawyers."

That was the last I saw of either of them. George had made another appointment. However, he called to cancel it, saying he felt fine. Jean flew to Germany to a spa she had frequented in the past while the lawyers fought out the terms of the settlement.

Jean was looking for someone to heal the wounding she received as a young child from her neglectful mother. She longed for love and caring and was constantly seeking this from others. However, she was able to understand love only as indulgence and adoration. Relationship beginnings have that aura of magic about them, and that is what Jean expected should last. When the normal flaws and shortcomings of the other person emerged, Jean felt personally betrayed.

Our experiences imprint within us, creating mental grooves of familiarity. When we remain unaware of the effects of a wounding experience on our personalities, we act out the created patterns. Jean was aware she had an inadequate mother. However, she did not know the nature of her mistaken assumptions and that she was confusing fantasy and mature love. She continued to fall into the same pattern much as well-worn tire tracks pull a wheel into the same rut. The less we are aware of these experiences, the greater the likelihood of our sliding into the track and the deeper the rut will be.

Many people experience this phenomenon at family gatherings when we feel pulled back into childhood roles and behaviors. I find myself embarrassed at times to notice that I have slipped into making statements to my own visiting adult children such as "Don't forget your umbrella," or "Did you put your dishes into the dishwasher?" This type of behavior is called teaching when the children are six and nine. Now that they are thirty-six and thirty-nine, it can only be called controlling. Attempting to watch my behavior is only a superficial answer. I have discovered that my children, like most people, sense when something is going on *under the surface.* Only when a person becomes conscious of what is going on internally can the pattern be changed.

Jean is a sad example of someone who had no idea of her own unconscious groove, and because of this, she selected for her fourth husband someone who, like all the others back to and including her mom, was unable to give her what she needed. Jean needed to learn what was appropriate love between people *and* how to select a partner who would be able to give.

We can heal a lack of mothering by mothering, but it is easy to misunderstand what constitutes good enough mothering. Jean knew more clearly than anyone that she had not received enough nurturing from her own mother. She was angry about this, blaming her mother for a myriad of injuries and wounds. She also knew that she needed mothering, but Jean lacked an understanding of what this involves. As a result, she looked for husbands and friends who would pamper and care for her. Each time she failed to find what she needed, she blamed the other person.

Jean, however, was a fighter. Without this strong drive to survive, she would not have lived through the level of neglect that was present during her early childhood. She not only kept trying with others, but she also spent a great deal of time attempting to mother herself. Her youthful-looking body was the result of a series of surgeries undertaken to give herself something she wanted—attractiveness. She also gave herself vacations, manicures, a cleaning woman, and other tangible things. Yet none of this was working, either. The self-pampering was not able to reach deep enough to the place of the injury.

Jean and many others fail to heal and grow because they see the problem and solution as external. Before she could heal, Jean needed to see what internal distortions existed as a result of her early deprivation. When she understood these clearly, she would know what she needed to do to heal. Until then, her behavior was like that of a spoiled and pampered child.

Jean had no idea that good mothering involves setting limits and being imperfect as well as loving and nurturing. She needed to first discover the distortion in her internal view of love. Then she would be able to begin to learn to tolerate frustration. When I saw her, she lacked any ability to impose and accept limits, even when those limits were in her best interest. Jean was good at giving "things" to herself, but she was still unaware of how to guide herself in her own growth. To become her own good mother, Jean needed to learn the word *no*. Her mistake was attempting to get 100 percent loving care with none of the balance provided by limits.

There are many ways the good enough mother sets limits for her child. Children, guided by this type of mother, begin to learn about the imperfect nature of life itself. These children are able to internalize an ability to tolerate the frustration of not always having what they want. Consequently, they learn to set appropriate limits for themselves. In contrast, children of excessively permissive or strict mothers grow up frustrated and anxious when something doesn't go their way.

Limits are one of those things that fall into the category of what a child needs rather than what a child wants. Most children will respond to a limit set by a parent with some amount of frustration or anger. The mother who can hold firm without responding in kind to the child's emotion helps the child mature. Maturation requires experiencing and living through frustration while understanding that the mother still loves and cares for the child. The relationship between them survives. Limits set by the good enough mother protect the child from physical harm, teach appropriate social behaviors, demonstrate the fallibility of humans, and teach the frustration tolerance necessary for reaching long-range goals.

These understandings are imperative in adulthood if we are to discover unconscious material we need to heal. Without the acceptance of limits, none of us could find meaning in the aging process, for that process itself is one where physical and external limits grow increasingly numerous and serious as years go by.

Clarisse was a young mother who was facing the consequences of an unrecognized internal groove. Clarisse's mother had been a strict, angry woman, and Clarisse vowed to be a nurturing, loving mother when her daughter Amanda was born. Every time Amanda cried, Clarisse responded at once. Nothing was off-limits as the baby learned to crawl and later to walk.

By the time Amanda was ready for preschool, she was a demanding, tyrannical little girl who was unable to cooperate or play with other children. Clarisse was aware others didn't like Amanda, and, if truth be told, she too was harboring a great deal of resentment toward the child. Any suggestion from Clarisse that Amanda behave more appropriately in public brought forth screams, tantrums, and hitting.

Clarisse worked hard and soon was able to understand the dynamic between them. First, Amanda did something inappropriate such as climbing on the living-room sofa with dirty shoes. Clarisse would then say in a sweet tone, "Amanda, dear, please take your shoes off if you want to play on the sofa."

"No!"

Clarisse would back off and begin to feel angry. As she watched the dirt accumulating on the sofa, her anger would mount. She would then either explode, yanking Amanda down and screaming at her, or she would leave the room, silently fuming. Either way she felt terrible. It seemed to her she was angry no matter what she chose to do. Clarisse was unskilled at setting limits. As a result, Amanda consistently defeated her. Both she and Amanda grew more angry with each failed attempt at mothering.

Clarisse's behavior with Amanda is the way many women also behave with themselves. "I really should watch what I eat," they will say, but the scales creep upward year after year as they continue to eat too much of the wrong foods. These women understand their behaviors are harmful but are unable to set effective limits. Limits all seem like punishment because their internal reference point is "love means having whatever I desire." They have not yet internalized the idea that a good mother sets an effective limit and then keeps that limit calmly and lovingly while the child inside fusses and fumes. Eventually the anger will abate. At that point the internal child will understand that a loving relationship is durable. The internal mother does not abandon her child.

One important aspect of good enough mothering is an ability to *contain*. The mother must contain the tension of the child's anger or frustration without either pretending nothing is happening or exploding and acting out her own or the child's frustration. Similarly, she must be able to say to herself or the internal hungry child, "No. You don't need milk and cookies. You are feeling bored. Take a walk!" As the internal child rants and raves, she must then have enough ego strength and determination to take that walk, talking firmly but gently all the while in her internal conversation. The message she needs to continue to give herself is that there is no blame; only a need to learn a new way.

The first part of containing, therefore, involves holding firm and saying no to something that is incorrect. Implicit is that the woman understands what is correct. The second step in containment involves helping the child sort through what is going on. Getting mad is only the beginning. The child must learn, understand, or change, or the anger will contribute to the development of one of those unconscious grooves.

In the example of milk and cookies, the sorting involves first identifying the source of the urge. Am I bored, hungry, angry? When we block an activity such as eating, other feelings and thoughts will rise to consciousness. Through a long process Janie discovered her constant eating had to do with wanting to be fat to keep men away from her. Because of traumatic experiences in her past, she was afraid of attracting men. Marsha and her dictatorial mother struggled over who was in control of Marsha. Marsha discovered that by refusing to eat an appropriate amount, she could defeat her mother's control. Lisa, by staying with her feelings, discovered she ate to avoid anger. Each woman has her own story and the feelings underneath the activity, when examined, can be the highways to meaning.

When a mother contains, she encloses and embraces what is fragile, tender, and vulnerable—protecting it from the outside world. Opal took up painting at the age of fifty. She always loved sketching but never pursued her talent. Now there was time. She thought she might be talented, but she also felt unsure and scared. For a long time she kept her paintings to herself. It wasn't until she had taken lessons for two years, developed her technique, and had some idea of her own direction that she showed any of her work. Opal understood the type of mothering she needed to provide for herself.

Past generations of people lived near the extended family. Parents, as they aged, moved in with adult children. If it was a happy and close family such as the one portrayed on the television program *The Waltons,* the arrangement worked well for everyone. Although there may not have been many families where intergenerational life was this happy, this arrangement remained for many generations as the collective social ideal.

We are currently living in the midst of a major paradigm shift. Extended families no longer reside in the same small town or neighborhood. Along with the outer shift caused by mobility and distance is an inner shift: the collective ideal is being replaced by individuality with each family member or small unit assuming responsibility for their own lives. We no longer expect a family to take in its aging members. Older parents, separated by miles from adult children, are moving into retirement communities. Eventually most of these seniors will receive some form of assistance from strangers.

We are no longer able to count on experiencing daily sustenance from our connection with children and grandchildren during old age. Meaning and satisfaction must come from within. This means we must work to develop our inner resources during our midlife period. The internal Good Mother helps us in this work, as "Mother Holle," a story from the Grimm's collection, illustrates.

This tale teaches about the nature of the Good Mother archetype and gives some direction about how to learn and internalize the needed attitude and skills. Our protagonist, Rosa, like many young heroines in fairy tales, is living with a stepmother who symbolizes a critical, rejecting mother. Rosa is in need of the experience of a Good Mother that she finds with Mother Holle.

~ Mother Holle ~

ONCE THERE WAS a young girl named Rosa who lived with her stepmother and stepsister. The stepmother made Rosa do all the work while her own daughter lay around most of the day. Rosa never complained and would work late into the night to finish the tasks assigned to her.

One day Rosa was sitting by the side of the well spinning when she pricked her finger on the spindle. As she leaned over to wash the blood away, the spindle fell into the well. Rosa went home to tell her stepmother what had happened.

"Go back and find it," her stepmother said in an angry voice. "Even if you have to go to the bottom of the well, do not return until you have found the spindle."

Rosa went back and jumped into the well. The next thing she knew, she was standing in a large field of flowers. Off to one side, near the road, was an oven. Rosa walked that way and as she came to the oven it spoke to her. "Please take out the loaves of bread before they burn."

Rosa stopped and removed the bread, then began walking down the road. Soon she came to an apple tree whose branches were bent low with the weight of the apples. "Please shake me before the apples break my branches," the tree said. Rosa stopped and shook the tree free of all the apples before continuing down the road.

Next Rosa came to a cow whose udder was filled with milk. "Please milk me," the cow said, and Rosa stopped and milked the cow. Then she continued down the road.

Soon she came to a little house. As she was about to knock, the door opened and Rosa found herself facing an ugly-looking old woman. The young girl turned to run, but the woman said, "Don't be afraid. My name is Mother Holle and I won't hurt you. You can stay here for a while if you will work for me. I need someone to shake out my mattress each day, for that is how the earth receives snow."

Rosa agreed and worked for Mother Holle for many days. She did all she was asked and Mother Holle was pleased with her. Finally Rosa began to grow sad and yearn to return to her home. When Rosa spoke of her homesickness, Mother Holle pulled a spindle from her apron pocket and gave it to Rosa. Then she showed her a door that Rosa had not noticed before. As Rosa went through the door, she was showered with gold, which stuck to her clothing.

When she arrived home, her stepmother was very excited about the gold and immediately sent her own daughter to the well. The girl threw in her spindle, jumped in, and found herself in the same field of flowers. However, as she met the oven, the apple tree, and the cow, she said no to each request for help and continued on her way.

Arriving at Mother Holle's, she accepted the invitation to move in but refused to do any work. After a day, Mother Holle said, "Perhaps it would be good if you left for home." This pleased the lazy girl and she accepted the spindle and walked through the door. As she did, instead of the gold she had been expecting, she was covered with tar. When she arrived home, both she and her mother tried to wash the tar away but it would not be removed by soap and water.

∽

In "Mother Holle," the storyteller uses four characters to illustrate four aspects of a woman's psyche. As the story begins Rosa's real good enough mother is absent. In her place is the negative stepmother. The stepmother represents that unconscious aspect of any woman that is demanding, insensitive, critical, and unrelenting.

As the central character, Rosa could be called the ego position. This ego position is the way any of us consciously think about ourselves. Rosa is hardworking and behaves in a caring manner, but her caring is extreme. She is unable to discriminate whether that response is appropriate or not. The stepsister would correspond to Rosa's shadow. Here are all of the traits that Rosa has but cannot consciously acknowledge: selfishness, laziness, envy. Rosa and her shadowy sister are mirror images of the two extremes within a human personality.

Rosa has a stepmother part as well. This story exemplifies the driven nature of that part as the stepmother pushes Rosa into work and negates her. This relationship between conscious good intentions and a driven controlling underbelly is seen in women who accept every committee job or request for help no matter how busy they are and then go home and are demanding with their husbands and children. The stepmother aspect arises when the woman has given away too much of herself.

When the conscious personality identifies with Rosa, the individual does not see herself containing a stepmother. Instead, she views the problem as pressure from some external source. Some years back we heard the term *superwoman* used for women who attempted to do everything. These women experienced themselves as driven. They, like Rosa, saw the source as external. A modern-day Rosa, driven by work, relatives, and commitments, has an internal stepmother. These Rosas describe themselves as unable to do anything else.

In a therapy session I will sometimes ask, "Why don't you just stop doing some of those things?" The response is often an incredulous look. "Who would do them?" they ask. "Perhaps no one. Would that matter?" When under the spell of the stepmother, constantly working in a frantic driven way, the thought of stopping seems impossible. Although there appears to be some logic driving the process (I have to do A, B, and C and then I can relax), this logic rests on an impossible premise: namely, that tying up all the loose ends and completing all the details is possible.

Jane, now fifty-six, had this problem. She taught school, was active in the community, often baby-sat for one of her several grandchildren, and kept a perfect house. She entered therapy for depression.

When talking about her childhood, Jane described her mother as strict. "My dad was the preacher. Mom always wanted us to be examples for other children. We lived in a small town so everyone knew everyone else's business. My dad was always busy. He left child rearing to mother and nothing escaped her notice. Grades, appearance, manners, and behavior were all scrutinized and any area needing improvement was always talked about before prayers each night.

My brother rebelled from a very early age. He was always in trouble. I tried to do what she expected."

"But you never felt her approval?"

"Not really."

It took a while, but gradually Jane began to understand the connection between her mother's constant expectations and dissatisfaction and what Jane was doing to herself through her overwork. She had internalized the never-satisfied mother.

Jane needed to stop long enough to experience her sadness at never receiving any sign of approval from her mother. She needed to see how she was duplicating within herself the childhood interaction she had had with her mother. She needed to experience her current fatigue and sadness at the minimal rewards she was gaining from her current behavior. By paying attention to these internal feelings, she, like Rosa, would go down the well into the unconscious.

Once Rosa descends, there is again work to do, but with two important differences. First, there is a nondriven quality to the requests and the work. This work originates from a different place, and the source of an action contributes to its meaning. A request as simple as "Pass the salt" can convey a message of desiring salt or a message that the person is selfish and thoughtless because he or she failed to notice another's need for salt. A request for work can have within it a driven quality or be natural and instinctual. Stepmother work conveys a driven quality.

Second, all three of these requests concern nourishment. To refuse any of this work implies that something would spoil. This part of the story reminds us of the Old Testament passage from Ecclesiastes.

> To every thing there is a season
> and a time to every purpose under
> the heaven.

Each of the requests that greets Rosa in this new territory gives information about what she—and we—must do to transform a driven feeling into one that is nondriven.

Rosa first passed the oven and heard, "Please remove the loaves of bread." While bread is a basic food, it also serves as a significant symbol in early religions as well as current ones; this indicates that we are looking at something more than ordinary physical nourishment. We find the symbol of bread in the New Testament. Jesus broke bread as the symbol of his body. The modern-day Christian continues this meaning by incorporating bread along with wine as symbols of the body and blood of Jesus.

Within the Jewish faith the unleavened bread provided sustenance in the desert and symbolizes the freedom of the Jews. Celebrants serve it still as part of the Passover dinner. According to Greek mythology, Demeter, an early Greek harvest goddess, exemplifies the connection of grain and bread to the earth mother.

To move from a driven to a natural place, one must search for sacred nourishment. This sacred nourishment is different from a simple understanding on the level of the ego. We find it within the unconscious. Once we relax and allow ourselves to open to the unconscious, this source of sacred nourishment will call out to us.

Rosa passed the apple tree next. Apples have a dual symbolic meaning. They are symbols of love, sacred to many early goddesses. The apple is also a metaphor for becoming conscious. It was the apple in the Garden of Eden that symbolized knowledge, the awareness of good and evil versus the previous innocence. To be innocent is to be unconscious. Spiritual nourishment and consciousness are both necessary to remove oneself from the domination of the psychological stepmother.

Milk, the third element, is also a basic form of nourishment, but its inclusion by the storyteller gives us additional information. When a person does not milk a cow, the milk will dry up. Just as neglect will cause the cow's udder to stop producing, it will cause our own internal ability to grow toward authenticity to atrophy.

This idea is easier to understand when we view it practically. Imagine a person who discovers as a child that she has a talent for music but does not work with this talent in any way. The musical ability will never develop. It will dry up like the milk of an unmilked cow.

Milk is also a spiritual symbol, letting us know that the storyteller is still focusing on the necessity of a spiritual connection in breaking the domination of the driven energy. We see milk used in this symbolic way in pictures of Jesus as a shepherd carrying a milk bowl.

In other belief systems there is also the concept that the gods themselves are in need of the nourishment which humans can provide, furthering the idea of a process that includes giving. Ancient Greeks offered milk, honey, oil, and water to the gods. In Siberia, the people poured milk on the ground during a thunderstorm as a way to appease the angry gods.

The source of this nourishment, the cow, initiates the contact with Rosa. Like the ancient Greeks and Siberians, Rosa is asked to perform a service, but is not invited to eat. To eat too soon would be a mistake, an easy answer. Although easy answers are tempting, we must move on. We move on, however, knowing that an abundance of spiritual food is available. Before she and we are ready for that food, we must do more work. Do not remain inactive, the storyteller is suggesting. This is a process where you will receive in a deep and spiritual way but only if you participate in the process.

This is a very similar situation to that of the old woman who entered the cave of the Oni in "The Old Woman and the Rice Cake." In order for her to receive the gift that the unconscious had to give, she needed to stay awhile and get to work. Simply entering the cave and seeing the Oni was not enough, any more than being down the well and seeing these first three symbols is enough. Often in our psychological work we gain an initial connection to some divine value or quality and then lose that connection. It is only after doing some required work that we again gain the value.

We experience the truth of this on a deep level as we try to become more spiritual, learn to meditate, or work for self-knowledge in therapy. Growing in wisdom demands commitment.

Rosa, by continuing her journey, arrives at the home of Mother Holle who asks her to do more work. To shake out a mattress, sending snow, is to invite in the cold, frozen, dormant period of the year. Snow comes in winter and is a symbol of new life being unavailable or covered over. This time is often one of depression.

People frequently respond to this type of inactivity and threat of depression by rushing into busyness. "Cheer up!" "Go shopping!" "Do something!" This can be appropriate advice but only in some instances. There are times in life when attempting to explore the unconscious is impractical. At those times there are external demands of a crucial nature that we must attend to. When a house is on fire, it is time to get the fire extinguisher. After the fire is out, we can contemplate the meaning of loss and flame.

At the beginning of the story we see the problem symbolized by Rosa's being under the domination of the stepmother. Some part or quality of her personality is driving her behavior beyond what is healthy or reasonable. What Rosa needs is not available externally but is present within her own psyche because the unconscious has a tendency to attempt to supply whatever is missing in order to provide a balance.

Rosa is in great need of the Good Mother archetype. Although Mother Holle still asks Rosa to work, there is an important difference between this work and the work the stepmother demands. The stepmother work that Rosa does in the beginning of the story is compulsive. The work Rosa does for Mother Holle is connected psychologically.

Rosa is no longer working for external reasons. She has withdrawn her energy from the old compulsive way of being. Now she must persevere. If she will stay with the internal connection, she will develop a tolerance for the ambiguity and tension surrounding this type of work. And tension there will be, because what is implied in this image is that Rosa must stop herself from all her old behaviors and notice her feelings so that she will become clear about what she needs to do for herself.

Anyone who had gone through the process of withdrawing from the superwoman role knows how difficult this is. Not only do the requests and pressures continue from those around, but there is an ongoing internal pressure that must also be resisted. This is a time of waiting just as the earth awaits the warmth of the spring thaw and the breakthrough of the plants.

The necessary task of waiting is very difficult. We find it difficult to trust that the unconscious will lead or teach just as the seed underground will germinate. It is helpful to find some internal or external good mother who is able to be kind, gentle, and nurturing, and will contain, as Mother Holle does for Rosa, by keeping her with her in the house. That good mother's job is to continue to be reassuring—to allow feelings to develop while we wait for insight.

At this juncture in therapy a client will also say, "But what do I do? Nothing changes. So I feel the feelings: So what?"

As Jane worked in therapy, she began to understand how much she needed a good mother. In the beginning, whenever these feelings would surface, she would take herself shopping, out to dinner, or treat herself to late-night snacks. She put on a great deal of weight and accumulated high credit card bills she couldn't really afford. It took a while before she understood that this type of nurturing or taking care of herself was not good mothering. She was like a little kid who is hungry and fills up on candy. Sometimes you have to wait to discover what you're genuinely hungry for—what you need. You don't forget you're hungry. You just don't act on it.

The important aspect of the Good Mother is her ability to understand our needs. She directs us in the way to go if we want meaning rather than busyness. Jane clearly knew that she had worked hard but still felt empty. She was working on what she perceived to be others' wishes. The internalized mother, created from her experience with the real mother, was driving her. This is the stepmother. She can drive but is unable to nurture because she has no connection with the individual. The stepmother sees the individual as an object to be used. Connection, caring, and understanding only come from our internal Good Mother.

The storyteller has also woven the number three into "Mother Holle." Remember the woman in "The Woman in the Vinegar Bottle" who had to turn around three times? As we learned from that story, we associate the number three with wholeness and completion. We remember we must continue until we realize our goal. Rosa is asked three times to harvest food. The storyteller is describing learning and relearning spiritual or psychological nourishment. This process of repetition is the way deep learning always is. We try something, get it, fail, try again, get it, fail again. Each time, the experience of "getting it" is a little deeper and a little stronger until finally we have internalized the insight. The process takes time.

Marian came to see me a month after she had retired. "I don't know what to do with myself," she said. "I am busy but I feel lost. Nothing really seems satisfying." Marian slid down her well and began exploring. Friends and previous colleagues offered her things to do, but nothing seemed right until Marian discovered meditation. This provided her with the link she needed to that deeper place where she could learn her direction.

At first Marian was elated. "I felt like I had come home the minute I walked into the class. It is exactly what I need to help me know what I must do."

I heard from Marian off and on over the next several years and each time she was at a different place with meditation. Sometimes she hated it; at other times she felt this was the only possible direction she could take. She would get it, then fail, only to pick herself up and get it again. It was a long process but one that seemed worth it for her. She was learning again that those things that are truly valuable take time.

During my years as a therapist I have met very few women like Jean who had no idea of how to give or nourish at least a little. Even the most angry women have had someone or something in their lives to care for: a child, a husband, an ailing parent, a puppy, an African violet collection. The task is to find the internal Good Mother. From her we will learn how to appropriately direct this nurturing toward ourselves.

"That sounds selfish," many women will say when first hearing the idea, but caring for oneself is just the opposite. It is the starving person who selfishly grabs for food. The well-fed person is able to genuinely concern herself with others' needs as well as her own.

Mother Holle, the archetypal Good Mother isn't beautiful. Instead of hugging Rosa and giving her milk and cookies, she asks Rosa to work for her. Our cultural image of the Good Mother is one of endless bounty. She has a warm, loving, comfortable appearance that invites us to move onto her lap. Once we are there, she will hug and sing. The popular image of the Good Mother is a female Santa. This image, imprinted during infancy, is the fantasy of the mother who never frustrates. The actual Good Mother archetype isn't as simple or one-dimensional. Her ability to frustrate makes her appear ugly to our untrained eye, yet it is this ability that teaches us how to work when things don't immediately go our way. To understand how to work with the natural cycles of our lives is indeed golden.

Francie came to see me on her fiftieth birthday. "It's a birthday present to myself," she told me. "I really don't have much to complain about except for an ongoing feeling of nausea."

"Have you been to a medical doctor?" I asked.

She laughed. "It seems like I've seen hundreds. I've had every test that's ever been invented. They all end up saying the same thing to me. There is nothing physically wrong. It's all in your head."

"What do you think?" I asked.

"I think perhaps they're right, although I honestly do feel ill, so I don't really know how this could be just imagination."

"I don't think it's just imagination, either," I said. "I think it must be an important metaphor. I think your unconscious is trying very hard to tell you something about your life and it is using your body to communicate. The task in therapy is to discover what the message is about so that you can decide how to respond. Do you have any idea what you might be sick of or what in your life you might want to throw up?"

Francie had no idea. Her life was full, with friends and family she loved and who loved her. Her marriage was satisfying. Although all the children were living away from home, they lived close and she saw one or another of them or her grandchildren daily. It sounded, as she described her life, as if she were the beloved family hub.

Francie's early life was a sharp contrast. Her father had been an enlisted man in the military and they had moved often. Her mother was a nurse who worked long hours to supplement their income. When she was a child, Francie was left at home alone for long hours each day. She remembered countless times when she hid under her bed, fearful that the house-creaking noises she heard were intruders who would carry her away before her parents returned from work.

When she met and married Joe, she was determined to provide a warm and loving family environment, and she apparently succeeded. Some years ago her father had died and her mother came to live with them. "That was good," she said. "It gave me a chance to get to know her."

"How long has she been here?"

"Let me think." Francie appeared to be counting silently. "About seven years I think."

"And when did your nausea begin?"

"Oh, not then. It's only been about"—again the silent counting—"only about two, maybe three years."

"What does your mother do with herself each day?"

"When she first came out here she was quite active. She volunteered at the hospital and became active in the church guild. Then, gradually she had to cut back. She became increasingly forgetful and confused. Didn't I tell you she has Alzheimer's disease?"

The connection to the meaning of the nausea took time for Francie to make. What finally began to emerge were feelings of rage that she had pushed into the unconscious. We do not completely understand how this mind-body connection works. We do know that emotions are able to impact and alter the chemical balance within our bodies. Francie was furious at her mother for all the childhood neglect that included so many hours of fear and terror. She was angry as well because the Alzheimer's allowed her mother to again absent herself. Francie repressed the rage because it conflicted with her value system of kindness and caring. "She can't help having Alzheimer's," Francie would say, but the intellectual understanding didn't change the feelings. They were real and they were literally making her sick to her stomach by causing internal physical changes which, in turn, were creating the nausea.

"What should I do?"

"Stay with the feelings."

"I want to scream at her."

"That's *doing* something. Just stay with the feelings. Write in your journal. Go to the woods and scream. Scream at me, but don't do anything to make the feelings go away and don't take it out on your mother."

This idea of there always being two extremes that are opposites to each other—an either/or—is an important concept. In Francie's case the extremes were denying the feelings and doing something to make herself feel better on one side or giving in and acting the feelings out by screaming or venting on the other. To do neither is to sit in the middle and experience the tension that exists between the two alternatives. It feels terrible to be there, but this is also the most productive place to be, for it is the gateway to insight and understanding.

To be able to stay with these feelings, Francie needed some time alone, away from constantly caring for her mother. She found a day-care center where she could take her mom each day. As she was able to focus on the feelings, they appeared to grow "worse." At least that was Francie's perception. "I hate her! I hate hating her! I hate that I dug all this stuff up. I can't help wondering what was the matter with her? She wasn't stupid. How could she have left me alone every afternoon? How could she have not known how terrified I was? I was a completely mousy little kid, scared of my own shadow! Why didn't she take care of me?" On and on through great pain Francie stormed. We continued to explore, and very slowly Francie's nausea diminished as she learned how to respect her own feelings of rage without behaving in ways that would produce guilt. As we worked, she was able to begin identifying what she needed and find options to meet her own needs. Slowly over the next months the rage gave way to compassion and understanding.

"I still occasionally have days when I feel the nausea," Francie said. "When that happens I remember how you said it is a metaphor, and I know I'm fighting against throwing something up that I'm stuffing. I actually am feeling grateful that I have this symptom. Once I understood its meaning, it has become a signal that I'm betraying myself in some way."

Francie's nausea came from the repressed feelings of fear and anger. Francie kept them repressed both because they conflicted with her value system and because she feared her own infantile response should she let the feelings out. We all have the potential for an infantile response that pops out when we act in an out-of-control manner—which I think of as an adult temper tantrum. These are the times when adults scream, say things they later regret, or become so overwhelmed by the emotion of the moment that they lose all perspective. It is exactly for these reasons that most people repress this type of anger. Francie was afraid that she would say cruel, awful things, hurting her mother with words that she could not take back.

These awful things, however, need to be felt and need to be expressed somewhere, whether in a journal, to a neutral third party, or to a therapist. Sometimes a new client will begin the first session announcing, "I had a terrible childhood, but I understand my parents did the best they could." I know that the client and I will have to work harder than usual because of this understanding. To intellectually understand that truth before the feelings emerge is to keep a psychic cancer beneath awareness where it can only spread. It is the opposite extreme of losing control.

Therapy was the container that provided Francie with the necessary limits, caring, and direction to successfully go to these internal places of insight and transformation. Without the container, Francie would have either acted out her rage toward her mother or been so frightened at this possibility that she would have stuffed it back below awareness again. Another story, this one from the Cherokee Nation of Native American people, tells of the value of containment.

⌒ Grandmother Spider Steals the Sun ⌒

ONCE, IN THE VERY BEGINNING, there was no light where the animals lived. The sun with all the light was kept on the other side of the world by selfish people who did not want to share. The animals met to plan how they could steal the sun.

"I will go," said the possum. "I have a big bushy tail and it will be easy to hide the sun until I return." Possum left and all the animals waited anxiously for his return. But possum had bad luck.

Oh, he found the sun without any problem and was able to put a piece of it under the fur on his bushy tail. The sun was so hot it burned off all the fur. Possum hollered and yelled in pain and all the people came and took back the piece of sun. Possum had to return with a skinny bare tail and no light.

"No matter," said Buzzard. "I will go. I am able to fly fast. Even if the people see sunlight balanced on my head, they will never be able to catch me." So Buzzard went to the land of the sun.

Buzzard's plan would have worked except that he forgot how hot the sun was. As soon as he put a piece of it on his head, it began burning his feathers. Buzzard let out a whoop and the people rushed over and managed to grab the piece of the sun. Poor Buzzard had to return to his village with a very sore bald head.

The animals felt very discouraged. They talked and argued among themselves as to what they could do. Finally a quiet voice said, "I will go." The animals looked and saw that it was Grandmother Spider. She was very small and they were sure she would not be able to do such a hard job, but no one could think of another plan so everyone agreed.

First Grandmother Spider made a clay pot to hold the sun piece when she had captured it, for she didn't want to burn herself. Then she began to spin a web to the other side of the world. She was so small and the web was so thin that none of the people noticed her.

Once there, she quickly grabbed a piece, popped it into her container, and scampered back along the threadlike web. Oh, how the animals all rejoiced when there was light on their side of the world.

Since then, there has been not only light but fire. And always since that time, there has been the knowledge of how to make containers.

～

This Cherokee tale, similar to many stories coming from land-based societies, features animals instead of people. Native Americans understand the kinship between animals and people and frequently tell animal tales to teach valuable human lessons.

Throughout the ages, animals have been used to symbolize human instincts. For example, we associate traits of unconditional love and loyalty with dogs. A story featuring a dog might be illustrating the importance of loyalty. In "Grandmother Spider Steals the Sun," three different instinctual parts of ourselves are represented by three different animals—possum, buzzard, and Grandmother Spider. None of these animals are as familiar in our modern urban culture as they were to the Cherokee society that originated the tale.

The story begins in total darkness. Darkness affects most people as evidenced by the increase in depression during the winter months. In Iceland and other countries to the far north where only a couple of hours of dusky light exist each winter day, the people have learned to install special lighting in their homes. People need light.

Psychological darkness symbolizes a lack of conscious awareness or insight. Intuitively we apply this meaning in such expressions as "I was kept in the dark," "shed some light on the matter," or "It was as if a lightbulb was turned on." We also refer to an "unenlightened" period of history as the Dark Ages.

The storyteller reminds us that achieving insight, the image of gaining the light or sun, is not an easy process. The animals had to make three attempts. By now we understand this symbolism of "over and over," which reminds us of the necessary trial and error that must occur to achieve understanding.

The first animal or aspect of the personality to volunteer was possum. A possum, or opossum, is a night animal, a creature of the dark. Along with other nocturnal animals, she moves and forages by night and sleeps through the light.

We need to know more about possums to understand why possum failed. To begin with, the possum is not a smart animal. With a braincase only one-fifth the size of a house cat's, a possum uses repetitious behaviors to aid in survival. The possum follows the same pathway night after night, and instead of discriminating certain foods as desirable, the possum eats anything it finds. This lack of discrimination extends to the fact that possums would even eat another possum if they found it dead in their own path.

This failure to discriminate occurs on a psychological level with people who become trapped in adopting whatever pop-psychology fad may be in vogue. While their search always comes from some legitimate need, these possum people fail to sort valid insights from the garbage or invalid nontruths. Unless we consume things of value, we will, like the possum, fail to transform.

The possum also has a behavior that we call "playing possum." The possum falls on its side, drooling from an open mouth and giving off the musk of the death scent. Menacing animals respond by walking away, exhibiting what appears to be confusion at the lack of a fight or chase.

We mimic the possum's collapse when we use denial as a defense. Some people play possum by not noticing what is or was happening around them.

"He was a good husband," Merle says.

"Mother, he used to hit us all. He was awful!" a daughter may reply.

Strange as it seems to someone looking in from outside, Merle either didn't notice or forgot.

Another way of playing possum, which also has origins in feeling threatened, involves making excuses. "Yes, he did hit us at times, but he really didn't meaning anything by it. He was just under pressure."

While avoidance and denial may help people keep away from conflict and confrontation, playing possum is an ineffective way to resolve whatever underlying issues exist.

Prudence is an example of someone who engaged in this ineffective behavior. Her husband teased their son continually. There
was a hostile edge to the teasing although the husband maintained it
was all in fun. The boy became more angry over the years. He was
only able to demonstrate the anger in passive ways, but these were
all effective in getting even with his father. Where dad was punctual,
the son was always late. Dad was an achiever, so his son failed. Dad
was responsible, so his son forgot. Prudence spent her life torn between her husband and son, attempting to protect the boy, calm the
father, and generally be a peacemaker. She was playing possum to
the underlying issue, frozen into a placating pattern of denial.

Another woman, Wanda, was also playing possum. She grew
up in a family that valued boys. The father and brothers considered
her, as the youngest and only girl, cute but incompetent. Wanda
never dealt with any of her feelings toward her original family. She
also married a man who, for years, treated her in the same way. At
fifty, Wanda found herself standing fixed and immobilized in the
headlights of her oncoming divorce. She was unaware of any feeling
beyond her fear of being alone.

Another interesting fact about the possum is that it was alive at
the time of the dinosaur. It is an ancient and primal animal. Similarly, within each of us are ancient and primal instincts. Any woman
who has given birth has experienced these raw instincts that are still
alive beneath our civilized veneer. We equip our hospitals with technologically sophisticated equipment to monitor, diagnose, and facil-
itate healthy new life. At the moment of birth, however, it is the
primitive instinct to push that new life into its separate existence
that causes the birth.

In spite of the possum's lack of intelligence and primitive nature, we must be grateful to it. Learning anything new is a process,
and possum is the point of beginning. We begin in a slow, waddling
manner, perhaps playing possum along the way. We begin our journeys toward insight with hesitant steps. Still, like the possum we can

keep on, night after night. We can return, going over the same land and gathering everything we can find. The possum is a primal determination that serves us as a firm beginning.

Possum burns her tail because she tries to carry the sun with the tail. To this day the possum has a bare tail. A tail is an extension of the spinal column that humans left behind as we evolved. This level of primitive development, while a necessary place to begin, will eventually burn us if we attempt to accomplish too much without gaining additional skills.

The primitive nature of the possum's mothering skills speaks to why remaining on a possum level is destructive to a person. The possum has two to three litters a year of young. When born, each baby is responsible for the climb to the mother's pocket where it then swallows a nipple. This reattaches the baby to the mother's body where it stays until it is larger. Later when the baby is free of this attachment, it must watch out for itself. As the mother waddles along the pathway each night, the baby waddles, too, climbing onto the mother's back and holding onto the tail for stability. Mother possum does not carry her babies around, herding them here and there like other mammals. For baby possums, the rule is very much survival of the fittest.

This aspect of laissez-faire mothering is something we are all capable of. We experience it when we do only the minimum for ourselves. When I wake, remembering dreams but neglect to write them down or work with them to increase my self-understanding, I am using possum-mother energy. Our new, fetuslike insights must eventually receive more than this type of minimal mothering.

Many older women of today grew up with minimal mothering. They lived on farms or in small towns where everyone worked. Their mothers had little leftover time or energy for nurturing. For some of these women, this type of minimal mothering worked because of the number of people around. Aunts, grandparents, older sisters, or cousins were also available to nurture when needed. There were no episodes of something going wrong that someone in the community couldn't handle.

In other cases, a possum-type human mother has a daughter who is creative or special in some way. This daughter needs more than the minimum that possum-mother is able to provide. If there are no other resources, this daughter is in trouble.

We also see a great deal of possum mothering these days from the number of young teens who are becoming mothers. Unless these girls can receive help themselves, there will be a new generation of young adults—their children—who did not receive enough mothering to grow into healthy adults. In our current world there are many children like Nona.

Having taken our first faltering steps toward insight, as represented by the possum, our storyteller suggests that buzzard energy is the next approach. The buzzard, like birds in general, can symbolize an intuitive thought that flies by.

The buzzards' view contrasts sharply with our own. As they soar high above the earth on strong wings, buzzards can see great distances and are able to gain perspective on what is below. Their eyesight is sharp, allowing them to distinguish the spot where they will find food. The buzzard serves as a metaphor for the internal strength that allows us to soar through our thoughts and feelings and for our ability to identify and zero in on something crucial. We need to experience the hopefulness as well as use that ability to get ourselves closer to the nourishment we are seeking.

Once a buzzard swoops down to an identified dead animal, its hooked bill allows it to tear apart what it wants to consume. This idea of ripping and tearing suggests the struggle to analyze and understand that we all go through in self-examination. However, what the buzzard is ripping and tearing at is carrion—something dead—and this aspect of the symbol serves as a warning. We must combine our ability to analyze—to rip and tear through the tough outer hide of something to reach an intellectual understanding—with the appropriate emotions. Pure intellect or thought without the humanizing influence of our feelings will produce only carrion.

Once Prudence had begun therapy, she fairly quickly recognized that she had been playing possum. She then questioned why she had allowed herself to remain in the middle for so long. "I wanted to protect my son . . . or maybe because I loved and understood my husband . . . or perhaps it was both." She was able to see clearly, using her sharp beak, that is, her ability to think through and analyze, to tear apart the possibilities. Something was missing as she worked. She just went around and around and made no progress.

"What are you feeling about all this?" I asked

"It was long ago. I don't really feel anything now."

She was chewing on dead meat and failing to find nourishment. What she was going after lacked the life force of feeling and therefore it was unable to transform.

The buzzard has an ugly menacing look. When I lived in South America, I would watch the buzzards line up along the riverbank, waiting for fishermen to dump unsold dead fish or the meat cutters to toss away spoiled pieces of an animal carcass. Smaller birds hopped, chirped, and flew up and down collecting seeds, crumbs, or whatever they could find while the buzzards sat waiting, their large, long bald necks retracted and their bald heads thrust menacingly forward. I had difficulty imagining that these ugly creatures were the same as the beautiful soaring birds I would see above.

As Prudence struggled, it seemed her disposition grew increasingly ugly. She blasted her husband for faults real and imagined, past and present. She was short-tempered with her son for transgressions committed or not. She reproached me for creating this unpleasant state of affairs. This is often one of the main reasons I hear from people about why they don't want to explore what is under the surface. Prudence complained of a friend who had been in therapy. "My friend really changed. She became grumpy, unpleasant, depressed, self-absorbed, really different, no fun. I'm afraid if I ever released the anger or sadness or grief, I would never be able to stop crying." Prudence's buzzard ugliness emerged as a lack of patience.

The storyteller understands that when we go through great periods of change, we will feel like the buzzard. She is also telling us that to stop there is to stop too soon. There is a third character. Buzzards ultimately fail, but their ability to soar above the mundane, to sight the needed goal, and to be patient while waiting for something to come their way is a valuable aspect of the process.

After possum and buzzard fail in the story, Grandmother Spider volunteers. Her first act is to form a thick-walled pot of clay in which to place the sun. She understands the importance of taking time to prepare to contain the heat and avoid being burned. So it is in our own process toward self-awareness.

Grandmother Spider is closer to our own humanness in this action. We have jars and vases, teapots and pitchers in every shape and design imaginable. We understand very well the necessity to contain things in our external world. As women, on some very deep level, we also understand something about internal containment. Our bodies themselves are the containers of new life, holding each fetus safe until it grows into a child able to survive on its own.

It is this understanding that we must expand if we are to begin to grasp the concept of containing our insights. Young children are perfect examples of people who have not yet learned much about containment. "Look, Mommy," a child will say. "That man can't walk."

Young children also fail to contain their emotions. This is easy to see in toddlers. Angry toddlers will scream, kick, turn red, bite, and hit. Their fury knows no bounds, and they are as much in danger of breaking a nearby vase as they are of throwing themselves down and hurting their own heads. It does not matter to them that this is occurring in the grocery story or on the front steps of the church on Sunday morning. What they feel pops out. Any containment that is necessary, to protect the child, the vase, or the ears of others, becomes the job of the Good Mother.

A lack of containment can also occur within adults. Even something as positive as insight can flood consciousness. One example of this is the fanatic who, having reached some wonderful internal light, allows this new truth or understanding to overtake his or her entire personality. We have lost many young people to cults for this very reason. Another example of this occurs in people I call "group junkies." These people are so impressed by their quick insights that they attend one group after another, dependent on the "high" they find there each day or week.

When we fail to contain our place within a context of belief or insight, we become obsessive and intolerant of others' views or their process of learning. We burn ourselves when our emotions become explosive. Feelings appear to come from nowhere, an emotional missile. "You're late!" we scream without asking why. "Damn it! I just washed that floor!" we respond to an accidental spill.

Sometimes it is only necessary for someone to say something to us and we burst into tears. There is a wonderful scene in the movie *Sense and Sensibility* where the young man finally declares his love to the character played by Emma Thompson. Emma's character bursts into loud, uncontrollable sobbing. She had been *stuffing* instead of *containing*. When we *stuff* a feeling, we pretend that what we are feeling is different from our real feeling.

There are several types of psychological containers. One type is the ability to hold on to and focus on the emotion. "Allow yourself to feel without acting," I tell clients. "We need to see what the feeling is about."

Usually we avoid doing that because, of course, the feeling, like a hot potato, is generally not pleasant and is hard to hold on to.

When we act out in some way, we manage to discharge some of the internal tension we feel. This is exactly how it would be if we drop the hot potato. Our hand will feel better, but the potato will smash and the floor will be a mess.

Finding a container for the feeling is the alternative. Many women keep journals as a way to fashion a container for their feelings. On those pages, during that time, it is safe to explore, feeling and saying anything. Since journals are private, there is little chance of being burned or burning someone else.

Therapy is another form of container. A therapist helps to *hold* the feelings by accepting them without judgment. We need others to hear what we are feeling. At the same time, family and friends may not be the best listeners. The people who love us often lack the needed objectivity.

A therapist, on the other hand, can help regulate the flow of information and contain the insight by slowing down the process with suggestions to *sit* with a feeling or idea for a while and explore it further before moving to the next thought. Therapists also add information and introduce alternative perspectives.

Therapy also helps a person contain by setting limits. At the most extreme, a therapist will contract with a client not to harm herself or will even hospitalize a client for her own safety. These events happen infrequently. A more common form of containing occurs when the therapist helps a client separate the feelings from contemplated behavior. This is the type of containment that Francie needed to learn when she struggled to know what to do with her anger at her mother. Francie—like most of us—needed to experience the difference between feeling and acting.

When a therapist and client contract to work on the client's feelings, they are agreeing to another form of containing. Our culture teaches blaming and externalizing feelings. "You made me do it. It's all your fault!" is a familiar refrain. The therapist in this instance acts as a director, continually pointing back to the inner world of the client.

Quiet time to *be* is another container. When we quiet ourselves we are allowing the psychic material to bubble and stew until something worthwhile comes into consciousness. In our noisy age many have gotten out of the habit of quiet. A woman at my fitness center reminds me of this whenever she and I are there at the same time. My center, like all fitness centers, I suppose, is a noisy place. There are televisions and music everywhere. To the side of the women's dressing room is a small sitting area. If I have had an idea while biking or walking, I will usually go to this sitting area with a cup of tea to write for a few minutes before showering.

A television in that room is constantly on whether anyone is watching or not. If the room is empty when I go in, I turn the set off. Whenever this woman is in the dressing room, she will come in to turn the set back on. "I want to hear," she will say. She then goes into the dressing room and begins a conversation loud enough to block any information from the television. I can only conclude that silence creates anxiety for her. Unfortunately we are raising an entire generation to be noise dependent.

This idea of valuing quiet as a way to go within and allow something to grow is a very old concept for women. In the New Testament the shepherds, having seen the baby Jesus, went abroad telling everyone what they knew. They were the external messengers. Mary, however, exemplified more of the feminine characteristic of internalizing. We are told: "Mary kept all these things, and pondered them in her heart." It is only when we go inward and ponder that we are able to reach first the feelings and then the meaning of those feelings for our own lives.

The web Grandmother Spider spun to reach the other side of the world was thin but sufficient to provide her with a clearly defined pathway. The outstanding fact about a spider's web is that it belongs to the spider who spun it. Unlike what the new generation of computer-wise people may think, all webs are not superhighways. Webs are, however, connections between things. A web will link one point to the next. A spider is able, from within, to put forth a resource, a substance, that will allow her to move from here to there. With this she is able to create and walk her own path.

Because each web comes from inside, it is the pathway from our own nature that is the one we are intended to walk. Women whose personalities suit them for a business world they have never entered, artists who have never created, or explorers who have never explored are all women who are not functioning out of their own inner webs. They need to spin their own webs.

A gift that comes with growing older is the freedom to discover our own paths internally as well as externally. It is no longer as crucial to meet the expectations of family, friends, or community. This becomes the time when women are free to discover that we are more loving, more irritable, more self-concerned, less there for others, less preoccupied with appearance, or less interested in graciousness and politeness. Many women have said or thought what Hilda said to me one day:

"I don't know how many years I have left but I know they are limited. I plan to use them to discover and be who I am, whether Horace or the children or grandchildren like it or not. If they have any sense, they'll do the same thing for themselves, but I can't worry about that. That heart attack scared me and I sure don't plan to meet my Maker and have to say I've spent my whole life being what others wanted me to be and don't have a clue who I really am."

To which I could only silently say, "Amen."

The story of Grandmother Spider reminds us that gaining awareness—getting the sun—is a long and difficult process. It is necessary to be willing to forage in the dark for a while. We must be willing to go to unfamiliar places halfway around the world. We will be able to gain our necessary insight if we follow our own pathway. We must allow all the time necessary to spin from inside and contain what we find. We must cultivate within us the nurturing and limit-setting mother. She is the one who will guide us as we develop our skills at perseverance, objectivity, and containing.

We can see another aspect of containment in "Rizpah," a story about a good mother who has patience and the ability to hang in. Any woman who has raised children understands the importance of having patience and waiting until something develops. This story comes to us from the Old Testament.

~ Rizpah ~

THERE ONCE LIVED a woman named Rizpah who was a concubine to King Saul. Over the years she bore two sons by this ruler. For years Saul's reign was peaceful but there came a time when he lost favor with Yahweh. His right to rule was challenged by a shepherd named David. David and Saul fought and eventually David was victorious. He then had Saul and one of Saul's sons killed.

A famine came to the land. For three years the famine lasted. David prayed. He received the message that Yahweh had sent the famine in retaliation for unjust deeds committed by Saul. David sought the seven remaining sons of Saul. When he found them, he ordered that all must be hung in retribution for Saul's deeds. Two of those hanged were Saul's sons by Rizpah. As further punishment, David ordered that the bodies of the sons be left unburied.

This deed occurred at the time of the spring barley harvest. Rizpah, seeing that the bodies were not to be buried, sat day and night by the rock where the bodies lay to keep away the vultures and predatory beasts. Finally, in October when the rains began, David heard of her long vigil. In compassion for her feelings as a mother he had the bones of Saul and his son Jonathan moved to the place where the other son's bodies lay and had all buried in a common family grave.

～

Rizpah is a symbol of the archetypal Good Mother who vows never to abandon those wounded or dead internal aspects. She is the mother who says, "I will always watch over you."

It is difficult to comprehend this level of devotion. When we think about applying it to ourselves it seems hard to imagine. Probably we can imagine aspects of ourselves that have been wounded or even killed. We remember a teacher in high school who said discouraging words that made us feel bad about ourselves. We remember the time mother or father said or did something that hurt or discouraged. However, we have long ago formed public images to cover these wounds. We have spent so many years with our "covers" that we have convinced ourselves that the wound has no more power. It lives only as a distant memory.

Certainly this would be what Gertrude would have said if anyone had thought to ask her. Gertrude's life was full. Her friends viewed her as a happy woman, and Gertrude certainly agreed. No one would have described her as wounded or neurotic. Then, at sixty-six, Gertrude became ill with cancer. Her family wanted her to live as long as possible although the doctor was sure she wouldn't live more than a few months.

In order to give her body every advantage to fight the cancer, Gertrude needed to swallow many pills per day and to eat balanced nutritious meals. Gertrude refused to do either. When the nurse gave her the pills, she would pretend to swallow them, removing them from her mouth when she was alone. Much of the food remained untouched on her tray.

Friends, family, and staff reasoned, pleaded, threatened, and begged. Gertrude would say whatever they wanted her to say, but when the pills and food arrived, she was unable to cooperate. Sometimes, when her family would stand over her hospital bed, threatening her into cooperating, she would swallow some food. Almost immediately the food would come back up in an involuntary vomiting. Everyone felt upset. The doctor finally felt the issue must be psychological and he called in a therapist.

When someone is this physically vulnerable there is a sense of urgency that those external to the situation always feel. One of the first things that Gertrude needed was some protection from the intense pressure she was experiencing from those who wanted to save her. She needed the therapist's help in creating a container around her to protect her from the external caring that was channeling all her available energy into defense.

The therapy sessions occurred during her meals. As Gertrude would look at the food tray, she would begin to cry. The memories that came, accompanied by fear and rage left from her vulnerable childhood, were ones of being force-fed by an angry matron in an orphanage. Her mother placed her there during the time she was fighting with her husband over divorce terms and custody issues.

Grandmother, an old Irish matriarch, finally rescued Gertrude from the orphanage. This woman's agenda was to raise the child in a way that would prevent her from becoming like her mother. The old woman had little that was nurturing or gentle to give to this frightened little girl. Dinner was the most unpleasant time of day. Each evening Grandmother would give forth with a litany of Gertrude's faults as well as a recounting of the faults of her parents. "She would always finish with, 'Sit up straight, chew with your mouth closed, clean your plate. You're lucky you have someone who will feed you.'

"Night after night until I wanted to die," Gertrude would sob. "I would choke down the food but half the time I would throw up afterward."

The therapist and Gertrude were Rizpah, standing watch over the small frightened child. Finally the child was willing to try some broth. The therapist made chicken soup. The little girl liked the noodles. They ordered ice cream and ate it together. Gertrude was too weak to write so the therapist brought in a tape recorder and Gertrude talked and talked and cried and cursed and spoke to the child and began to love her.

It was a healing of the soul that the body was unable to accompany. Gertrude died, at peace with herself and her family, including the old matriarch and the parents.

Gertrude was too weak to stand alone, but she and the therapist together were able to be Rizpah. They became that internal aspect of the Good Mother who is there to stand watch. Together they were able to keep away the well-meaning relative predators who would steal the feelings before meaning became clear.

Few of us have to endure what happened to Gertrude. However, we all have people in our lives who want to steal away our feelings. Those people who love us are often the most aggressive about moving us away from negative feelings. For most of us this distancing began in childhood. I remember Uncle John—perhaps there was an Uncle John in your life, too. I think there was more than one. Whenever Uncle John saw I was crying or pouting, he would begin to tease.

"There is a smile there," he would say. "I see it! It's right there. Your mouth is just starting to twitch at the corner. You can't keep the smile inside much longer." On and on he would go until the absurdity of the situation brought forth the smile. As for the original feeling—it was gone, buried somewhere.

Now we do that to ourselves. "No time," we will think. "I have to go to work. There is dinner to prepare. The laundry needs doing.

Cheer up." We have lost the feeling. There was a chance for insight, but the only highway to real insight is the feeling and it is no longer around. We need the internal Rizpah, the Good Mother archetype, to protect those initial fragile and often ambiguous feelings.

Sometimes we become caught in the trap of thinking we need to pay attention only to important feelings. We are willing to stop for rage or grief or passion but not for something as simple as hurt feelings or a mood. We may understand that the past is important, but it is difficult to locate the feelings that go along with past events. They feel dead. Rizpah reminds us that those things that seem as if they are a "dead issue" or some feeling without importance are feelings we must honor. We must keep watch without distraction or failure until the October rains if necessary. We need to feel the moods and everyday hurts. Then we will, like Rizpah and Mary and Gertrude, ponder these within.

The second half of life is an internal journey to find the nature and meaning of our lives and to discover in what ways our own life or essence connects within the universe. To do so we have talked about accepting our own mortality and discovering how the losses within our lifetimes have become part of the fabric of our individual lives. We have identified how both those qualities we have rejected and repressed into our shadow and aspects of the Dark Feminine must be made conscious. And now we see that we have a Good Mother archetype that can be called upon to go with us on this journey toward wholeness.

The Good Mother, like all archetypal energies, is internal. She is experienced through our instinctual energy and through our emotions.

We know that she may show up first as possum energy, coming to us when we are in the dark and waddling along to meet our needs. She will come to us as buzzard energy, helping us to back off and gain perspective. She will show us ways to contain and control until we have understood and grown. She will help us reflect, often sending us messages we don't want to hear through our dreams, our emotions, or our mistakes.

The internal Good Mother understands about caring and about limits, and it is from her that we are able to learn balance. She also promises us spiritual nourishment but requires that we do the necessary work to gain what we need. This is internal work and involves withdrawing energy from external goals and following our emotions to their internal source.

6

~

Islands and Falcons

THE MASCULINE WITHIN

The night air had the gentle warmth of late spring; the rains were over; and the sun was warming deeper into the earth each day. Cerina had died some weeks back. In the spot where her body had been buried, a newly planted yellow rose was budding for the first time. Elsewhere in the village the redbud and pear had finished their blooms; and on the village trees what had been only baby leaves the week before were now unfolding into a green canopy.

It had been dark for over an hour. The people were gathering underneath the blue-gray leaves of the ancient, gnarled oak. The Old Woman looked around, sensing the direction of the people's spirits. Her eyes came to rest on her grandson—or was it her great-grandson? She couldn't remember. He was leaning against a tree, his eyelids slightly lowered, his lips parted to allow in the necessary air. She followed the direction of his look and saw his gaze settled on Meda, a girl who had entered her woman-nature three moons ago.

A half smile was on Meda's lips as she returned the boy's look. The musk scent was traveling between them. The Old Woman sighed a remembering sigh.

Her eyes continued around the groupings of villagers. Couples long together sat closer this night. She watched the reaching out and touching that was rippling back and forth throughout the group. The warm, gentle feel of the night was mirrored by couple after couple.

But not by everyone. Gwenlyn sat next to her husband, but her presence was across the clearing with Sean. Gwenlyn had been married for more then a hundred moons. When Sean came to town a few moons ago, her eyes turned away from her home. Indeed, she was not the only one. Nona also was fascinated with Sean, and the Old Woman had seen several other village women watching him hopefully. Sean had a type of magic. His dark eyes sought women, promising what they had never before dared to dream. Without saying a word, he invited adventure.

The Old Woman remembered this man. When he had come into her life, his eyes had been gray, his stride longer, and his name had not been Sean. Even so, he was the same. The look, the magnetism, the way he had of drawing oxygen away so that you felt your breath pulled from your body; these were all the same. An adventurer was always around when something within the woman called for him.

When the Old Woman looked at Sean, she saw little on the surface that would appeal. When she looked beyond the shell of his appearance, it was all there. She watched him now as if she were seeing the man and his reflection on blue pond waters—one image solid; the other fluid and elusive. She brought the images together in her mind's eye as she focused on the meaning learned from her past. Her relationship had ended as Gwenlyn's relationship with Sean would end. But the important inner purpose of this type of relationship does not lie in "happily ever after."

As the primal energy passed around and through her that night, she knew the story she would tell. She also knew that Gwenlyn would listen but probably not hear. Sometimes the story must be told only out of hope that it might be remembered when needed.

⁓ Ariadne ⁓

IN A LAND FAR AWAY and in a time long past, there lived a King named Minos. This king had a son who had died when visiting a nearby land. Minos had always held the king of that other land responsible for his son's death. As retribution, he required that seven youths and seven maidens be sent to him every nine years.

Minos also had a stepson who was born half bull and half human—a terrible monster called a Minotaur. The youths and maidens sent from this nearby land were sacrificed to the flesh-eating Minotaur.

Because the Minotaur was so dangerous that he could not live among men, King Minos had the architect Daedalus build a labyrinth from which no one could escape. It was here that the Minotaur was placed, and it was into this same labyrinth that the young victims were sent.

King Minos also had a daughter—a beautiful young girl named Ariadne. When she was young she was very devoted to her father, but now that she was growing older, she found her feelings were changing. One day as she was looking out of her window, she saw the new group of sacrificial youths arriving from the nearby land. There was one young man among the group who seemed to her the most beautiful youth she had ever seen. His name was Theseus, and she fell in love with him at first sight.

Since this was clearly a relationship that would be forbidden by King Minos, Ariadne knew she must work in secret. Somehow she must save the life of Theseus and gain him for herself. To accomplish this, she waited until dark and then went to Daedalus in order to learn the secret of escape from the terrible maze of the labyrinth. Once she knew, she sent for Theseus.

"I will tell you the secret of escape," she told him, "if you will take me with you when you leave, for I want to be with you more than anything I can imagine."

Theseus promised, and she gave him a ball of twine.

"Attach one end of the twine to the door as you enter," she told him, "and unroll the ball as you go. When you are ready to leave you must only follow the string."

Theseus took the twine and did as Ariadne had instructed. He found the Minotaur asleep at the end of one of the pathways, and fell upon the monster to kill him. A terrible fight followed. In the end, the Minotaur was dead. Theseus then picked up the ball of twine, which had fallen to the ground, and, rolling it up, walked back to the entrance.

Ariadne was waiting for him and the two of them, together with the other youths and maidens who had escaped death because of Theseus's bravery, ran to the ship and set sail. They sailed all day. By nightfall the sea had become rough, so they put into a harbor. The two lovers went ashore where they made love for most of the night. Finally Ariadne fell asleep, awakening only when the morning sunlight crossed her face. She reached out for Theseus, then opened her eyes. The soft leaves next to her showed the indentation where his body had lain, but he was gone. Ariadne looked out to the sea. In the distance she could just make out the sails on Theseus's ship, sailing away without her.

There are different versions to explain why Theseus left and never returned. Some say he intended to return for her but was prevented by the gods. Others say he forgot about her once he left. In either case, Ariadne waited and grieved for many months, hoping for what was not meant to be. She felt sure her life was over—she could not return to the father she had betrayed, and she had been abandoned by her lover. Just when she was ready to give up all hope of finding any way to continue her life, a young man, a Greek god, discovered her on the island and they fell in love. He took her away with him. How they lived together is another story, but I will tell you this—his love for her was true for the rest of her life.

⌒

This ancient myth is from Greece. It tells us of one woman's experience with a father, a monster and a Seanlike man named Theseus. The men in these stories could be actual men in our lives, but they also represent energies that are internally available to women. Another task necessary as we age involves developing a conscious connection with our own inner masculine nature. Jungian psychologists call this masculine energy *animus* or "man within." Those familiar with Eastern thought refer to this energy as yang.

All humans are born with internal *contra sexual energy*, that is, energy that is the opposite to the dominant orientation. For women the dominant orientation is our feminine nature and masculine is our contra sexual aspect. We need a clear awareness of our masculine energy not only because it represents a large aspect of who we are, but also because it constitutes a reservoir of strength and skill, especially for women in midlife and beyond.

It is important to begin by identifying those qualities labeled masculine. The Chinese idea of yin/yang helps to define the masculine and illustrate the difference between it and the feminine. The Chinese describe the masculine as yang energy (the white side of the yin/yang icon); it is active, ordering, rational, and associated with images of the sun, daylight, and the Hero who brings order to the realm. Feminine or yin energy (the black side of the icon) is passive, chaotic, and nonrational. The moon, nighttime, and the primal darkness of the forest are yin images.

There are two major difficulties that many of us encounter as we attempt to understand this idea. The first is that we have been told that the qualities of feminine and masculine are each the exclusive property of one sex or the other. Although this exclusivity is psychologically impossible since feminine/masculine connect to each other like the two sides of one coin, we still hear statements such as "Women are emotional and men are logical." This mistaken view has crippled both sexes.

There is a second difficulty in understanding the relevance of identifying some of our attributes as feminine and others as masculine. A value judgment has been placed on the qualities within each category. Characteristics associated with the masculine have been identified as superior while feminine attributes have been viewed as inferior. Many of us remember hearing women ridiculed for being "too emotional" or have had a point of view disparaged because it was emotional rather than rational. Those of us who grew up in a society that artificially separates the feminine/masculine attributes by assigning them in an either/or fashion, feminine ones only to women and masculine ones only to men, must work to change our understanding. Those of us who internalized the inferiority of feminine attributes must accept that our task includes healing this wound.

Our culture, historically, has frowned on women who move too far from traditional female roles without male permission. Julia Morgan, the wonderful early twentieth-century architect who designed much great California architecture, had to study in Europe because no American school would admit a woman. Novelist F. Scott Fitzgerald's wife, Zelda, was unable to persuade anyone to take her writing seriously. For those of us who lived through similar early conditioning and then through all the subsequent changes that came with the women's movement, there is a great deal of unfinished business.

Our task of recognizing and accepting our masculine qualities as an inherent aspect of who we are includes reaching the understanding that feminine and masculine attributes exist in relationship to each other, both as a complement and as an opposite. Breath is an example of this type of complementary opposite. Each inhalation is matched by its opposite exhalation. Day and night, hot and cold, sweet and sour are all complements of each other. We automatically gravitate toward hot soup on cold days or crisp, cool salads in summer.

Feminine/masculine are opposites, and opposites create tension. For example, it is difficult, when we are feeling passive to remember that we are also active. It is difficult to learn how to make a decision using both our heads and our hearts. It is easier to view ourselves as one or the other. Yet when we attempt to be only one part of a whole, we frequently find ourselves in the midst of an uncomfortable situation. Gina was a case in point.

"I have worked so hard," she told me. "I really wanted to be a sweet, kind, loving wife, I suppose because my mother wasn't that way. I know for a fact that she didn't respect my dad. He was a workaholic and she was a nag. She criticized him for not spending time with us. 'Act like a father,' she'd always say. She nagged him about not repairing things around the house. She maintained that she nagged because he seldom came home, but I thought he stayed away because she nagged. I vowed to be sweet and loving to my husband so that he would want to be home and do things with me and with the children. Guess what?

"I have been married twice. Neither of my husbands would participate in family life. My first husband was an alcoholic—oh, not when I married him, but that's where he ended up. He was physically home, but he might as well not have been because he wasn't really there. My current husband doesn't drink, but he's not present, either. He watches TV, plays golf, goes fishing. He knows I hate all three, but it doesn't seem to matter. I never nag at him, but even when I very sweetly ask him to do things, he ignores me."

Gina believed that the roles and acceptable behaviors between husband and wife should be sharply divided. She wanted to be all soft and feminine in some fairy-tale manner while her husband was to be the Father/King who was able to always be in charge.

The following week at their first joint appointment the husband said, "I think Gina should look in a mirror. She's a nag—exactly like her mother. 'Do this, do that. Why haven't you painted the closet doors? Why is there no gas in the car?' On and on and on. She says all of this in her little girl whiny voice—I guess she thinks I will feel better if she doesn't shout."

Gina interrupted. "But honey, you know how many things there are to do, and I just can't manage to get them done even though I really try not to bother you. Some things are too hard for me. I don't think asking you to do just a few little things to help us is asking for too much."

On and on she went, in a whining voice that only thinly covered her anger. Gina saw herself as maintaining her feminine mask against great odds. It was clear, however, that her parents' example had affected her. Her mother's split view of appropriate female and male roles had been passed on to Gina.

First her mother and then Gina had married men who appeared lopsided. Their husbands initially appeared to be men who had little to no feminine and enough masculine to provide for everyone. When the men were unable to sustain this role, both Gina's mother and then Gina became Minotaurs. Their internal ability to step back from a rapid emotional decision to apply logic to feelings had failed. They lacked this skill. Then, once in difficulty with their partner, they found their internal ability to problem solve, act in an assertive manner, or explore new ways of thinking undeveloped and deformed.

The split between appropriate behavior for girl children versus boy children begins at birth for children in all cultures. Although we are currently seeing values change, components of the past still exist. We still view infant girls as sweet and innocent and their brothers as rough and tumble, We talk to girls in softer tones and touch them with greater gentleness. This is the beginning of the subtle message that little girls are a bit more fragile. Remember the nursery rhyme

> What are little girls made of?
> What are little girls made of?
> Sugar and Spice and everything nice
> That's what little girls are made of.

The spice implied is something like cinnamon—never cayenne pepper.

We are given conflicting messages as children; advised to be whatever we want to be while at the same time told to repress aspects of who we are. It should not be a surprise that our masculine side is unhealthy or negative. What occurs, given the conflicting messages, is that all the masculine potential exists but it becomes distorted. Instead of being rational, the person grows rigid, holding opinions but unable to entertain new ideas. She becomes stuck. She, like Gina, honestly believes her version of the situation is true. However, the people around her feel attacked and defeated. What begins as a conversation will end with a feeling of having run into a brick wall. No information, no logic can shake the conviction of a woman who has no conscious relationship with her own internal masculine. That woman believes that she knows and understands perfectly.

The myth of Ariadne helps our understanding of the negative inner masculine. As the story begins she is at a turning point in her life. Ariadne now needs to change and leave. While this is an appropriate and normal stage of development, the storyteller lets us know, by Ariadne's use of subterfuge, that she has not internalized that ability in a healthy way.

Everything in life reaches a point when it must renew itself. A summer flower will bloom only so many times. Then it must produce seed, die, and begin again. When I lived in New England, I always assumed that it was frost, the external cold, that caused the plant to stop blooming and die. When I moved to a warmer climate, the same flowers stopped their bloom after time, even though no frost killed them. The need and ability to renew are internal. It is the nature of life.

The Father/King energy must also be renewed, but Minos has lost that ability. The heir to the throne, the next generation, Minos's son, is dead. A deformed stepson remains alive, but he can never rule the kingdom. King Minos is bitter and demands victims for revenge. He brings in youths and maidens from a neighboring kingdom. Once they arrive, he kills them. Youth, once positive, is now a painful reminder of what he cannot have.

Anyone who reads this story without understanding that a story is a metaphor will understand only that Ariadne is an adolescent who must make the break from her family of origin. What we are able to see, however, by focusing on the symbolism is a King Minos aspect of a woman's psyche. This King aspect represents internal masculine energy. In this story, unfortunately, it is masculine energy that has become rigid and is in need of renewal.

There is no age limit for discovering that an internal aspect of our masculine energy has become rigid, bitter, and vengeful. King Minos is often present when we face a great change. We cling to old ways, wanting to kill whatever is representative of the change. A son marries before we are ready to let go, and we dislike all the new ways he and his wife are doing things. A relocation occurs to a different part of the country, and we notice the inadequacies of the new location. We face a loss and want to find someone to blame. King Minos energy, while it *once upon a time* was a wise ruler, has turned into something quite different.

We see this rigidity of masculine energy in women who have stayed too long in the same job. They move through the work in a stiff and inflexible manner. We see King Minos operating behind the mask of the overcontrolling mother. She imprisons her child's spirit within a labyrinth of her vision of what life should be. We meet this bitter King in women who live only in the past, unresponsive and unappreciative of life's newness and renewal.

We see this type of negative masculine energy in women's behavior. We also experience the energy attacking us from within. We call it guilt, fear, or anxiety. The energy seems to emerge whenever we challenge a long-standing tradition. The woman who marries outside her family tradition or begins to practice a different version of her spirituality or who does anything in a manner different from what the childhood family believes is correct is betraying this Father/King principal and is in danger of being attacked by the emotions. The Father/King wants law and order and tradition.

The solution for negative energy is clear from the story. Minotaurs must be killed. We cannot do that with logic, reason, or authority because these are aspects of the Father-type masculine. We need something more than rationality, intellectual insight, or authority. Whenever we try to use Father energy we may end up telling ourselves not to feel whatever we are feeling. Or perhaps we find ourselves able to analyze the situation but unable to do anything different in spite of our insight. Repeatedly we discover that our Father/King energy, once solidified, will not work to change itself. It was Minos who hired Daedalus to build the labyrinth as a way to keep the monster-son alive. King energy, once negative, feeds and protects our internal monsters.

There are other resources internally available. The psyche includes another type of energy that, in this story, is the energy of the Hero. Heroes are able to provide a situation with a fresh perspective. Theseus is the energy of the Hero—bold, daring, and willing to take risks. Often before we locate our internal energy, we find it by projecting it onto another person. We see the necessary courage or free spirit as an aspect of another person's personality. We allow the other person to rescue us. The traits we see in the outer man are the traits we need in our inner selves.

"My marriage was dead, but I couldn't seem to find the energy to do anything," Barbara told me. "Then Bill came along. We fell in love, had an affair, and I got a divorce. We were happy for a while but then . . . ."

This form of projection can be a good way to learn, but it also has its limits. We may believe that this energy is the complete man. We become angry when he falls short. We may assume that we are incapable ourselves of achieving whatever traits he possesses. If that happens, we feel dependent on him to provide them for us. In either case we fail to recognize that the needed energy can also be found internally within our own psyches.

In searching for renewal, we also need to use the feminine within. It was Ariadne who found the way Theseus could escape from the labyrinth. Until that time, anyone not immediately killed by the Minotaur died anyway because there was no escape from the labyrinth. By combining the emotional (feminine) energy with the aggressive Hero (masculine) energy, the task was accomplished.

Many women have become trapped in a labyrinth. Children of some successful actresses have written of how career and public image became all-important to the mother. What often began as wonderful creativity grew into a need to maintain success at almost any price. In this example the Minotaur was the woman's obsession with success. This obsession killed the emotional connection between the mother and child. This obsession destroyed the mother's ability to comprehend what she or the child needed. The family structure and the emotions (the youths and maidens) were sacrificed to the obsession (the Minotaur).

Closer to the experiences of some of us are the perfect house-wives of the 1950s. Doris Day and June Cleaver became role models, advocating makeup, high heels, and clean kitchen floors. A novel by Ira Levin, *The Stepford Wives* tells of a town of women captured by a Minotaur. This particular Stepford monster was an obsession with perfection.

In exploring the Father/King energy through the figure of King Minos, we have seen what can happen when our internal masculine energy becomes rigid. However, we must be careful to see that this energy is also healthy at other times. The books of Samuel and Kings tell of the succession of rulers of Israel. In each case, the king begins to rule from a need of the people, evidenced by chaos and disorganization. The energy of the organizing Father/King is needed to pull the people together.

Saul is an example. The people were threatened and "lifted up their voices, and wept." Saul used what might appear to us as an extreme amount of authority in responding. He cut oxen into pieces and threatened that anyone who did not accept his leadership would have their cattle destroyed in this manner. We are told: "they came out with one consent. And when he numbered them . . . the children of Israel were three hundred thousand." The people were in need of a leader with strong abilities to organize and control. Saul was that healthy leader.

In thinking back to the days when my own house was filled with noisy children, I remember feelings of love and laughter and pure delight. At the time I truly believed my children were the most delightful, wonderful gift I could have been given. I was filled, much of the time, with an excess of emotion.

I also remember that in the midst of the noise and fun, there was a need to brush teeth and do chores. Children need to be loved as much as mothers need to love. We all, however, also need structure and direction. Our family would not have been able to survive without both feminine emotion and masculine structure. It is the job of one or two parents to each provide a mixture. To rule without compassion is to rule with rigidity and without the softening of the feminine. To rule with only emotion is to advocate chaos. Either parent can provide both, and many children in single-parent homes are growing up with a healthy mixture.

We are told that King Saul understood the need to bring order into chaos through structure and authority and to rule with compassion. Yet, by the end of his reign, Saul had become rigid and there was trouble in the kingdom. The young Hero David replaced him. David, in turn, matured from Hero into King and, in turn, was replaced by his son Solomon.

The image of the late actress, Audrey Hepburn, was one of a woman who had internalized this healthy Father/King masculine energy. She spoke of her feelings in a soft and sensitive manner. Her major concern during the second half of her life focused on the needs of children around the world. She felt deeply that the world community must learn to respond to the hunger and illness and poverty of children.

Her level of emotional sensitivity was melded with an ability to organize and act. She was a major force in the development and implementation of programs that would feed and heal. She publicized the plight of children living in countries most Americans had not heard of before her talks and films. If she had just *felt* without acting, she would have been split with only the feminine energy available. If she had *felt* but only complained and criticized the lack of caring of others, she would have been caught in a negative masculine. Her ability to *feel* and *take risks* and *structure and organize* indicates an integration of the feminine energy with the Hero and Father/King masculine energies.

Both types of internal masculine energy, Father/King and Hero, live within the psyches of all women. They do not appear, however, at the same time. When the psyche is operating in a smooth and healthy manner, these two different types of energy will rotate or function cyclically. We know that all energy, including Father/King energy, is in danger of becoming rigid with time. When this happens, we know that a change of some type is needed. There is an emotional need for a shift from the previously stable, structuring energy into the risk-taking energy. Once that has happened, we must then stop and allow that young risk-taking aspect of ourselves to settle down and internalize this new place where we find ourselves.

No one can live with constant change without a price tag. I have seen many clients over the years who have spent their childhood in constant motion because of a parent's job or some other factor. Many of these children moved yearly. One child I saw recently had been living on the streets with her mother. She had moved daily. Part of the cost for these individuals has been difficulty with aspects of their lives that require commitment. It is difficult to make a commitment to a task or to another person when you may be gone tomorrow. These are individuals who have developed skills at coping with change but who must find ways to heal the lack of structure and stability.

During the years when I was a child, very few people changed their location. I remember, still, the names of both children who entered my elementary school class as newcomers during the six years we attended. One moved into the neighborhood during fourth grade and one during sixth. It was an era of stability. Our task was to find our internal Hero energy. We needed the courage to take risks and ride off to kill dragons.

In stories it is always the hero who slays the dragon. It is always the hero who wins the kingdom. By winning the kingdom, the hero takes his turn as Father/King. In time he will be in need of renewal and Hero energy must enter again. It is important that we look at how well we continue to allow the cycle to spin around and around.

Some women have not developed the authority aspect of the Father/King energy except in areas concerned with homemaking and childbearing. Risa, a woman who found her husband rigid and dull, was one of those women.

"We've been married twenty-five years," she said. "Now I want out."

"You're planning a divorce?"

'No. I want to leave him, but something stops me. It's not love because I haven't loved him in a long time. I think it's fear. I don't know how to live on my own. I got married young and moved from living with my parents to living with him. I can't even begin to imagine what it would be like to live by myself."

This is a story I have heard in many variations. Sometimes there is a slight love that remains. Sometimes there is a feeling of caring, but neither of these change the underlying reality that there is really no relationship between the woman and her husband. Sometimes the factor that appears to hold a woman back is money, and sometimes she stays "for the good of the children." The consistent factor, however, is an internal masculine so undeveloped that the woman cannot figure out how to stand on her own.

The fear that exists for many of these women is this: If I learn to take care of myself, I will not want to be in a relationship. The opposite appears to be true. Once a woman learns the skills necessary to take care of herself, she is free to *want* to be with someone instead of being there because there is no choice. These skills, however, are not easily gained.

～ Inanna ～

ONCE IN ANCIENT Sumer, there lived a goddess named Inanna. Although she was destined to rule her kingdom, Inanna had not yet gained the necessary powers. The knowledge she needed was kept by her father Enki. So, she journeyed over the sea to meet with him.

Now Inanna judged correctly that Enki would be reluctant to part with the powers so she took spirits with her to get her father drunk. As they drank Enki began to offer one power after another and Inanna accepted each. When she had all that she needed, Inanna jumped into her boat and sailed away.

Soon Enki sobered and immediately regretted that he had given these powers away to his youngest daughter. He set out at once to recover what he had given, but each time they met Inanna defeated him in their struggle.

When Inanna's boat reached the shore of her kingdom, she had all the powers from her father intact. Having these, added to her feminine traits, Inanna was ready to rule. When Enki saw this he gave her his blessing.

⌒

Enki is like many good real-life fathers. The good father passes on traits to the daughter. "The world is like this," he says to her. "I will give you everything that I know. Take it and go."

Fathers do not give these things consciously. This is the meaning of the metaphor of Enki becoming drunk. Fathers give this gift primarily through how they are rather than what they say. A father who is direct and respectful in his communication and is able to settle conflicts without attack will pass that along to his daughter. She will understand how to behave in this way because of who her father was rather than anything he may have tried to teach her.

Enki also lets us know one way we can expect our inner masculine to behave. The psyche also does not give these gifts in a conscious way; we cannot sit down one day and demand that the unconscious energy will be there for us. To have the necessary contact and to receive the gifts, we must travel to the unconscious; work to get what we need; and then escape, fighting to keep what we have worked to achieve.

When the time comes in our external family life for a daughter to leave, many fathers have difficulty. "Come back," they tend to say. "Did you remember to put gas in the car? Are you sure you have purchased the right amount of insurance? Have you set up a retirement plan?" They are Enki, pursuing the daughter.

The psychological reason Enki pursues, and why the daughter must flee, is to strengthen the daughter. Internally we find there are parts of our minds, our emotions, and our resulting behaviors that attempt to steal away what we have gained. If a particular insight is valuable to us, we must be willing to fight to keep it. When we decide something is worth fighting for and we actually struggle, we become stronger. Not everything a parent or a psyche offers is right for a particular daughter. Only the daughter can make that decision.

"When my husband was alive," Enid said, "we had a good life. We played golf, traveled in the summer all around the country, and it seemed as if everything just flowed in an easy way. I think that happens when a couple is together for a long time.

"After he died, I continued many things the way we had always done them. Then I began to discover something very strange. There were things I had always done that I really didn't want to do and that wasn't just because I was alone. Of course, there were those things, too: I didn't really enjoy traveling in the RV either alone or with anyone else the way I had with him. But I'm talking about something different.

"Getting up at seven, would be an example. We always woke and got up at seven. Then we'd have coffee and read the paper before showering and dressing. Now I find I like to get up and get going. I walk every morning, rain or shine. It is so wonderful—almost like being in church. There have been quite a few of those types of things.

"What I realized was that I had never really thought much about what I had wanted or liked. I just agreed with whatever he wanted to do. I went through a really rough time trying to figure out what I really wanted to do with myself once he wasn't here. Now I wonder why I waited so long. I followed what my father and mother wanted and then what my husband wanted. Now I have to be responsible for myself."

Enid had not developed her inner masculine. She had not asked herself what she wanted. Since she did not know, there was no need for her to exercise any authority to protect what she wanted. When her husband died, she was on her own. Then she found her inner masculine. That was when she found she needed to struggle to find and claim what she wanted and needed for herself.

In much the same way that Enki pursues Inanna, an emerging aspect of the masculine will pursue us as we practice our skills for the first time. "Did I remember to . . . ? Let me make lists to remind myself. Perhaps I should consult another person or read another book before I . . . ." All of these are ways to decide if something is really right. All of these are ways to help us slow down and develop a structure for our new behaviors.

Another way to look at this internal masculine energy is to view it developmentally. We understand that children go through developmental stages. In a similar manner, our internal masculine energy will function at various times on different developmental levels.

One of the least developed or primal stage of masculine energy occurs when it manifests physically. An example of this occurs in a video I recently saw for the first time. The movie, *First Blood,* stars Sylvester Stallone as Rambo and Brian Dennehy as the sheriff. It is an excellent example of this type of physical masculine energy.

Rambo interacts with the world and solves problems physically. During most of the movie he does not speak. The crucial dramatic situation of the movie would not have occurred had he verbally communicated with the sheriff, but that is not who his character is. The sheriff is also a man who operates on the physical level. He is the upholder of the status quo, yet his only technique for implementing authority is physical force. He also could have averted the conflict had he only responded with less rigid authoritarian action.

At one point in the film the sheriff points out that once the law breaks down there is chaos. Of course, he is correct. What he does not see is that law (masculine) without compassion and empathy (feminine) is inhuman. The sheriff expects blind obedience to his authority and when that does not come, he acts in a physically punitive manner.

Another example of this first physical level of masculine development occurs in Tennessee Williams's play *Cat on a Hot Tin Roof.* The protagonist, Biff, is a discouraged young man whose identity has been in his physical masculine nature. His glory days were in high school when he played on the school football team. Since that time, his life has paled. In order for his life to have meaning or value, he would need to advance to the next level or stage of masculine development. For many reasons Biff cannot leave his glory days behind. He feels intense anger and sorrow and is medicating himself with alcohol that deadens his physical energy and feelings of frustration.

Anyone who enjoys spectator sports experiences this first level of physical masculine development. As one example, we pay football players a great deal of money to be physical, joining them by screaming encouragement from the stands.

What is helpful about this physical level of the masculine is its ability to move into action automatically when it is needed. This primal physical response is the energy we use when faced with a crisis of some sort. This is the energy that makes something work through physical action. It is pragmatic.

Your daughter calls in tears. "Stay there," you say. "I'll be right over." You arrive and find the new baby screaming with colic, the dishes undone, the house a disaster, and the other children glued to the television set. You turn off the TV and send the ten-year-old to the kitchen to load the dishwasher while you instruct the eight-year-old to pick up the toys scattered over the living-room floor. You start a load of laundry, collect the garbage—especially the smelly Pampers—and take the trash outside. Meanwhile you have started water for tea.

Within an hour, supper is started, the house is at least orderly, the two older children are working on their homework, and the baby and your daughter are napping. You take a deep breath, thanking the Powers that Be, both that you are no longer in that phase of life *and* that there is such a thing as this masculine physical energy to call on in time of need.

The Hero energy that we saw in Theseus is energy developed beyond the primal or physical level. Theseus in our story volunteers to be one of the nine young men. He goes to Minos's kingdom for the express purpose of killing the Minotaur. Hero energy allows us to be purposefully active and to respond to challenges. When we use Hero energy, we find the courage we need to face difficult hazards. This is the same behavior we see in stories when the hero goes out to kill a dragon or rescue a town from a monster.

During the sixties I knew several families in which the father was a Theseus. These men dedicated themselves to fighting the dragons of racism. The work they did was important, and they were able to slay many dragons. The men were heroes. At home, some of the wives were unhappy; they were raising children, driving car pool, supervising piano practice, and calling plumbers alone. They had become married single parents. While the Hero had appealed initially, many of these women had moved on to another aspect of life, while the husbands continued the Hero's journey. Some of these marriages were able to find ways to bridge the gap. Remember the story of Ulysses who left to fight in the Trojan war and stayed away ten years? His wife, Penelope, was able to wait patiently for his return. There were women during the sixties who had the qualities of a Penelope. Others could not maintain this connection; the Hero went his own way while the wife and children searched for a different type of man.

Of the marriages that failed, the women who were able to understand what internally had propelled them toward this man, who was now a disappointment, were able to make much better second choices. The women who instead of understanding what went wrong placed the blame on the character of the man often found they were disappointed in their second choices as well.

This is a trap that many of us fall into when things fall apart. We project the failure onto the man; we identify the problem as his fault. We blame him for the sad state of affairs: "My husband was so stuffy and boring" or "rigid and controlling" or "unfaithful and a real louse." None of this does more than ventilate some feelings of the moment. The questions that will help us are ones like: How does this person with these characteristics fit perfectly into the big picture of my life? How is this choice meaningful rather than a mistake? What in me sought out another who was stuffy or boring or controlling or conservative or unfaithful? Where is that same energy in me? What did it allow me to be or do? What have I been ignoring in myself? On and on, the helpful questions can go, leading us toward growth and transformation.

The internal energy we search for occurs in various ways, personified by different masculine fictional characters. One type of personification seen in our lives, as well as literature, is the cycle of the calcified Father/King replaced by the Hero.

There is also the image of the wise old man; another source of our internal masculine energy. This level is an ability to tap into a higher level of wisdom, personified by the wise old man. He is the mentor. In the Star Wars movies there was a wizened old man, Yoda, who taught the young hero about a type of energy called "The Force." Yoda was the sage, the wise old man.

This aspect of our energy does not go into battle. That is the job of the Hero. Nor does this aspect of our energy uphold the authority and laws. That is the job of the Father/King. This wisdom energy, balanced by the wise old woman within the feminine, helps us transcend the everyday level of life to the spiritual level. Our internal Yoda helps us find meaning.

Each of the internal aspects of our masculine energy has both a positive and a negative pole. The positive pole of the Father/King involves stability, reliability, good judgment, sureness, and a comfortable reliance on our own internal judgments. The negative pole takes these very traits into their extreme with stability becoming rigidity and reliability becoming inflexibility.

Our Theseus or Hero energy may help us to break away from a situation that is stunting our growth or to develop an ignored aspect of ourselves. Our Hero journey may be one of dragon slaying. The positive pole of the Hero energy creates the fresh air that allows us to see a way to create change from a different perspective. The negative pole comes if we get stuck in the energy of the Hero for too long.

The Hero can become the eternal youth, the *puer aeternus* who lives forever chasing dragons. This is difficult for real-life men and for the women who relate to them. When Ulysses, the hero of the Trojan war, stayed away for ten years, his wife, Penelope, had to stitch by day and unraveled her work at night to postpone the time she would have to wed one of her many suitors. Ulysses was young. When he grew older, he took shorter trips.

Our Wise Old Man energy imparts wisdom about our journey and its meaning. This energy, when stuck, becomes the lecturing, rambling, and pedantic side of us that puts us and others to sleep rather than illuminates.

Often we must work to regain lost or injured aspects of our masculine. In stories the necessary work to develop this awareness is symbolized by tasks that the heroine must accomplish before she finds the prince. In the well-known tale "Cinderella," it was necessary for the heroine to sort peas and lentils from ashes. The following Russian tale tells of different types of tasks.

∽ The Feather of Finist the Bright Falcon ∽

ONCE UPON A TIME three girls lived with their father. The two older girls were very vain and self-absorbed while the youngest spent her time caring for the house. It was the youngest who was her father's favorite.

Whenever the father went into the town he would ask the girls what they would like for him to bring back for them. The two older would say dresses or handkerchiefs or earrings, but each time, the youngest would ask for a feather of Finist the Bright Falcon.

The father was always able to buy the older girls' presents. However, trip after trip, he returned without the feather. Then one day he met a little old man as he passed through the gate of the town. The man had a box in his hand, and in the box was a feather of Finist the Bright Falcon.

"How much do you want for the feather?" the father asked.

"A thousand," answered the old man.

The father paid the sum and went home with the present for the youngest girl.

That night when the girl was alone in her room, she opened the box. The feather flew out of the box and turned into a handsome prince. The prince and the young girl talked and fell in love. The sisters heard the noise and began to knock on the door.

"Who are you talking to?"

"No one. I'm talking to myself."

"Then let us come in."

The prince immediately became a falcon and flew out of the window, leaving one feather behind. When the sisters came in, they could find no one. The next night the same thing happened, but this time the sisters went to the father.

"Little sister has someone in her room," they said. But before the father and sisters could enter, the prince turned into the falcon. Again he flew away, leaving only the feather. When the father found no one, he scolded the older sisters.

On the third night, the sisters were determined to catch whoever was sneaking into their sister's room. They put sharp needles and knives on the windowsill since they thought the visitor was entering in that way.

The girl, not seeing the prince, went to sleep. When Finist the Falcon tried to get into the room, he cut his wings. Although he called to the young girl, she did not hear. However, in her dream, she heard a voice saying, "If you want to find me, you must wear out three pairs of iron shoes, break three cast-iron walking sticks, and gnaw away three stone wafers for I will be in a land beyond thrice nine lands in the thrice tenth kingdom."

When the young girl awoke and saw the blood, she immediately had the iron shoes and walking sticks made, gathered the three stone wafers, and set out on her journey. Along the way she was given gifts of silver and gold by three old women. There was a silver spinning wheel and golden spindle, a silver dish and golden egg, and a silver embroidery frame and golden needle. She was also given a ball. "Roll the ball," the first old woman said. "Follow it and it will take you where you need to go."

The girl followed the ball for long day after long day. When she had finally worn through the three pairs of iron shoes and iron walking sticks and gnawed away the three stone wafers, she arrived at the town where Finist now lived with the baker's daughter.

The girl bartered each of her three gold and silver treasures for three nights with Finist. The baker's daughter, however, had drugged him so that he slept on, never realizing that his love had come for him. Finally, with nothing left to barter for another night, the young girl began to weep. A tear fell onto his cheek, and Finist awoke. The two of them returned to the young girl's home where they were married.

⌒

This story provides us with information about another aspect of our inner masculine, our spirituality, and tells us something about the way to find this aspect of ourselves.

We and our young heroine must go through a process. The process begins because the youngest daughter *wants* this energy. She gets what she wants, only to lose it, and then to have to work very hard to regain it. In this way, the story reminds us of Inanna, who must fight for her leadership abilities. Those internal aspects of ourselves that are valuable demand work on our part.

In the beginning of this story, we have a father and three girls. The youngest girl is the story's main character. Symbolically this youngest represents a version of our feminine ego. The two sisters represent an unknown part of her—and us—the shadow. This shadow is all of the unconscious greed, vanity, and jealousy. On a conscious level this youngest girl appears to be free of these traits. She presents herself as a caring, thoughtful family member who takes care of the others by keeping house. Unlike her sisters, she requests only a feather as a gift.

As the story reminds us, our ego is seldom aware of traits that are incompatible with how we consciously perceive ourselves. In chapter 3 we explored the way we push our unpleasant qualities into the unconscious. This is what our young heroine is doing. She sees herself as "nice." Her greed or "not nice" aspects are shadow or sister parts. The story points out what most of us have experienced: our shadow or not-so-nice parts can become very active and troublesome.

When we act out of this unconscious place, we are in danger. It is our capacity for relationship that suffers from unconscious jealousy and envy. In this instance, the young girl is not able to maintain a connection with Finist the Bright Falcon, her spiritual self, because he is constantly under attack from her unconscious shadow. The two sisters are able to injure Finist the Falcon, her emerging spirituality.

It is easier to see how this works in the external world. We have seen other women, and perhaps found ourselves, making "slips" that were sharp, cutting, and damaging. "Where did that come from?" we wonder. "How could I have said that? I'm much nicer than that." Of course this is leakage from the shadow. The less we claim those parts of ourselves by forming conscious relationships, the more we will experience these parts creating havoc. Certainly the story warns that there will be damage to our attempts to grow spiritually.

The following example is one of countless similar incidents that finally motivated Ed to seek marriage counseling. He was a very successful businessman. His wife, June, had given up the idea of a career when their first child was born. When the children left home, she did not go back to school or work. She enjoyed her life as it was. She was unaware of any feelings of envy or jealousy toward her husband. There were many times when she would comment on how she hated alarm clocks and wouldn't trade places with Ed, her husband, for anything. Listening to June's assessment of life, we might think that all was well, except . . .

June had a habit of verbally stabbing Ed. The most recent episode occurred at a party in his honor. A guest, who was also a prospective client belonging to a large firm, said, "Congratulations on landing the Browning account."

June interjected, "With all the moaning and groaning I had to listen to, you would have think it was a whale instead of a simple business deal. He was lucky I was there . . ."

Her voice trailed off when she saw Ed's glare. "I was just making a joke," she said later as they argued over the episode.

Ed, however, was wounded by June's split-off and unconsciously stabbing jealousy over his success. Once the slip had occurred, June then transferred the attack onto herself through guilt. "I feel awful," she said, over and over. "I never meant to hurt him. I love my husband."

Because June's internal masculine energy was underdeveloped, she was unhappy and seemed abrasive to others. She wanted to control others instead of lead them and was very critical of her husband. June needed to develop her own masculine energy in order to heal her competitive jealousy.

The only masculine energy available as our Falcon story opens is the father. As father, he is the authority figure, a projection of the Father/King archetype. This is the source of decisive action, power, and control. This particular father falls short. The shadow sisters are vain and materialistic. He feeds this vanity by buying whatever they desire. They are jealous and envious. He does nothing to put a stop to this.

This is one type of external father. This is the masculine exemplified by a type of man I remember from the South of my childhood who, surveying an injustice, will say, "Now sugar, never you mind. Just don't you pay any attention." This apparent comfort functions as an injunction against taking action out of a desire to avoid conflict.

There are moments in my current life when that voice kicks in and implores me to "be nice!" I have learned to stop and listen before I take my own advice. I must evaluate the message. This aspect of my masculinity has its own agenda. It proposes inactivity not because doing nothing would be appropriate, but because activity is difficult or perhaps even painful. If I acted in that situation, this inner voice is afraid I might "blow up." This inner voice that is my capacity for action does not want to deal with whatever would result if I weren't "nice." This is the same internal voice that inappropriately advises us to "look the other way" or "to count to ten," and always "to understand."

In many ways our story father is the traditional television father of the 1950s. He is kind, brings presents, and loves his children, but beyond those behaviors, he does not become involved. That fifties father did not take decisive action and had little insight into his children.

Our story heroine suffers from a father who does not act more assertively in facing the dynamic that is occurring. Like June, she was in need of internal discipline.

Our heroine is very focused on her need to grow. We know because she keeps requesting a feather of Finist the Bright Falcon. The storyteller selects the falcon to symbolize spirituality. Falcons are hunters; a quality they share with the Hero. The trained falcon soars high, spots prey, and dives. When he catches the prey, he returns to the one who released it. This is a symbol of an ability to move above the earthly objects while staying connected, for the falcon is focused on its goal and bonded to the arm where it will return.

Within the Christian religion this trained bird is a symbol for a convert or holy man. It is always the converts and holy men who are the most aggressive about the practice of their religion, and the image of the falcon certainly fits that truth. Falcon handlers must wear leather protection against the falcon's sharp claws. This idea reinforces the image of aggressiveness, for in this manner, the falcon, like the convert, grasps tightly.

The falcon is also a central figure in Norse mythology. Freyja, a major fertility goddess in the Norse pantheon, owned a falcon skin. Whenever she put it on, she was able to become spirit, travel to the underworld, and come back with knowledge of what was still to come. The falcon's skin and feathers could transform and transcend by changing a person and taking her into other worlds or dimensions.

The gift of the feather in our story brings contact with an ability to transform and transcend. This is the gift of spirituality, of understanding our lives in spiritual or metaphysical terms. It is the ability to soar while still connected and to see from above.

We are told, through our story's symbolism, that this energy—the falcon's feather—is very difficult to locate. Our heroine perseveres. Eventually, with persistence, she—and we—receive the gift from a wise and deep place within. The storyteller pictures this center of our energy as a wise old man. This image of old men being the embodiment of wisdom is so familiar that even God, when pictured, is an old man with a flowing white beard.

This spirituality is very dear. The old man's price was a thousand. The thousand brought the young girl and the feather, a tiny part of the bird, together, but there was more to do before the spirituality was hers. Even after waiting, remaining constant and unwavering in her desire, and paying this costly price, she has only sporadic contact before losing the connection. If we want to be able to claim a connection with an internal spirituality, we, too, must wait, remain diligent in our desire, pay a price in the form of self-discipline, and rely on some internal source to make things available. Even then, we will receive only a glimpse. There will be more work to do.

The type of contact that the girl has with the falcon is paralleled by many of us in our own spiritual contacts. We have a moment of deep communication with another person that is so true and honest, we feel transformed. The moment passes, leaving us with a memory and a yearning, yet we puzzle how to have more of those moments. We enter a cathedral or stand on a beach and feel the presence of an energy. Later we return to the same place, but our mind is on other things and whatever we felt is gone. We call those moments in time numinous. They are gifts from the old man at the gate. We hold them, but then they are gone.

Maintaining any consistent contact with the world of the spirits or the divine takes a consistent and firm discipline in dealing with issues of the unconscious. This is the father energy that was weak in the story. The father does not prevent the sisters from injuring the falcon.

When Finist is injured and calls to the young girl, she does not hear him, but she does learn how to find him through her dream. The information about how to proceed was given to the young girl by the unconscious. This is an interesting and exciting concept. What we are hearing is that someplace within the unconscious wants to be found and connected with as much as we, as conscious ego, desire the connection. We have heard this message before. The wise old man at the gate appears to the father. The moments we have experienced on the beach, in a church, or with another were gifts from somewhere. We do not force this connection on a conscious level.

In looking at the information given to the young girl by the falcon, we must understand that the unconscious is providing a way, not an end product. "You must do this and this and this," he tells her. "You must do these things repeatedly until you have worn down any resistance."

The information is a gift. Even the young girl is not clear how she knows. This is the type of knowing that we have when we wake up in the morning and we know what we should do about a problem we had no solution to the day before.

What the girl knows is that she will have to wear out three pairs of iron shoes and three iron walking sticks and gnaw through three stone wafers before she can even arrive at the place where she can see clearly what she wants.

Iron represents a Father Spirit archetype that often appears as a small iron man in folktales. This archetype has qualities of hardness and durability that are aspects of the masculine missing in the story's father. These are necessary elements in developing the discipline of a spiritual quest.

Iron also has magical qualities attributed to it, perhaps because people once believed that it came to earth from the otherworld of the stars of heavens. Iron could drive away witches and other evil. Mothers or midwives placed iron nails into babies' cradles to keep the children safe. People drove iron stakes through the heart of a suspected vampire to ensure permanent death. This attribute of iron is a metaphor that tells of the need for firm authority blended with goodness.

In working to gain access to our own spirituality, we, like the heroine, must learn to incorporate the discipline, structure, and firm authority of the Father/King masculine. We must also work hard to ensure that this energy works for good.

The image given by the storyteller or the unconscious also suggests a way to ensure that the masculine stays grounded and utilized for good. The suggestion is given through the use of the symbol of shoes. Shoes in several ways are used as a symbol for the feminine, and so the suggestion is made to keep the inner masculine (iron) integrated with the inner feminine (shoes).

We see shoes as a symbol of the feminine in their ability to connect with the ground or mother earth. Shoes have qualities of nurturing—keeping us warm, dry, and protected from cuts and bruises—and other qualities of holding and containing that are all mother attributes.

A shoe is also a fertility symbol. It is from this meaning that the custom arose of tying shoes to the bridal couple's carriage or car. "We wish you fertility in your marriage," the symbol suggests. And remember the old English rhyme:

> There was an old woman who lived in a shoe
> She had so many children she didn't know what to do.

The instruction to wear iron shoes can be translated as this: Add some authority and structure to your existing masculine energy. You will not be able to pursue the growth of your spirituality without a firm discipline. Make sure, however, that this inner masculine does not lose touch with your feminine or fertile, nurturing nature. This is needed in order to keep the masculine from becoming punitive, hard, or nonredemptive.

There is a further instruction regarding iron: The heroine is required to take three iron sticks on her journey. Through this she—and we—are reminded of the need to constantly keep our balance and stay on course. We must guard against falling and utilize the strength of external support to keep us upright on our task. The walking sticks will also help us find a way to achieve an internal balance.

Recently I was shopping with my young granddaughter. We wandered into a store where there were gyroscopes on display and spent a happy time watching and attempting to understand how this device could keep moving while maintaining the same direction. The sales person provided us with a minilecture, including the information that this was the same principal used to stabilize ships. I'm not sure either of us really understood by the time we left, but her six-year-old mind seemed more comfortable with the idea than mine did. I began to think, afterward, of the symbolism of this story. The walking sticks were needed, I thought, because we do not have a consistent internal gyroscope that keeps us pointed in the appropriate direction. We humans are always falling off the side of the hills and landing bottom-side up. This story warns of this danger, telling us to take care.

The third item our story protagonist takes with her on her journey is stone wafers. Her task is to gnaw through three of these before she will reach the land where her spirituality is hopefully waiting. Stone is a container of divine power or the life force. It is a symbol of wholeness. Christ called himself the spiritual rock while he identified Peter as the rock upon which he would build his church.

Many societies also believe that stones contain life energy. When such people wanted to commemorate a person, they made stone statues of their likeness in the belief that an aspect of their spirit would remain with the statue. There are also many societies that place stone above a grave site of a loved one, a custom that has the same origin.

The storyteller combines stone with the image of a wafer, that symbol of communion with the transpersonal or divine. Our heroine needs to chew on what this means in order to internalize it. This is an ancient antecedent of the Christian communion where the wafer transforms into the divine. When a believer swallows the wafer, she has incorporated divine energy. The story's symbolism states that in this task we must learn to avoid the quick, easy, obvious, or superficial understanding. We must spend as much time as we need to claim, understand, and internalize. In seeking our own individual spirituality, we must gnaw and chew until our truth is ingested.

It is the ball, given to the heroine by the first old woman, that provides the direction. In Jungian theory, each person contains something called the Self. This is our internal guiding factor that is able to direct us psychologically in the ways we are meant to grow.

We have become comfortable with the idea that many aspects of our physical future are programmed in our DNA before our birth. We will have blue eyes, red hair, light complexion, and be a certain height because those genes are present from the moment of conception. Even a vulnerability to certain diseases is programmed in our genes, although whether we manifest a disease depends on our actions within our environment.

In a similar way, the Self holds the key to our emotional or psychological growth. While it certainly is possible to thwart our innate psychological potential (in the same way that malnutrition can thwart our physical potential), there nonetheless is an underlying emotional blueprint that exists and continually unfolds. If our ego— that part we usually think of as ourselves—is willing to listen, the guidance is there. It is the ball, thrown out. We only need to follow.

How will we know what the direction is to be when we cannot see it in the way we see a ball and its path? We are living in a time in history when we have come to believe that the only true things are those which we experience through our concrete senses. If we can see, hear, touch, smell, or taste something, we are willing to believe in its reality.

Slow down, the storyteller suggests. You have gifts available— gifts of gold and silver or masculine and feminine. You have inner resources. Listen! Spin! Roll your ideas and feelings around! Keep what you are learning about your healthy masculine (gold) connected with your healthy feminine (silver). And make sure—very, very sure—that you apply the emotion to the task. When you reach the goal, it will be the emotion, the tear, which will join you with your own spiritual nature.

A marriage between our feminine and masculine does not guarantee "happily ever after." It is, however, one more piece of the puzzle that we put together to create our own wholeness. It is also a necessary internal marriage that must occur as we search for our own spirituality.

7

A Golden Bird

THE SEARCH FOR MEANING

Almost a year had passed since that gathering night when Elizabeth, surrounded by her own shroud of grayness, had sat listening into the late hour until the stories ended. This night, as the village families left quietly for homes and sleep, the Old Woman decided to stay with Elizabeth instead of returning to her own home. When they reached the cottage, the Old Woman lit a fire, and the two of them sat together in silence throughout the darktime. Not until the sky began to lighten did Elizabeth rise and begin walking toward the door. It was a slow, deliberate walk as if she were navigating through water. Her angular arms swung back and forth in a jerky, nonrhythmic motion, reminding the Old Woman of the stick dolls that the children made. At the door, Elizabeth stopped and turned. She looked at the Old Woman for a long moment. Her mouth opened, as if to speak, then closed as she turned, walked through the door, and disappeared into the forest.

There were some nights during the intervening time when the Old Woman thought she could hear Elizabeth's cries from the lake's edge, but the sound might have come from coyotes. Some from the village thought they caught sight of her as they hunted, but no one was sure. Then, eleven moons later she was back. She strode into town with a sureness and lightness of foot learned perhaps from forest deer. Her hair, pulled back in a single braid, had turned completely white. Her skin was burned dark olive. By her side was a tall white-haired man she called Cormac.

They moved into the same cottage that had been her home all the years, but now she lived more outside than within. She would disappear at times for a day or two. When she returned, she brought roots and seeds that became part of her emerging vast garden. Each plant, after settling into its new place on the earth's surface, would begin somehow to flourish under Elizabeth's care until it was able to provide leaves, seeds, flowers, and roots that could comfort and heal. Elizabeth, as brown as the earth she worked in and as willowy and supple as white yarrow, had left the village near to soul death and returned both healed and healer.

As we prepare for our own old age, we look for our scattered parts. We, like Elizabeth, must go into the forest. Our forest is the unconscious. There we find pieces from our shadow, our masculine, and our feminine; we find these and other parts we lost, or perhaps never knew were ours. We also find there the guidance and wisdom we need.

The guiding aspect of our unconscious, the Self, this deep inner core, has been with us since our beginning. Because the Self knows our true nature, we are able to discover from this center both our direction and meaning. It is a discovery, however, that is characterized by listening rather than talking. This is often difficult for those of us who are most comfortable when we are active.

Many religious or spiritual practices speak of the same phenomena using different terms. Instead of the psychological description of a Self, some understand it as the manifestation of the God within. Some call this inner source a higher power. Some call it spiritual life energy. The Israelites of old, in the story of Moses and the burning bush, identified this as fiery energy called I Am that I Am. The Persian Sufi poet Rumi speaks of this energy in this way:

> My eyes gleam because there is Another inside
> if water scalds you, there was fire behind it—understand?

The psychologists and religious people are all identifying an experience of inner energy. All describe this energy as all-knowing, greater than the individual, and outside of the individual's control. All suggest that the only way this energy is contacted is experientially.

As we look ahead toward becoming old women within the culture, we see we have still another task. We need to discover the meaning of our lives. After we have become conscious of those characteristics that have been lost and after we work to hold the tension between our opposite parts, we need to know even more. We need to know the way to find the significance of our lives. It is necessary to use more than our conscious ego to accomplish this task. The search will take us deep within, to the Self or Another. We wonder again about the nature of this journey.

It is wounding that starts us on the road to this type of deep work. Elizabeth's wound became conscious and painful enough that she could no longer teach the children but needed to go into the forest to heal. Elizabeth experienced herself separated from her emotions. Each of us has different wounds, but any wound can become motivation for the journey. As we grow older, many of us begin to experience a need to heal what needs healing. As we grow older we experience an urgency to discover our own unique significance. The poet expresses the intensity of this feeling in the Book of Psalms.

> As the hart panteth after the water brooks
> so panteth my soul after thee, O God.

The story of the golden bird tells us about this process. We see that although meaning is desirable, obtaining it is not a simple task.

~ The Golden Bird ~

ONCE UPON A time a king and his three sons lived in a palace. An apple tree outside the palace bore golden apples. One morning an apple was missing. The king sent his oldest son out to sit beneath the tree and watch, but when night came the boy fell asleep. The next morning another apple was missing.

The second night the king sent his second son to guard, but he, too, fell asleep, and another apple was missing by daylight. There was nothing to do but send the third son on the third night. This son stayed awake and saw a golden bird come just at midnight. The boy shot an arrow at the bird knocking off one golden feather. The bird escaped.

The next morning the son took the feather to the king and told him what he had seen. The king was dazzled by the beauty of the feather. He decided he must have the bird and immediately sent his oldest son off in search of it.

The boy rode off and soon came to a fox who was sitting at the edge of the wood. The eldest son was about to shoot when the fox held out his paw saying, "Stop! Do not shoot me and I will give you some good advice on how to find the golden bird." The eldest put down his gun.

"You will come to a town," the fox said. "In the town you will see two inns. In one there will be people singing and dancing while the other will look empty and meager. Stay away from the one where there is merriment and go into the other." With that, the fox ran away.

The eldest went into the town and found everything as the fox had described. The meager inn, however, looked too bleak, and the eldest went into the merry one where he soon forgot his task of finding the golden bird.

After a while the king decided his son was not returning. He sent the middle son to find the bird. The same thing happened with this young man, and he ended up in the merry inn with his brother.

By now there was nothing to do but send the youngest. He, too, met the fox. This son, however, followed the fox's advice. After a good night's sleep in the meager inn, the youngest set off. Again he met the fox.

"Get up on my back," said the fox. "I will take you to the castle."

The youngest did. He held on tight. Soon they stood in front of a large castle with sleeping soldiers in front. "Go past the soldiers," said the fox. Inside you will find the golden bird in a wooden cage. Beside this cage is an empty golden cage, but you must leave it and bring the bird with the wooden cage.

The youngest thanked the fox for his help. Once inside, however, he was dazzled by the beauty of the golden cage. He opened the cage door so that he could transfer the bird, but as he did so, the bird shrieked. The soldiers awoke and rushed in to capture him. They put the youth into prison.

The king of that castle, however, said he would pardon the boy if he would find the golden horse and bring it to him. As a reward, along with his life, he would also give the boy the golden bird.

The youngest rushed off to accomplish this task and again met the fox who helped him. When they reached the stables where the horse lived, the fox gave him this advice: "You will see two saddles. One is of wood while the other is golden. Do not put the golden one on the horse. If you do, it will go ill with you."

The youngest, however, could not resist the temptation when he saw the beautiful golden saddle gleaming in the sun. As he put the golden saddle on the horse's back, the horse began to neigh, waking all the palace grooms who seized the youngest and threw him into prison.

The king of this castle agreed to free the boy if he brought back the beautiful princess who lived in the golden castle. He also offered the golden horse as reward for this deed.

Again the fox was waiting. The youngest rode on the back of the fox to the golden castle. The fox advised him to go in and give the princess a kiss and she would follow him. "'Do not," said the fox, "allow her to say good-bye to her parents, or there will be trouble." The youngest agreed, but the princess wept and pleaded, and finally he gave in. The fox's prediction came true, and the king had the young man thrown into prison.

It was again the fox who aided the young man in obtaining his freedom and the princess. The young man finally had learned his lesson. From this point onward, he listened to the fox. Thus he was able to regain the golden horse and finally, the golden bird.

～

The story begins with golden apples stolen from the tree by a golden bird. Stealing is an important metaphor. Any type of stealing that occurs in our lives wounds us. Something we value, perhaps a part of who we are, is being stolen or taken away and the story uses the symbol of the disappearance of golden apples to alert us to that loss.

There are many ways to steal and many interpretations. Stealing in daylight is transparent and visible. Psychologically, this type of stealing would correspond to an obvious self-betrayal. The golden bird, however, comes to steal in the dark of night. This type of stealing comes from the unconscious. It is a raid by the unconscious on the conscious. In the story, the metaphor of the golden bird taking the golden apples tells us that the unconscious is taking away something of value. What does this mean?

A golden apple is stolen when we lose our connection with some feeling. We experience something disrespectful and have no awareness of a feeling.

"How did that make you feel?" I often ask a client.

"The person was upset when that happened."

"Yes. I think you are right, but how did that make you feel?"

"I understand what was going on."

"Good. But where is the feeling?"

This may go on for a short or a long time before finally, the client declares, "I'm angry!"

Now we are beginning, but we're not there yet. There is more work to be done and the process may be long or short before we discover what is buried beneath the anger. In our example, our mythical person might find she felt hurt at the disrespect. Usually, we hide our hurt because we feel vulnerable when it is around.

The hurt isn't the end of our search. We sit with that feeling for a while, not trying to *do* anything to make it go away. Then our mythical person probably begins to make some connections with the roots of the hurt. Perhaps she finds early events, rules, or conclusions that convince her that she has no right to feel hurt. The right to have her own feelings has been stolen, not by who or what was disrespectful, but by something within. The ability to be consciously aware of her feeling has been stolen. There was no human thief in the night, but an internal bird that flew away with what rightfully belonged to her.

The first attempts to detect what happened to this valuable treasure are not very successful in the story. The first two sons are sent out to watch. They sleep instead of doing the work needed to solve this puzzle.

This is the lazy part of each of us. We know something is not quite right. We have, for example, strong feelings of anger toward another person. The work of staying awake to discover what is really happening is difficult. *Staying awake* means that we continue to feel the feeling. *Staying awake* means that we resist the temptation to distract ourselves.

We must stay with the feelings to learn what there is to learn about ourselves. Instead, we gossip or eat or go shopping. These are the drugs of our modern generation. We have learned to deaden ourselves with food and distraction. We fall asleep emotionally under the tree and fail to see for ourselves who or what is stealing from us.

This is the same part of us that chooses the fancy inn. We begin a journey to find what was stolen but stop before we have gotten very far. In our example above, these are the times we get far enough along to realize we are angry. Then, as if a switch were pulled, we move from the internal to the external. We project and blame. We become litigious. We are caught in a swirl of activity that fools us into thinking we are dealing with whatever is occurring, but in fact we are avoiding it.

This is a difficult concept for most of us. After all, someone did do something to us. We are in touch with the feeling of anger. And we are doing something in return. Often, just to ensure that we can live with what we are doing, we package our behavior in the box of "righteous indignation." We are ridding the world of this external evil. What could be more of an active journey? How could this be a failure to do something to recover the stolen apples?

I recently heard on a TV news show a story about a school bus accident. The bus was transporting children from a small town to a nearby sports event when it went off the road. The bus driver and many of the children were killed. It was a tragedy of great proportions.

Lawyers rushed into the town soon after the accident and lawsuits erupted. The bus company, school system, tire manufacturer, seat belt manufacturer, family of the driver, superintendent of county roads, and others were all sued. As a result of all the litigation, many families became millionaires. After several years some families were still in court. One of the commentators raised the question of grief.

It was a good question. One mother, who had two lawsuits still pending, said there had been no time to grieve. She remembered the old days before the accident. Back then, she said, whenever tragedy would strike a family, everyone would come together. Everyone would remember and cry. Everyone would talk and tell stories. Everyone would help. But this time, she told the interviewer, everyone was busy with the lawyers. Everyone was very busy with the anger. There was no community to grieve with her, and she did not grieve with others. She said she didn't know about the others, but she had achieved no peace, even though the accident took place three years before.

The lack of peace occurred because there was no meaningful transformation. In our earlier example of the disrespect we saw that anger is a necessary first feeling. But these families stopped with the anger. They mistook that first feeling to be something of permanent value rather than a signpost. They ended up in the fancy inn, mistaking action for meaning. Loss and grief had been transformed into something even worse—hate, blame, and greed.

We need to remember that the flashy inn can be a type of hypermaterialism or it can be an equally compelling external search for a resolution of another type, such as our village parents found with the lawyers. When the parents began these lawsuits, they saw their actions as "righteousness" in that they were preventing the same thing from happening to others. In fact, this type of behavior is really revenge, and revenge has little healing salve within.

Involvement in lawsuits created the illusion that they were doing something. The real labor of grieving and struggling to understand how such a terrible loss was an aspect of the meaning of each life, had been missed.

It seems there are many reasons people choose to avoid this type of task. Neurotic forces such as greed and blame may block awareness of alternatives. In other cases a woman appears to neither need nor desire this type of journey. My aunt Martha is a good example of someone who had no interest in any walks into the forest.

Aunt Martha lived her old age quite contented with almost no self-insight as far as I could tell. She cooked for her family the three meals a day she knew they needed. When the family was gone, she still cooked for herself. She cleaned her house as she always had. She did her laundry on Monday, and on Tuesday she ironed. Wednesday she began her housecleaning. She divided the tasks so they occupied the rest of the week, and Sunday, of course, was church.

When she became quite old, I would ask her if she would like to have some help. "No," she always answered. "I wouldn't know what to do with myself if someone else were doing the work the good Lord intended for me."

Aunt Martha had no interest in discovering her shadow or animus. The Self within would have seemed silly to her. Her God was up there in heaven, and her work was her home. Sometimes I would sit in her big old kitchen drinking a cup of tea while she baked. I would talk about some of these ideas and she would respond with, "That's nice, dear. Would you hand me the pot holder, please." Aunt Martha was a good woman who lived her life honestly and generously. She was happy with her life as it was. There were many times over the years, as I struggled in the forest, that I envied her.

I have come to believe, however, as I grow older, that the *correctness* of either position is not determined by us, but instead by the Self. It was correct for Aunt Martha to live without the struggle of self-knowledge. It was not who she was meant to be. There are many of us, however, who have been placed on a different path. If we want to live our lives as they are meant to be, we must search the forest.

The youngest son in the story is the energy of the Hero who is willing to search. He wants to know more. He is that aspect of ourselves willing to stay awake to discover what the problem may be and then go on the journey.

This Hero energy within each of us does not have to travel alone. We also have a fox waiting for us. Fox is the instinctual energy that guides and directs us with an amazing accuracy if we know how to listen.

Learning to listen, however, is not easy in our culture. Women are inundated with external standards, fads, or values. The lines of communication with this instinctual information are down. A woman may hear a message clearly, only to discover that it is difficult to find others who will listen and take her seriously. I once had a discussion with a physician friend of a friend. The location was an informal gathering in L.A. and the topic was the shift in doctor-patient relationships. Someone in the group had made the point that individuals were becoming more informed about their own bodies. The M.D. expressed concern that this might undermine the authority of the physician. "After all," he had said, "people don't really understand. Disease and medicine are extremely complex."

While I didn't disagree with his assessment of complexity, I saw the issue as more one of a collaboration in which the different type of knowledge a patient has will be taken seriously and utilized. To illustrate my point, I described a recent experience I had with my own body. I suddenly became ill. Instinctively I knew it was my gall bladder. Although I had never had any previous symptoms of gall bladder disease, I knew exactly which part of my body was affected.

"Perhaps you remembered something from anatomy or physiology courses in school," he suggested.

"No. I never took those courses."

"Did any family member have this disease?"

"No."

"Obviously you're more educated then most people would be. Or perhaps it was a lucky guess."

As far as he was concerned that was the end of the conversation—his tactful way of dismissing my idea. He did not believe there was such a thing as an instinctual way of knowing.

In my experience, this doctor is not unique. I have heard other women relate similar stories about their instinctual ability to understand what is occurring in their bodies. Unfortunately most of them also encounter disbelief when they talk about what they know. One woman I know began having symptoms that included headaches, confusion, and vertigo. She went to the doctor and was told she had an inner ear infection.

"I don't think so," she told the doctor. "The problem is in my brain. It's the right temporal lobe."

But inner ear infection remained the diagnosis. Medication was prescribed. She took the medicine, giving it a good faith effort, but returned with the same symptoms. "I need a brain scan," she suggested. "I can tell the problem is in the right temporal lobe."

It was not until all else failed that the physician ordered a scan.

There was a tumor and guess where they found it? In the right temporal lobe.

Certainly I am not suggesting that the advances made by medical science should be abandoned. Alongside of objective and rational science, however, stands the fox. It is necessary to cultivate and validate our own instinctual energy despite the fact that most people do not believe in the reality of an internal fox.

This ability does not extend to all areas of my life. I find myself unconscious at other times or in other areas. This is true for most of us. We must work for a continued awareness of our instinctual wisdom. Otherwise we fail to hear what we are being told. We wander into places we don't belong, failing to smell a rat.

Once the youngest son, our Hero energy, is on the journey, he makes mistake after mistake. His instincts tell him to take the wooden cage. Instead, he chooses the gold and loses the bird. Next his instincts tell him to take the wooden saddle. Instead, he chooses the gold and loses the horse.

This young Hero energy of ours is very human. In it is our tendency to move too quickly. In it is our perception that we will be able to achieve what we want in a short period of time. In this Hero energy is our proclivity to make decisions based on external clues, enchanted by the external sparkle. Our young Hero energy often responds in ways similar to the Prince of Morocco in Shakespeare's play, *The Merchant of Venice.* If this young prince correctly chooses from among three boxes, he will win the maiden Portia. He passes over the lead and silver boxes and selects the gold. When he opened the box, instead of the likeness of Portia, which would have allowed the union, he finds a skull with the following message:

> All that glisters is not gold;
> Often have you heard that told
> Many a man his life hath sold
> But my outside to behold.

Our storyteller is reminding us of the danger of quick judgments based on what is externally obvious. Our young hero, like the Prince of Morocco, is dazzled by the gold. He is not able to trust his internal instinctual energy. We see this same warning over and over, in stories and in life itself. It is difficult to trust that anything good will come from selecting a lead box or a wooden cage or saddle.

Finding the Self and the meaning of our lives is a long process fraught both with difficulties and opportunities to make the wrong decisions. If we move too rapidly, if we are blinded by the gold's sheen, we will neglect the necessary steps and end up with screeching birds and kicking horses. Most of us have had a few of those in our lives. Like the little wooden puppet Pinocchio in the story of the same name, we continue to fall into the trap of believing we can turn our four pieces of gold into thousands by simply burying them overnight in the Field of Miracles.

The youngest son in our story picks himself up after each mistake with the help of the fox, or his internal instincts, and moves on to the next task. He learns he cannot have the golden bird until he has the golden horse and he cannot have the golden horse until he has the princess. There is a process that must be followed.

In a similar way, there are steps that each of us must go through to discover the meaning of our lives. I have discovered that every time I manage to take a shortcut, congratulating myself on my cleverness, I end up either in some difficulty or at least back where I started.

Stella was a woman I knew who was working to allow herself enough time to go through the steps even though her children wanted to hurry her.

Stella's adult children became very concerned for her after their father died. Stella and Joe had been living in the same two-story house for fifty years. They had watched the neighborhood change to such an extent that, for the past few years, neither of them went out after dark. Still, Stella loved the house and her rose garden. This was home.

One of her sons found an apartment that would have been ideal for her in a retirement complex. The buildings were new and in good repair, unlike the old home where Stella lived. Her son and his family lived nearby, and they would be able to visit and keep an eye on her.

Stella went with her son to look at the apartment but would not agree to move. "It's sweet of you to have found this for me dear," she told him, "but I don't know yet."

Stella's daughter Patsy had a home with several acres of land. "I want you to move here, Mom," she said. "Bud and I will build you a cottage behind our house. You will have your own home and room for your roses. You can even design the cottage if you'd like."

"Thank you, dear," Stella said. "But I just don't know yet."

Stella's sister had retired to Florida. "It's wonderful here," she wrote. "You could move here and we'd be together. Remember how much you've always liked Florida?"

Stella wrote back: "Thank you. I do like Florida and I do love you. But I just don't know yet."

Over the years Stella had developed a friendship with her fox. He had given her good advice on many occasions. So far, it appeared, he hadn't formed an opinion. Stella was willing to wait. If she decided to sell her house and move, she wanted to be sure that she was not jumping too quickly into someone else's idea of a good place for her. Stella had learned to avoid fancy inns and glittering cages.

The youngest son in our story did not have Stella's wisdom. He disregarded his instincts. He wanted the gold. He fell into the trap of thinking that if one is good, then two are better. The golden bird is great, but why not *also* have the golden cage? The golden horse is wonderful, but why not *also* have the golden saddle? Whenever we become blinded by the external, we lose the message from the fox. We disregard our instincts. This will always lead to trouble.

This golden bird is the symbol for the internal place where we will find meaning and wisdom. The storyteller is letting us know that this search is a process filled with trial and error. We cannot rush this process. There are no shortcuts. We cannot earn the golden bird with one insight. Only with continuing work can we find meaning. At the end of the story, the youngest son gets it. He arrives back at the castle with the princess, the golden horse, and the golden bird.

This century is ending. At those midnight moments, a golden bird is always available for anyone who wants to stay awake. We are women living in a time when we are able to find a voice. As we heal ourselves, we may begin to speak about healing. We are becoming the old of society at a time when society needs female wisdom and elder wisdom. There are many ways to become a Wise Old Woman.

The Sufi poet Rumi said:

It's simple. You thought you were dust
and now find you are breath.
Before you were ignorant, and now you know more.

Exactly what more each of us may know remains to be seen. What we do know is that our truth is about who we are, who we have always been, and who we are meant to be. What is also known is that our truth is filled with paradox. It is universal and personal. It is outside ourselves and within. It is found but not sought. If we become conscious enough of our darkness, there we will find light. This is the way of the Self.

Epilogue

The Old Woman had been busy most of the day with preparations. Tonight at sunset the weeklong ritual would begin. She tried to think back. The ritual occurred each June. This would be—was it forty? Maybe forty-one. She sighed. However many, they marked the deepening layers on her journey.

Tonight there would be three new women from the village joining the ritual circle. So young, these new old women. Perhaps, many years ago, she had looked as they do now; hair scarcely flecked with gray, backs still straight. Still, their blood had stopped its flow, and it was now their time to join the circle and journey with the other women into the hills for the week.

Altogether there were thirty-two—no, thirty-three—now that Elizabeth had returned. The oldest of the village old women, Zeta, was still alive, although the Old Woman had feared for her this past winter. Zeta had lived more than twelve hundred full moons, and for five hundred of those she had been part of this circle of old women of the village. The Old Woman paused, thinking of all she had learned from Zeta, and a contented smile crossed her face. "More than Zeta," she said out loud, "I've learned from them all, and they from me." That was the way of the circle.

Tonight she had no need to prepare a story. Indeed, the week would pass before she would tell another. This week, deep within the hills where an oak grove sheltered animals and birds, the women would stay. They would talk, those older ones and the new ones just beginning.

Each woman, now that she was a part of the circle, was on a sacred journey to discover the story of her own life. In many ways each story would be the story of every woman's life. In even more ways each story would be unique. No two women had walked the same path. No woman had seen all there was to see. Some women had seen shadows, some storms. No woman arrived here without knowledge enough to begin. Within each there lived the divine, and within each there existed a thirst for meaning.

The Old Woman carefully folded a heavy wool covering, for it was cold in the hills. She remembered the year this wool had been taken from the sheep. She had helped birth this one as a lamb. He had been turned wrong and in danger of breaking his neck on the passage out. She had put her hands and arms up into the warmth of the mother and managed to grab hold of legs and head. He popped out then with all the verve of any newborn. She had felt a special closeness to this one, perhaps because of the birth, and thought of him whenever she used the blanket.

Her large pot would go, but she would take no food. The food they needed would be easily found in the hills. There would be wildlife, and the woods and hillsides were covered with fresh greens. Fiddle fern were up, and dandelions were tender. The abundant sorrel would make greensauce for whatever animal offered itself. The fragrance of hyssop would fill the air where they slept. She could feel and taste and smell the goodness of this week already.

Putting her blanket on her back, she went out to meet the other women for the walk to their place in the hills. The full moon would be out tonight as they began adding to the pool of knowing. It was into this pool that each woman looked in order to see what needed to be seen. Into this pool was wisdom placed and from this pool was wisdom reflected back. Every woman who passed through her moon blood time to join the circle would have the responsibility to provide wisdom where it was needed. This is the meaning of the circle of the wise.

And so it is, even until today. Becoming an old woman is to join the circle with all the ancient ones who have gone before. Becoming an old woman is to do the work to find one's own life's story and from it draw meaning and wisdom. This is the job of all who no longer use the blood to create new life. For we are the ones who are becoming the ancient ones for the coming generations.

Index

A

Abandonment, 28–29
Acceptance, 114
The Aged Mother, 48
  interpretation, 48–61
Aging, *see also* Death
  abandonment during, fear, 28–29
  body and, 9–10, 14, 137
  limitations, 64–65, 66
  loneliness in, 120–121
  pathways, 4–5
  preparing for, 75–76
  repression and, 96–100
  task, mothering as, 182
  women's role, 3–4
Alice in Wonderland, 13
Anger, 23
  Dark Feminine and, 143
  recognizing, 108
  repressed, 106–107
Animal motifs, *see specific animals*
Animus, 229–231
Aphrodite, 42
Apples, symbolism, 196
Archetypes, *see also* Energy
  Dark Feminine as, 150
  definition, 38
  Father Spirit, 256
  Good Mother, 191, 198–200, 201,
      219, 222–223
  Jupiter as, 38–41
  Mercury as, 38–41
  power of, 39
  self, 58–59
Ariadne, 227–229
  interpretation, 229, 233–236

B

Athena, 97, 165–167
Aunt Essie, 106
Aunt Martha, 270–271

Baba Yaga, 89, 175, 178
Baucis and Philemon, 35–37
  interpretation, 37–44
Beans, symbolism, 80
Behavior, destructive, 83–84
Bess' history, 130–131
Beth's history, 118–119
Betty's history, 97–98
Bible, *see* New Testament; Old Testament
Body
  aging and, 9–10, 14, 137
  knowledge of, 271–272
Butcher, internal, 160–161
Button-pushing, 100
Buzzard, 211, 213

C

Campbell, Joseph, 156
Cat on a Hot Tin Roof, 244
Cedric death, 45–47
Cerina, 225–227
Certainty, 62
Childhood
  deprivation, 183
  emotions, 213–214
  limits, setting, 187–188
  loss of, 54
Child image, symbolism, 16–17
Christopher Columbus, 29

Chrysaor, 166
Cinderella, 87, 88–89, 248
Clarisse's history, 188–189
Codependent relationship, 118–121
Cold, symbolism, 65, 104
Compassion, 109
Connections, 217
    feminine/masculine, 230–321
Connie's history, 112–114
Conscious, 56
    awareness, symbol for, 207
    metaphor for, 196
Containment, 189–190
    emotions, 213–215
    lack of, 214–216
    therapy as, 215–216
Contra sexual energy, 229–231
Creativity, 16–18, 22
    symbols of, 16–17

D
Danger, personal, 154
Dark Ages, 207
Dark Feminine, see also Witch
    acknowledgment, 163
    as archetype, 150
    directness of, 147
    dual function, 167
    emergence, 142–145
    energy from, 156
    exploring, 163–164
    ignoring, 161–162
    incarnations, 151–152
    intuition and, 148–150,
        157–158
    reflections of, 165–166
    relationship with, 164, 179
    truth and, 156–157
Darkness, 114
    depression and, 207
    symbolism for, 207

Daughter
    relationships
        father, 241–242
        mother, 74–75
Day, Doris, 236–237
Death, see also Aging
    accepting, 43
    fear of, 8–10
    as metaphor, 5–6
    midlife crisis and, 5
    preparation for, 34
    realization of, 5–6
    realization of, importance, 33–34
    symbols of, 31, 122–123
Deception, 79–81
Demeter, 46, 135, 196
Denial, 138
Dennehy, Brian, 243
Depression, 132–135
    darkness and, 207
Destructive behavior, 83–84
Disappointments, 122
Divine power, 258
Divorce, 59–60
Dream of Three Women, 24–25
Driving Miss Daisy, 49
Dualities, 18–19
    uniting, 44

E
Ecclesiastes, 195–196
Ed's history, 251–252
Ego, see Conscious
Either/or situations, 13–14, 203
Elizabeth, 93–94, 261–263
Elizabeth's history, 29
Emotions
    accepting, 108–110
    childhood, 213–214
    containing, 213–215
    insulation from, 66–67
    symbols of, 65

Energy, 80, *see also* Archetypes
    contra sexual, 229–231
    Dark Feminine, 156
    Father/King, 234–235, 237, 238–239,
        239, 252, 255–256
    Hero, 235–236, 238–239, 239, 245,
        271, 273
    inner, 263
    internal, 73
    masculine, 229–231, 243–244
        physical, 243–245
    Wise Old Man, 247
    witch, 142
Enid's history, 242–243
Entitlement, 155–156
Eros, 82–83, 163
Essie, Aunt, 106
Eve, 82
Extended families, 190–191
External solutions, 68, 70
Extroverted women, 152

F
Fairies, symbolism, 73
Falcon, symbolism, 253
Falsehoods, *see* Deception
Families, extended, 190–191
Farmer's wife fantasy, 50–53
Father/King energy, 234–235,
    238–239, 239, 246–247, 252,
    255–256
Fathers
    –daughter relationships, 241–242
    traditional television, 253
Father Spirit archetype, 256
Fears
    abandonment, 28–29
    death, 8–10
The Feather of Finist the Bright Falcon,
    248–250
    interpretation, 253–258

Feelings
    in midlife, importance,
        30–31
    reclaiming, 127
    unconscious, 100–102
Feminine
    dark, *see* Dark feminine
    –masculine
        connection, 230–321
        as opposites, 231
        unification, 42–43, 79, 259
Fertility symbols, 257
First Blood, 243
Fish, symbolism, 135
Fitzgerald, F. Scott, 230
Fitzgerald, Zelda, 230
Florida woman, 69
Francie's history, 201–205
Frankl, Viktor, 163
Frau Trude, 152–153
    interpretation, 154–156, 163–164
Frigga, 42
Frustration, tolerating, 164–165

G
Gaia, 39
Gandhi, 109 110
Gertrude's history, 219–222
Gina's history, 231–233
Glass, symbolism, 65
The Golden Bird, 264–266
    interpretation, 266–267, 274–276
Golden bird, symbolism, 275–276
Good enough mother, 182, 187–190
Good Mother archetype, 191, 198–199,
    201, 219, 222–223
Grace's history, 53–57
Grandmother Spider Steals the Sun,
    205–206
    interpretation, 207–213, 216–217
Gratitude, psychological aspects, 73

Grimm's Fairy Tales, 48, 147, 152
Gwen's history, 171–172

H
Hades, 163
Hansel and Gretel, 175
Head, symbolism, 31
Healing of meaning, 58–59
Heat, symbolism, 65
The Hedley Kow, 85–87
    interpretation, 87–88
Hepburn, Audrey, 238
Hero energy, 235–236, 238–239, 239,
        245, 246–247, 271, 273
Home, symbolism, 70
How a Worm Destroyed a Tribe, 115–117
    interpretation, 117–125
How Do I Look, 10–12
    interpretation, 12–15
Human figure, symbolism, 117
Hypermaterialism, 269–270

I
I Have Sent Them My Death, 26–27
    interpretation, 27–30
Inanna, 240–241
    interpratation, 241–242
Inauthenticity, recognition of, 99–100
Infantile response, 204–205
Inner energy, 263
Inner voices, 9
Insulation
    emotions, 66–67
    loss, 71
Internal butcher, 160–161
Internal energy, 73
Introverted women, 151
Intuition, 147–150, 157–158
Inuits, about, 117
Iron, symbolism, 256–257

J
Jane's history, 194–195, 199–200
Janet's history, 120–121
Jean's history, 183–187
Jesus Christ, 37, 80, 135, 196, 216, 258
Joan of Arc, 144
Joan's history, 59
June Cleaver, 236-237
Jung, Carl, 104, 129
Jungian psychology, 38, 258
Jupiter, as archetype, 38–41

K
Kali, 19, 151, 175
Kindness, universality of, 37
King Arthur, 43, 80
King David, 218–219, 238
King Minos, 227–229, 235
King Saul, 218–219, 237–238
King Solomon, 238
Kitchen fire, 131
Knowing, *see* Intuition
Knowledge
    body, 271–272
    symbols for, 196
Kobrin, Shoshana, 92

L
Lawsuits, 268–270
Levin, Ira, 237
Life force, 258
Limitations, *see also* Loss
    aging, 64–65, 66
    marriage, 60
    recognizing, 55, 57
    setting, 187–190
    symbolisms of, 84–85
Linden tree, symbolism, 42
Loneliness, 23–24
    in aging, 120–121

Loss, *see also* Limitations
  childhood, 54
  experiencing, 49–51
  grieving, 51
  insulation from, 71
  mothering, 53–54
  types, 49
  via divorce, 59–60
Love, symbol of, 196

M
Magic paddle, 131–132
Marian's history, 200–201
Marie's history, 158–160
Marriage, limitations, 60
Martha, Aunt, 270–271
Mary's history, 89–90
Masculine
  energy, 229–231
  –feminine
    connection, 230–321
    as opposites, 231
    unification, 42–43, 79, 259
Masculine Energy, *see also* Father/King
  energy
Masculine energy, 243–244, *see also* Hero
  energy; Wise Old Man energy
  physical, 243–245
  women with, 234–235
Masterpieces, 176–177
Materialism, *see* Hypermaterialism
Maude's history, 29–30
Meaning, healing of, 58–59
Medusa, 166–167
Memory, *see* Muscle memory
Menopause, Ode to, 90–92
The Merchant of Venice, 273
Mercury, as archetype, 38–41
Midlife
  death and, 5
  feelings during, importance, 30–31
  shadow in, 110–112

Milk, symbolism, 196–197
Morgan, Julia, 230
Mortality, *see* Death
Moses, 263
Mother–daughter relationships, 74–75
Mother earth, qualities, 256
Mother Holle, 191–193
  interpretation, 193–194, 195–196,
    197–198, 200–201
Mothering
  as aging task, 182
  archetype, 191, 198–200, 201, 219,
    222–223
  good enough, 182, 187–190
  inadequate, 185–186
  minimal, 210–211
  prevention of, 53–54
Mother Teresa, 163
Muscle memory, 129–130

N
New Testament, 37, 196, 216
Nona, 181–182
No One Lives Forever, 6–8
  interpretation, 8–10
Nourishment, symbolic, 196–197
Nurturing, need for, 51–52
Nyanbol, 173–274
  interpretation, 174–179

O
Oak tree, symbolism in, 42
Ocean, symbols of, 17
Ode to Menopause, 90–92
Old Testament, 195–196, 218
The Old Woman
  Cedric death and, 45–47
  Cerina and, 139–142, 225–227
  Elizabeth and, 93–94, 261–263
  at the hearth, 1–6

The Old Woman, *continued*
Nona and, 181–182
Zeta and, 277–278
The Old Woman and the Rice Cakes,
125–126
interpretation, 126–138
The Old Woman Who Lived in a
Vinegar Bottle, 63–64
interpretation, 64–68
Oni, 127–128, 130–132,
134–138, 197
The Owl, 145–147
interpretation, 147
Owl, symbolism, 147

P
Paddle, *see* Magic paddle
Palm tree, symbolism, 177
Paradoxes, 13–14
Pegasus, 166
Pele, 151
Penelope, 246–247
Perfection, 38
Persephone, 135, 163
Perseus, 165–166
Personal danger, 154
Physical activity, 129–130
Possum, 208–211
Processes, importance, 72
Prudence's history, 209–213
Psyche
kitchen fire in, 131
losing touch, 117
Psyche and Eros, 82–83, 163
Psychological shadow, *see* Shadow
Psychology, *see* Jungian psychology

Q
Quiet, valuing, 216

R
Rambo, 243–244
Rebirth, symbols of, 105
Recognition of inauthenticity, 99–100
Regeneration, symbols of, 105
Relationships
codependent, 118–121
with Dark Feminine, 164, 179
father/daughter, 241–242
mother–daughter, 74–75
with shadow, 114–115
with unconscious, 127–129
Renewal, times for, 18
Repression, 96–100, 130
anger, 106–107
symbols of, 104–105
Righteousness, symbols of, 177
Rightness, sense of, 25
Risa's history, 240
Rizpah, 218–219
interpretation, 219–222
Rose's history, 132–134
Rules, obeying, 137–138
Rumi, 263, 276
Ruth's history, 19–21

S
Security, symbols of, 70
Self, 258–259, 262
acknowledgement, 34–35
archetype, 58–59
cross-cultural manifestations, 263
–renewal, symbols of, 177
separation from, 22–23
Sense and Sensibility, 214
Shadow
definition, 103–104
denying, 138
emergence, 112
in midlife, 110–112
recognizing, 123

relationship with, 114–115
responses to, 124
Shakespeare, William, 273
Shoes, symbolism, 256–257
Skull, symbolism, 31
Sleeping Beauty, 87, 150
Snake, 102, 115
metaphorical aspects, 111
symbolism, 104–105
The Snow Maiden, 15–16
interpretation, 16–17, 19–21, 26
Snow White, 150
Sore spots, 100–102
Sorting, 88–90
Spells, casting, 142
Spirits
life, finding, 43
role, 12–14
Spiritual symbols, 197
St. George, 126
Stability, importance of, 239–240
Stallone, Sylvester, 243
Star Wars, 247
Staying awake, 268
Stealing, as metaphor, 266–268
Stella's history, 274–275
The Stepford Wives, 237
Stone, symbolism, 258
Stories
importance, 1–5
metaphorical aspects, 37–38
unconscious and, 102–103
Stream, symbols of, 17
The String Bean that Went through the Roof of the World, 76–79
interpretation, 79–85
Superwoman, 194

T
Tandy, Jessica, 49
Tarot, 72

Tennyson, Alfred, 87
Therapy, as containment, 215–216
Theseus, 227–229, 245–246, 247
Thompson, Emma, 214
Three, symbolism, 72
Transformation, 135–136
meaningful, 269
symbols of, 135
Trees, *see* Linden tree; Oak tree; Palm tree
Truth, 156–157

U
Ulysses, 87–88, 246–247
Unconscious
feelings, 100–102
grooves, 185–186
guiding aspect, 262
physical activity and, 129–130
relationship with, 127–129
repressed aspects, 96–99, 104–105, 130
self archetype in, 58–59
stories and, 102–103
worms in, 123–124

V
Valuing quiet, 216
Victimization, 120
Victory, symbols of, 177
Vinegar
necessity of, 67–68, 71
symbolism, 69
Vinegar bottle
bitterness of, 74–75
wholeness of, 79
Violence, 126–127
Voices, inner, 9

W

Waite, Terry, 163
Waiting task, 199–200
The Waltons, 190–191
Water, symbolism, 17
Webs, 217
We'll See, 61–62
What the Snake Had in Mind,
    94–96
  interpretation, 96–115
Wholeness, symbols of, 79
Whuppie, Molly, 87
Williams, Tennessee, 244
Winnicott, D.W., 182
Wise Old Man energy, 247
Witch, *see also* Dark Feminine
    energy, 142
  symbols of, 147
The Witch's Shoes, 167–169
  interpretation, 169–173

Women
  aging, role, 3–4
  angry, labeling, 23
  extroverted, 152
  inner voices, 9
  introverted, 151
  with masculine energy, 234–235
  mothers, *see* Mothering
  old, *see* The Old Woman
  super, *see* Superwoman
Worm, 118–121
  symbolism, 122–124

Y

Yin/Yang, 105, 229
Yosemite rock climbers, 128–129

Z

Zeta, 277–278
Zeus, 46